Legal Leadership

A Practical Guide for In-house Lawyers

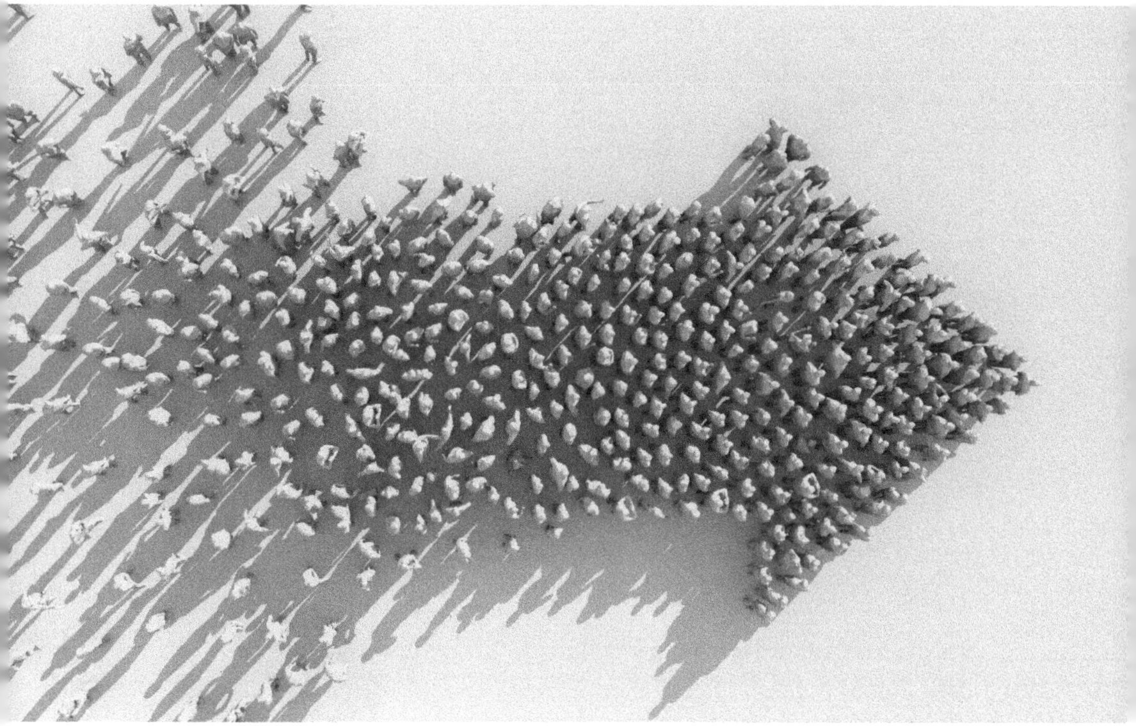

DR THOMAS LOEST

Commissioning editor
Alex Davies

Managing director
Sian O'Neill

Legal Leadership: A Practical Guide for In-house Lawyers
is published by

Globe Law and Business Ltd
3 Mylor Close
Horsell
Woking
Surrey GU21 4DD
United Kingdom
Tel: +44 20 3745 4770
www.globelawandbusiness.com

Legal Leadership: A Practical Guide for In-house Lawyers

ISBN 978-1-83723-179-9
EPUB ISBN 978-1-83723-180-5
Adobe PDF ISBN 978-1-83723-181-2

GPSR Compliance: EU Authorised Representative: Easy Access System Europe – Mustamäe tee 50, 10621 Tallinn, Estonia, gpsr.requests@easproject.com

Contents

Executive summary

The legal industry stands at a critical juncture. The global landscape has undergone profound geopolitical shifts, making the world we once knew hardly recognizable. In this context, legal leaders are required to prepare for the unpredictable and to train their teams to respond with agility, often stepping into leadership roles themselves.

Simultaneously, rapid technological advancements, most notably in artificial intelligence, are poised to disrupt legal services in unprecedented ways. This presents legal leaders with immense opportunities. By focusing on core deliverables and allowing systems to handle routine tasks, legal teams can enhance their effectiveness and strategic value.

Part one looks at culture as the foundation for success, positioning legal leaders as culture builders. In chapter 1, the author defines the cultural building blocks as the firm's essential values and behaviors. Thomas outlines the key elements for a successful team culture – including empathy, excellence, initiative, transparency, and integrity.

Chapter 2 then looks at how to build a winning culture. Legal leaders must articulate a common purpose that defines and unites the team. They must address common team cultural challenges such as lack of trust, fear of conflict, low commitment, avoidance of accountability, and inattention to results to build effective teams. In addition, legal leaders must accept – and learn to value – failure as a necessary step towards success.

Part Two then moves on to purpose and direction, outlining how legal leaders must be strategists and planners.

Chapter 3 creates a vision for the legal team. This chapter underscores the critical role of a business vision as both a guiding principle and an aspirational objective. The vision statement is particularly strong and relevant if built on the team's purpose.

Chapter 4 then provides a vision statement for the legal team. Building upon the team's purpose as its foundation, this chapter develops in detail a vision for legal teams as practical case study. It introduces the statement: "We are the business advisors of choice; we grow and protect the business," and discusses its practical implications.

In chapter 5, Thomas introduces how leaders are required to formulate a robust strategy and implement this through well-structured plans with clearly defined deliverables. This chapter recommends that the legal team's strategy address five key elements – supporting business growth, protecting the business, integrity and compliance, governance excellence, and people. Chapter 6 then emphasizes execution via comprehensive planning and visual management tools.

In chapter 7, the focus is on how strategic direction informs organizational design, specifically the allocation of resources required to achieve the vision. The chapter elaborates on the mechanisms and foundational components involved, drawing from practical experience.

Chapter 8 then looks at legal operations. Recognized as an emerging discipline in legal team leadership, Legal Ops plays a pivotal role as the GC's principal support and as a strategic partner, especially in advancing the (AI-driven) technology agenda.

Part Three looks at the practice and techniques of legal leadership.

Chapter 9 asks the question, what is leadership? It introduces the concept of leadership and highlights its significance for teams, exploring its various facets and forms.

Chapter 10 then leads the team with mission tactics. Drawing from proven military mission-command strategies, the chapter presents agile and decentralized decision-making within a set framework, offering practical advice on enabling fast but accurate team decisions while maintaining overall leadership control.

Chapter 11 looks at operational leadership – keeping the team on track. Expanding on the previous chapter, Thomas outlines how leaders can effectively direct and guide their teams toward their objective through well-structured leadership bodies, meetings, and other communication methods, building strong connections within the group.

Chapter 12 then looks at leadership in successful talent acquisition. This chapter provides insights for legal leaders on recruiting exceptional legal talent who embody the core values and behaviors discussed in earlier chapters.

Chapter 13 then provides a case study on navigating the VUCA world. Continuing from earlier material, this case study offers techniques to help legal teams operate effectively in volatile, uncertain, complex, and ambiguous environments, which are a reality in most rapid growth markets.

Part Four looks at how legal leaders can make themselves fit for the future – particularly in respect of the artificial intelligence challenge.

Chapter 14 outlines the current state of play in AI. As well as clarifying terms often used (and confused) in the discussion on AI, Thomas explains the technology behind it as well as its capabilities and limitations. Understanding the technology is key for impactful leadership, preparing the team for the challenges and opportunities ahead.

Chapter 15 looks at how prompting is the new drafting, and showcases the multiple opportunities AI can have in operating and leading legal teams.

Chapter 16 then looks at how we can be legal leaders in the AI battle. This final chapter details what legal leaders must address when introducing AI from a security, strategy, change management, and governance standpoint.

To Ciara – exceptional in law, extraordinary in life. With all my love and gratitude.

And to Johannes, Klaus, Maximilian, and Philipp – all formidable leaders but more importantly lifelong friends through every season.

About the author

Thomas Loest is an experienced international general counsel and strategic business partner within executive leadership teams. A modern thinking inspirational leader, his track record of building high-functioning legal teams, delivering legal transformation and excellence in business advice speaks for itself. He is German qualified with 30 years' experience, 18 years with international corporations. A lawyer by passion, Thomas considers himself a solution provider, utilising the full suite of legal, advocacy, ESG and compliance process tools.

Introduction

Leadership extends beyond technical proficiency; legal leadership is more than mastery of the law. Once entrusted with the responsibility of managing others, a leader's role expands to ensuring the team achieves outcomes and generates collective value surpassing individual contributions. This principle applies equally to private practitioners and corporate counsel alike. Many leadership principles outlined in this book are broadly transferable. However, since this book is grounded in my personal journey, the primary emphasis is on leading in-house legal teams.

Legal leadership presents distinctive challenges. Legal professionals often possess extensive academic training, deep specialization, and are accustomed to independent work. Teamwork often does not come naturally to lawyers. In law firms, siloed working patterns and the protection of knowledge can sometimes become a path to advancement. Conversely, in-house environments necessitate true collaboration for success. Legal leaders must cultivate teamwork within a profession where such skills are seldom emphasized. The objective is to foster a team environment characterized by shared purpose, rapid information sharing, routine collaboration, and effective utilization of the team's collective expertise. The old joke "three lawyers, five opinions" serves as a warning – coherence in legal advice from any member of the legal team is critical. "Think as thousands but speak with one voice" is the winning mantra for corporate legal teams. Without a unified approach, a legal team's relevance within an organization is severely compromised.

I often draw a parallel between in-house legal work and the high-stakes context of a surgical theater. Legal leaders assume the role of the chief surgeon. Their role is to oversee the theatre, coordinate processes, overcome complications, and train junior surgeons on the most difficult operations, driving both excellence and efficiency. Much like a surgical team, each member of a legal team must understand their responsibilities and support one another to maintain consistent performance under pressure.

Routine assignments and transactions, comparable to standard medical procedures, are delegated to junior staff, thus building their capabilities and confidence while freeing senior lawyers to address complex matters requiring advanced judgement and strategic vision. When less experienced colleagues encounter uncertainty or reach the bounds of their knowledge, they escalate issues transparently and without hesitation, seeking guidance from seasoned colleagues in a culture that values open communication. A clearly defined escalation process further facilitates swift and effective knowledge exchange shaped by the team's working culture.

Senior members are not expected to assume junior duties or micromanage but rather to offer expert mentorship and intervene only when necessary. This empowers junior staff and ensures all team members operate at their fullest potential. Regular updates and transparent internal communication help mitigate surprises and maintain alignment, which is a practice akin to surgical teams' constant coordination to pre-empt complications.

The hallmark of successful legal leadership lies in designing, implementing, and sustaining such collaborative systems. By establishing robust frameworks and fostering environments where escalation is encouraged and information flows freely, leaders ensure their teams perform with agility and resilience. Should a leader become preoccupied with routine matters best handled by others, it can impede both the team's growth and the leader's strategic influence. Thus, the legal leader's pivotal contribution is the ongoing refinement and improvement of operational frameworks to drive quality results while cultivating future talent.

Leadership is a dynamic process – continuous learning, adaptation, and improvement are fundamental. There is no universal solution. Certain strategies will prove more effective than others. Failure is normal and part of a legal leader's life. The most adept leaders draw from diverse tools, experiences, and insights, tailoring their approaches to fit specific contexts. Foundational concepts remain constant, but their execution must be pragmatic, agile, and context-sensitive.

This book is intended as a practical guide, derived from lived experience, research, and reflection. Leadership centers on impact and value creation. Legal leaders are accountable for ensuring their teams surpass general expectations through well-crafted and effectively executed strategies and plans while taking good care of every member of the team throughout this journey. Leading a high-performing team requires clear direction and defined deliverables, alongside providing meaningful support to achieve these objectives sustainably.

This book is written by a legal leader for legal leaders. It speaks the language of the profession, understands its pressures, and offers a vision of leadership that is both aspirational and achievable. Whether you are a chief legal officer, a group general counsel, a chief counsel, a senior team leader, newly appointed to a leadership role, or aspiring to become a legal leader, this book will help you to develop your own leadership framework and style. While the foundational elements of legal leadership, as developed in this book in detail, are widely applicable, authentic leadership is achieved by tailoring these components to maximize value for both your team and organization.

Readers will find an actionable, experience-based framework for legal leadership, grounded in practical challenges and solutions. In the opening section of this book, I lay the groundwork by exploring the essential concepts and theoretical frameworks that underpin effective legal leadership. I conduct an in-depth examination of these foundational elements, delving into why each is vital to the development and sustained success of legal teams. By thoroughly researching and analyzing the reasons behind their significance, I aim to clarify what makes these principles indispensable in both the practice and management of law.

Following this conceptual exploration, I transition to hands-on guidance, demonstrating how these principles can be applied to real-world scenarios. Through detailed case studies, I illustrate the practical implementation of these leadership strategies, highlighting both the challenges encountered and the solutions employed. This approach ensures that readers not only understand the theory but also see its relevance and impact in everyday legal contexts, providing actionable insights for aspiring and established legal leaders alike.

What I share here is my own journey, my personal viewpoints and opinion. I am not speaking for any organization or company with which I have been affiliated through my career. Confidentiality is rigorously maintained. Rather, I share my observations based on three decades of experience with the intent of distilling the key qualities underpinning successful legal leadership.

My journey into leadership began during my military service in Germany in the late 1980s, where I served as a paratrooper, having volunteered for a two-year term. This formative period proved instrumental in shaping my understanding of what it truly means to lead. In the military, leadership is never optional but the inherent duty and the very foundation upon which every officer's role is built. The expectation is clear – leaders must build a high-function team, develop and execute a working plan to accomplish the assigned mission, while simultaneously safeguarding the wellbeing of the team's members.

During my time in service, I was introduced to the leadership principle known as *Auftragstaktik*, a concept I examine in depth later in this book. *Auftragstaktik*, or mission command, places emphasis on giving clear objectives and then empowering team members to determine how best to achieve them. This philosophy aligns seamlessly with the demands of both military and civilian leadership. Establishing a purposeful direction, entrusting those under your command with autonomy, and fostering an environment where every individual understands their role in the collective success.

Reflecting on those years, it is evident that the disciplined environment and high stakes of military operations honed my ability to lead and build trust within the team. These lessons have served as a foundation throughout my career, influencing my approach to leadership across sectors. The principles of accountability, mutual respect, and clarity of purpose that I first encountered as a young officer remain just as relevant in legal practice and organizational leadership. In the chapters that follow, I draw on these early experiences to demonstrate how *Auftragstaktik* and other foundational concepts can be applied to create agile, resilient teams with a strong sense of mission, particularly in volatile, uncertain, complex, and ambiguous environments.

At its heart, leadership begins with mindset. You must recognize the fundamental importance of leadership and be intentional about developing it. The challenge is to strike the right balance between engaging in the technical aspects of legal work and investing adequate time and energy in leading your team. Leadership must be visible and embodied – the team needs to see and feel your presence and commitment.

Effective leaders must also be prepared to have difficult conversations. A CEO who I know well told me recently that about 80 percent of conversations he has are difficult and challenging in nature. While I have never quite reached that proportion, it underscores the point – as leaders, we cannot shy away from difficult conversations. Proactively addressing issues, planning for the future, and making timely adjustments are all part of the job and central to responsible leadership. It is vital to confront problems directly rather than letting them fester. Difficult conversations are not only necessary but a sign that we are fulfilling our responsibilities as leaders.

Yet, leadership is not all challenge and adversity. It is equally a powerful source of motivation, personal development, and shared accomplishment. There is immense satisfaction in witnessing your team evolve. Seeing the seeds you have planted flourish into something much greater than their individual parts, into a real team connected through a common purpose, is highly rewarding. This growth fosters a profound sense of belonging and pride, not just for team members but for the leader as well.

Leadership is also about recognizing and celebrating achievements, both big and small, and ensuring that moments of success are shared and enjoyed together. Creating an environment where accomplishments are acknowledged and joy is part of the journey helps to build camaraderie, resilience, and flow within the team. When leaders approach their role with openness and enthusiasm, leadership itself becomes a highly rewarding experience. Let's begin our journey.

Part One: Team culture as foundation for success – legal leaders as culture builders

Leadership is a multifaceted discipline, comprising several critical components, but none are more vital than culture and strategy. These two elements are inseparable – each dependent on the other to achieve meaningful, sustainable outcomes. To use an analogy, strategy and culture can be likened to hardware and software within a system or organization.[1] The hardware represents the tangible framework that legal leaders establish – the structures, defined roles and responsibilities, key initiatives, tools, and systems. However, without the right software – namely, the culture – this infrastructure remains inert. Culture animates the structure, shaping how a team interacts, collaborates, and ultimately delivers results.

While it is tempting to view strategy as merely the organizational hardware, in reality it is more than that. Strategy is directive. It sets the course, defines priorities, and identifies the path towards the team's goals. There is an oft-quoted phrase: "culture eats strategy for breakfast", but in truth, both are indispensable. A high-performing team cannot succeed with culture alone. Without direction, even the most motivated team is like a powerful engine with no steering. Conversely, the most meticulously crafted strategy is futile without the right culture to bring it to life. Culture is the enabling force that ensures the strategy is executed effectively.

Think of strategy as the team's long-term navigation system – a compass, or better still, a GPS that charts the route towards the desired destination. There are various ways to reach the goal – navigating motorways, meandering along country lanes, taking detours, or making well-timed stops. Strategy provides the multi-year framework, with operational plans marking the milestones and steps along the way. Yet, it is the right culture that ensures the journey is both successful and sustainable. For instance, a culture that values safety and accountability encourages regular pauses, check-ins, and course corrections, while a culture of proactive thinking allows the team to adapt plans in real time, avoiding traffic jams or bottlenecks and overcoming unexpected obstacles as they arise.

Ultimately, culture determines how results are achieved, especially within a legal team where collaboration is paramount. If forced to prioritize, I would argue that culture edges out strategy in terms of importance. Once a positive, empowering culture is established, it begins to shape the organizational structure itself. When leaders clearly communicate their expectations and foster a collaborative environment, empowerment follows naturally. This sense of ownership and engagement encourages team members to take initiative, contribute ideas, and work together towards common goals. It is a far more effective approach to build the structure collectively, rather than imposing a rigid framework and expecting unquestioning obedience.

I recall a business leader once saying, "Ownership is personal. You only truly own what you help to build. When you see your contribution reflected in the outcome, you feel a sense of pride and responsibility."

This insight rings true in my experience. Harnessing the collective intelligence and energy of the team is essential when defining strategy. Begin with culture – set clear behavioral expectations and cultivate an environment where everyone feels valued and empowered to participate. When you do so, you not only create a high-performing team but also lay the foundation for lasting success.

References

1 See also McKinsey, "Agility: It rhymes with stability", *McKinsey Quarterly*, Dec 2015. Bjarne Tellmann, *Building an Outstanding Legal Team*, Globe Law and Business (2017).

Chapter 1: Cultural building blocks – essential values and behaviors

Values, sometimes referred to as virtues, represent the internal convictions or guiding principles that shape how individuals and organizations perceive the world, interact with others, and make decisions. They are the deeply entrenched beliefs that inform one's sense of right and wrong. In contrast, behaviors are the tangible, outward expressions of these values. Behaviors are observable patterns of action that provide evidence of what is valued within a team or organization. While values are inherently abstract and philosophical, behaviors are practical, visible, and measurable manifestations of those ideals.

Take, for instance, the value of "integrity". Integrity is not simply about adhering to legal or regulatory requirements. Rather, it is about doing the right thing even when no one is watching. It is a commitment to honesty, fairness, transparency, and ethical conduct, regardless of external pressures. The behaviors that stem from integrity might include refusing to cut corners for expediency, resisting the temptation to misrepresent facts, and steadfastly avoiding dishonest practices. A famous business leader once said, "Humility and integrity forbid what the law may allow" – which is apparently a quote from Seneca. While I have not been able to verify the attribution to Seneca (and neither were the AI agents I had at my disposal), its sentiment remains relevant – true integrity goes beyond mere compliance, demanding a higher ethical standard. Ethical conduct, therefore, becomes the visible behavior that springs from the value of integrity.

Beyond integrity, a high-performing legal team is built on a foundation of several other key values. These often reflect the broader organizational values but can be tailored to emphasize qualities particularly relevant to legal professionals. For example, humility is a trait that distinguishes exceptional leaders. The most accomplished individuals often attribute their success to diligence and perseverance rather than talent or privilege. Humility, in this context, involves recognizing both one's strengths and limitations, giving credit to others and openly acknowledging mistakes. It means allowing others to shine, celebrating their achievements, and fostering an environment where everyone feels respected and valued. Leaders who are genuinely humble do not see themselves as infallible but as part of a collective effort, willing to learn and grow alongside their teams.

At the heart of a successful legal team lies an unwavering commitment to teamwork and collaboration. These are qualities that are perhaps even more critical in legal teams than in others. The nature of legal work often demands a unified approach, as the consequences of inconsistency or miscommunication can be far-reaching.

When lawyers interpret the same set of facts in divergent ways and consistently arrive at differing or even contradictory conclusions, they risk undermining the very purpose of their role. Such inconsistency does not merely create confusion, it can significantly damage the credibility of the legal team as a whole. Clients and colleagues begin to question the reliability of legal advice when it appears fragmented or at odds with itself, leading to a gradual erosion of trust. This may even lead to business clients directly engaging outside counsel, clearly manifesting the loss of trust in the in-house legal team. Consistent, unified advice is essential for instilling confidence, enabling sound decision making, and preserving the integrity and influence of the legal team within the business.

The responsibility for fostering this spirit of unity rests squarely with legal leaders. Leaders set the tone and are shaping the team's culture through their words, actions, and attitudes. Humility in leadership goes beyond simply acknowledging one's own limitations. It involves actively seeking input from others, listening, recognizing the contributions of the whole team, and being open to feedback and new ideas. By modelling these behaviors, legal leaders encourage collaboration and empower individuals to contribute to the team's goals and achievements. When humility guides those at the helm, it creates a ripple effect – leading to greater trust, stronger relationships, and a team that is truly greater than the sum of its parts.

The journey towards embedding desired values and behaviors often begins with a practical focus on behaviors. While shared values contribute to shaping the overall culture, it is the consistent display of right behaviors that truly drives cultural transformation. Misalignment between stated values and actual behaviors can signal a disconnect, undermining trust within the team. For instance, if "courage" is promoted as a value but team members routinely avoid difficult conversations, the credibility of that value is diminished.

From a pragmatic standpoint, building consensus around behaviors tends to be more straightforward than attempting to define core values. Values are usually established by organizational leadership and may not always align perfectly across different teams or functions. Attempting to promote unique values within a sub-team can create confusion or suspicion. Behaviors, on the other hand, can be adapted to fit the specific needs and developmental stage of a team. By identifying and prioritizing the behaviors that best support the desired outcomes, leaders can foster a culture of continuous improvement and alignment.

Behaviors are generally easier to define, observe, and measure than values. For example, if "collaboration" is a core behavior, one can assess its presence by tracking how frequently team members engage in knowledge-sharing sessions, contribute to group problem-solving, or participate actively on internal communication platforms. Observable signs of collaboration might include colleagues supporting one another, volunteering for tasks outside their immediate remit, or offering expertise to solve complex challenges. These behaviors demonstrate the team's commitment to the value of collaboration and provide clear indicators for leaders to reinforce and recognize.

Ultimately, a successful legal team is one where values are lived through consistent, visible behaviors. Leaders should focus on both articulating clear values and actively encouraging the behaviors that bring those values to life. Regular reflection, feedback, and recognition help bridge the gap between aspiration and reality, ensuring that the team's culture remains strong, resilient, and attuned to its goals.

Empathy and care

In recent times, empathy has become a much-debated concept, often carrying political overtones. Yet, empathy and the principle of care that naturally stems from it is at the very heart of effective teamwork and collective achievement. Genuine empathy underpins the behaviors that lead to outstanding results within a group or organization.

Weakness or virtue

Despite its prominence in contemporary discussions about corporate culture, empathy cannot be taken for granted. Some, such as Elon Musk in a 2025 podcast,[1] have controversially described empathy as "the fundamental weakness of western civilization". In certain organizations, success is ascribed to individual brilliance paired with a kind of raw, competitive instinct. I recall a friend's early experiences in investment banking, where he was told that, although he was performing well, he lacked the necessary "greed" to truly excel – a notion reminiscent of Gordon Gekko's infamous "greed is good" speech in the 1987 film *Wall Street*. This sounds like a message from a time long gone. The notion that greed can be celebrated as a virtue, or as a driving force behind the advancement of humanity, feels entirely out of step with modern values. While Adam Smith's (1723-1790) theories on self-interest suggest that individuals pursuing their own advantage can contribute to the common good, this concept has evolved significantly since his era. However, to characterize a vice such as greed – one of the classic seven deadly sins – as a positive force for societal or human progress is both misguided and antiquated. Greed, by its nature, prioritizes personal gain over collective wellbeing and can easily lead to destructive behaviors and outcomes. History and experience have repeatedly shown that when greed is allowed to dominate, it can undermine trust, damage relationships, and erode the very foundations of community and cooperation.

In today's context, the emphasis is shifting towards values such as empathy, care, and shared ambition, which foster collaborative and hence more successful teams and societies. Rather than championing unrestrained self-interest at the expense of others, we should recognize that genuine progress comes from advancement as a collective. Rooted in empathy and a sense of shared purpose, this emphasis truly drives sustainable growth and development, both within organizations and across society at large.

The science behind an empathetic civilization

There is a scientific explanation behind this, as Jeremy Rifkin proclaims with his hypotheses of an "empathic civilization".[2] Rifkin contends that humans are not fundamentally self-interested but are instead hard-wired for empathy. He draws on advances in neurobiology, notably the discovery of "mirror neurons", to support his assertion that empathy is an intrinsic part of human nature. According to Rifkin, these mirror neurons demonstrate that we are biologically predisposed to care for and connect with one another.

It is important to distinguish between sympathy and empathy. Sympathy involves acknowledging another person's feelings from your own perspective – feeling for someone, rather than with them. In contrast, empathy allows you to step into another's shoes, to perceive and experience the world from their vantage point. For instance, when my neighbor's young daughter lost her pet hamster, I sympathized with her sadness, recognizing her grief even though I had never owned a pet myself. However, when my own son later lost his goldfish,[3] I experienced the situation through his eyes – witnessing his care and affection for the animal, and in turn, developing my own emotional connection to the pet. This deeper, shared sense of loss was true empathy – it was not simply "I am sorry for your loss", but a genuine feeling of shared grief.

There is a fascinating story at the heart of our understanding of empathy. In the 1990s, Professor Giacomo Rizzolatti and his team from the University of Parma embarked on a series of experiments with monkeys,[4] aiming to observe how their brains responded to various positive and negative experiences. The tests seemed straightforward, designed to measure neural activity while the monkeys performed different actions.

One day, after a session had ended and the team was tidying up, an apparently ordinary moment sparked an extraordinary discovery. A researcher entered the room, sandwich in hand and took a casual bite. Unexpectedly, the monitoring equipment – still attached to the monkey – flared to life, recording a pattern identical to that seen previously when the monkey itself had eaten. At first, the scientists were baffled: surely the animal hadn't moved? Yet the equipment told a different story. Driven by curiosity, they repeated the experiment, each time observing the same mysterious phenomenon.

What they found, in essence, was a remarkable mirroring: when the monkey watched another being perform an action – such as eating – the same neurons fired in its brain as if it were doing the action itself. These "mirror neurons" revealed an uncharted neurological bridge between seeing and experiencing, blurring the boundaries between self and others. The implications were profound. Mirror neurons are the biological mechanism underpinning our ability to understand, internalize and even share other's emotions.

The existence of mirror neurons explains a broad range of social behaviors, suggesting that our primary drive is not self-interest but the need for belonging, connection and affiliation. Throughout history, this instinct has shaped our capacity for sociability, compassion and companionship. Empathy has evolved over time, expanding from familial and tribal bonds to broader societal affiliations.

Today, in the 21st century, it seems inconceivable that executions of death sentences were once public entertainment. The crowd cheered and reveled in the event, treating it as an occasion for communal amusement rather than feeling sorry for the poor soul who was to be killed in the most brutal way. It is tempting to blame the lack of cable television or the internet for this unrestrained appetite for violent performance happenings. The real question lingers – how could entire crowds, despite mirror neurons and the biological set-up hardwired for empathy, fail to feel pity for a fellow human being facing such a fate?

The answer lies in the way the condemned were perceived. To the assembled masses, the unfortunate soul on the scaffold was not seen as a neighbor or kin, but as a stranger – outsider, a wrongdoer, almost stripped of their humanity. They were cast as a problem to be eradicated, rather than a person capable of suffering and redemption. In this light, the absence of empathy becomes a matter of exclusion. The crowd could not see themselves in the condemned and so their hearts remained untouched.

Rifkin goes beyond our understanding of empathy today. His thesis is that as technology connects us on a global scale, we have the opportunity – and perhaps the obligation – to broaden our "empathetic tribe". He envisions a future where technological advances foster a planetary sense of empathy, enabling us to address the fundamental challenges of the 21st century through collective understanding and care.

Empathy as core value behind effective collaboration

Empathy is essential for successful teamwork and should be a key criterion in recruitment[5] of legal talent. However, building a culture of empathy and care requires more than simply hiring empathetic individuals – it demands empathetic leadership. Leaders must prioritize empathy as a core team value and recognize its vital role in effective collaboration. This is not just about promoting expected behaviors and measuring them through KPIs or annual assessments. It is about nurturing an emotional culture where care and connection are genuinely felt and expressed, forming the underlying fabric that binds a team together and powers its sense of shared purpose.

To foster such a culture, leaders must work to create a deeply rooted sense of unity: a "band of brothers" or "circle of trust" within the team. This connection is most powerfully forged through shared experiences "in the trenches", particularly in challenging or high-pressure situations. Whether working late to close a critical deal, preparing and delivering a crucial presentation to senior management, or facing adversaries in the courtroom, these collective efforts build trust, respect, and solidarity. The impact is amplified not only by shared successes, but also by the collaborative preparation and mutual support leading up to key moments. As legal leaders, our responsibility is to create opportunities for these shared experiences, ensuring that every team member feels part of something greater than themselves.

Ultimately, empathy and care are not just desirable qualities – they are the essential pillars of high-performing legal teams. By embedding these values into our day-to-day interactions and leading by example, we lay the groundwork for a resilient, connected, and truly effective team – one that thrives not in spite of, but because of, its empathy and collective ambition.

Legal excellence and quality

Excellence and superior quality are not just corporate jargon but essential values for our commitment to do a better job than our competitors. Technical mastery is fundamental – striving to be the best lawyer in our field, possessing a deeper understanding of the law than others, and being able to devise innovative yet robust and practical solutions. Our competitive advantage lies in our superior legal knowledge, the precision of our assessments, and our ability to present arguments that are not only more persuasive but also more resilient under challenge. Excellence means refusing to settle for merely adequate solutions. It is about going further and always pursuing the optimal outcome while never losing sight of business realities and pragmatic outcomes. While excellence is a relative concept, it is ultimately anchored in an unwavering commitment to continuous improvement, whether that progress is rapid in times of transformation or incremental through steady, ongoing refinement.

This ethos manifests itself in various practical ways. For example, we constantly update our contract templates to incorporate new learnings, ensuring that our documents reflect the latest best practices. We are diligent in sharing knowledge across the legal team so that every member is equipped to succeed. We keep our client alerts, executive briefings, and training materials current, so that both our team and our clients benefit from the most up-to-date insights.

This pursuit of excellence is both an individual and collective endeavor. The team is only ever as strong as its least prepared member. I once sought advice from a business leader whom I greatly respect, asking what she most valued in a lawyer. Her answer was unequivocal: "Above all else, you must be truly excellent at what you do. There is no substitute."

We must aspire to be what Phil Knight, founder of Nike, calls "damn good lawyers",[6] embodying not only competence but distinction in every aspect of our practice.[7] We must never lose sight of our primary purpose and our central mission to create value. While our roles are expanding and we are continually developing enabling skills and taking on additional roles, as members of the legal team we must remember that providing *legal advice* is the core product we offer to the business. This is an area where only true excellence will suffice.

Excellence is not a destination but a continuous journey. It is about setting a standard that drives us to seek better ways of working, to learn from every experience and to empower our colleagues to achieve collective success. By embedding excellence at the heart of everything we do, we ensure that our legal advice remains not just relevant, but indispensable to the business.

Initiative, accountability, and ownership

We seek team members who embody an entrepreneurial spirit – a mindset that extends far beyond simply performing assigned tasks. We want individuals who genuinely care, not only for one another, but also for the wider team, the organization, the company, and all its stakeholders. This includes our people, customers, shareholders, partners, brands, assets, communities, and everyone who plays a part in our collective success. Just as entrepreneurs pour passion and energy into nurturing their own venture, so too should our employees treat the business with a sense of ownership and pride. We value those who feel personally accountable for outcomes, results, and doing the right thing for the business at every turn. We should award this exemplary conduct with equity in the company through long-term incentives.

This ownership mentality is most evident when team members proactively volunteer for projects or, even better, identify opportunities themselves and take the initiative as self-starters. It is not enough to be adept at spotting problems or articulating what is wrong. As President Obama has observed and often shared in his speeches, many people excel at analyzing issues and can explain to the last detail what went wrong or didn't work. But instead of taking decisive action and bringing the matter to resolution, they simply escalate them up the hierarchy, waiting for guidance or instructions. This approach is insufficient in high-performing legal teams.

What we truly seek are colleagues who, whenever they see an opportunity to improve something – no matter how big or small – are willing to take the lead and drive positive change. In some instances, particularly with complex challenges, it may be necessary to develop a plan and seek approval before proceeding further. The critical trait is a willingness to assume full ownership of an issue, committing to its resolution and demonstrating a "leave it with me" attitude. This is not a superficial reassurance, but a sincere commitment to take responsibility for a problem and see it through to completion. Such an approach requires tenacity, discipline, and resilience, especially when obstacles arise.

As legal leaders, we greatly appreciate those lawyers who consistently follow up on matters, provide regular updates, and keep everyone informed of their progress. While there will inevitably be occasions when escalation or input from leadership is necessary, the expectation is not that team members simply hand off unresolved issues. Instead, when seeking support, they should come prepared with a well-considered analysis and proposed solutions –transforming the conversation from "What should I do next?" to "Here are several initiatives I have identified; I would value your input and backing to move these forward".

By fostering this culture of initiative, accountability, and true ownership, we empower every member of the legal team to contribute actively to our shared success. This, in turn, strengthens our resilience, agility, and competitive edge – ensuring that we do more than simply react to challenges, actively shaping our future as a high-performing, trusted legal function within the business.

Transparency

Transparency stands as one of the most vital and desirable behaviors within any high-performing team, particularly in the legal profession. It is the rock upon which trust is built, facilitating genuine collaboration and a culture of accountability. By fostering an environment where information is shared openly and freely, we enable all team members to comprehend the context behind decisions, understand shifting priorities, and keep abreast of project statuses and challenges, whether at an individual or collective level.

When a legal leader demonstrates transparency, sharing their intentions, the rationale behind decisions, or even acknowledging mistakes, it sends a powerful signal that there is nothing to conceal. This openness not only reduces suspicion and the spread of rumors, but also creates a culture where gossiping is discouraged. Most importantly, it lays the foundation for psychological safety[8] – a climate where individuals feel secure to voice concerns, take calculated risks, and admit errors without fear of negative repercussions. Such an environment is crucial for surfacing innovative ideas and addressing potential issues early, both of which are essential for effective problem-solving and the provision of sound legal advice.

Moreover, transparent practices help to break down information silos and minimize the risk of miscommunication. When team members have access to up-to-date project reports, clear timelines, and real-time developments on significant matters, they can better synchronize their efforts with the broader goals of the team. This is especially important when striving to create a "team of teams"[9] structure, which operates as an interconnected network rather than a rigid hierarchy. In such a model, individuals do not have to rely solely on top-down communication of strategies or plans. Instead, they benefit from access to the latest information, which empowers them to act decisively and align their work with the wider mission.

However, while transparency is of overwhelming importance for both team effectiveness and institutional integrity, there are practical limits to its application within a corporate environment. Certain information such as confidential M&A activity, sensitive litigation, or personnel matters must be managed on a strictly need-to-know basis. Such restrictions are not only prudent but legally necessary, as the indiscriminate sharing of material, non-public information could expose the company to regulatory risks, including allegations of insider trading due to inadequate safeguards.

The other extreme is the concept of "radical transparency", as championed by organizations like Bridgewater Associates, an American investment management firm specialized in hedge funds, under its CEO and founder Ray Dalio.[10] The company pushes openness to an extreme. It is recording and archiving nearly all meetings, making them accessible to all employees. Allegedly, employees carry "baseball cards" that show their strengths and weaknesses, more like a personality profile so that people know to how to best approach their colleagues. And there are other data collection processes (to the delight of every European data protection officer) to drive data-based transparency. While this approach aims to eliminate internal politics and foster a pure meritocracy, it can be highly disruptive and may not translate well to every organization, especially in regions with a more introverted culture as observed in many Asian countries.

Take, for example, the disclosure of salary information. Sharing such data without explanation, as seen in some law firms, can create tension and distract teams for weeks. Similarly, expecting team members to watch every meeting recording is impractical. Here, technology can offer solutions – AI-powered tools, for instance, can summarize content and distribute relevant updates efficiently.[11] Just as remuneration figures of board members are often published at a group rather than individual level, so too can meeting notes or project summaries be shared with those working on related matters.

Personally, I have valued transparency as a principle since studying legal philosophy under Professor Robert Alexy at Kiel University in 1990, whose teachings continue to influence me.[12] Alexy argued that procedural safeguards such as transparency, justification, and reasoned decision making are essential to the rule of law. The clearer and more open our processes for creating laws and delivering judgments, the stronger our commitment to material justice.

In the corporate world, the advantages of promoting transparency far outweigh the potential downsides, provided that we manage legal risks and other limitations sensibly. As legal leaders, it is important to discern whether information is "ours" to share (meaning originating within our team) or whether it has been entrusted to us in confidence by others. Breaching that trust by sharing news prematurely can quickly erode relationships and cut off valuable information flows. Instead, we should always clarify, at the earliest opportunity, what can appropriately be communicated to the wider team.

A practical approach is to classify information by its sensitivity and relevance, much as we do with personal data under the EU General Data Protection Regulation (GDPR).[13] For example, in the early stages of a deal, there may be no need to involve the entire legal team. However, on a need-to-know basis, it is prudent to include the M&A specialists as well as the commercial and IP lawyer supporting the most affected business units. Their expertise and knowledge of the business context make transparency within this core group particularly valuable, as it ensures that the legal advice provided is both timely and highly relevant.

In conclusion, while transparency is not without its challenges, its role as a fundamental pillar of effective and ethical legal practice cannot be overstated. By navigating its practical boundaries with care, we can create a culture of openness that empowers our teams, strengthens trust, and enhances our collective ability to serve the business with distinction.

Integrity and ethical conduct

Integrity is the value that leads to ethical conduct. Integrity is more than simply adhering to rules or avoiding breaking the law. Integrity is about consistently doing what is right, even when it is painfully difficult or when no one is watching.

Integrity is the cornerstone for enduring and sustainable business success. When it is genuinely embedded and actively upheld within a corporate culture, integrity acts as a safeguard against unethical shortcuts and questionable practices. By fostering an environment where doing the right thing is not only expected but celebrated, organizations are less likely to tolerate individuals compromising on their ethical standards, even when faced with pressure or temptation. Moreover, an unwavering commitment to ethical conduct cultivates an admirable reputation for honesty, reliability and principled decision-making. Such a profile is invaluable, attracting partners, customers, and talent who share similar values and aspire to work with businesses renowned for their ethical conduct. Over time, this commitment to integrity not only enhances the organization's standing in the marketplace but also reinforces trust and credibility among stakeholders such as investors and governments.

Moreover, when integrity permeates every level of the business, it strengthens resilience and adaptability. Teams are empowered to speak up, challenge assumptions, and collaborate openly, knowing that their contributions are valued and respected. This collective commitment to ethical behavior creates a virtuous cycle, where transparency and accountability drive continuous improvement and long-term success.

In essence, integrity means aligning our actions with our values and principles, regardless of external pressures or temptations. To bring ethical conduct to life, legal professionals must lead by example, acting as the unwavering guardians of integrity within the business. We are often the final checkpoint in the decision-making process, the last line of defense when ethical questions arise. This responsibility demands that we not only uphold the highest standards ourselves but also encourage and support our colleagues in doing the same. Integrity is not a solitary pursuit. Rather, it is a collective endeavor that thrives in an environment where transparency and constructive challenge are actively encouraged.

Yet, it is vital to recognize that holding ourselves and our teams to rigorous ethical standards does not mean striving for unattainable perfection. True integrity demands intellectual humility. This is the acknowledgement that, despite our best intentions, errors are inevitable. What distinguishes an ethical legal professional is not infallibility, but a willingness to admit mistakes openly, to learn from them and to foster a culture of continuous improvement. A story comes to mind – my priest in Brussels would annually thank his fellow priest at Christmas for helping him avoid the seven deadly sins. It became an annual ritual and I was touched by this public admission that none of us is immune to human frailty. In much the same way, legal teams benefit from humility, mutual support, and honest feedback, ensuring that we remain vigilant and accountable.

Importantly, integrity and ethical behavior cannot be sustained in isolation. The strength of a legal team lies in its ability to support one another, to hold each other to account, and to maintain a shared commitment to integrity. When we weave integrity into the daily fabric of our professional interactions, by being transparent about our reasoning, inviting challenge, and remaining receptive to constructive criticism, we transform ethical conduct from a theoretical ideal into a practical reality. In doing so, legal teams go beyond mere compliance, embodying both the letter and the spirit of the law and serving as trusted advisors and stewards of integrity within their organizations.

References

1 www.youtube.com/watch?v=sSOxPJD-VNo&feature=youtu.be
2 Jeremy Rifkin, *The Empathic Civilization: The Race to Global Consciousness in a World in Crisis* (2010).
3 RIP Luke. The Horsley heron got him.
4 www.researchgate.net/profile/Giacomo-Rizzolatti
5 See chapters five and 12 on talent acquisition.
6 Phil Knight, *Shoe Dog* (Scribner, 2016).
7 Nike calls this "master the fundamentals" which is the ninth of Nike's "11 Maxims", its business philosophy.
8 See chapter two on creating psychological safety.
9 See chapter ten on creating a team of teams.
10 Ray Dalio, founder, chairman, and co-chief investment officer of Bridgewater Associates, in conversation with Charles Duhigg, *New York Times* Event 2017, available on YouTube.
11 See chapter 14 on the state of play in Artificial Intelligence.
12 Robert Alexy, *A Theory of Legal Argumentation* (1976). For Alexy, the procedural requirement of transparency is the only workable safeguard protecting what is just. Substantial test will always be challenged and not accepted. There will aways be reasons why this case is different from others and should be treated differently. Procedural safeguards, however, are neutral and absolute.
13 Regulation 2016/679 of 27 April 2016, https://eur-lex.europa.eu/eli/reg/2016/679/oj.

Chapter 2:
The endeavor of building a winning culture

Culture does not simply emerge by itself in a positive form. Whilst some sort of culture will inevitably develop, leaving it unchecked is akin to neglecting a field and allowing weeds and undesirable growth to take over. Without careful cultivation, a workplace can quickly become dominated by unproductive or even toxic behaviors. Therefore, creating a robust, sustainable, and high-performing culture demands ongoing effort, intention, and conscientious stewardship.

Legal leaders play a crucial role in shaping this environment, not only through their actions and personal example but also by clearly expressing what is expected of their teams. They must actively communicate standards, values, and aspirations, ensuring these are understood and embraced by all. Furthermore, it is essential for legal leaders to design and implement incentives that reinforce positive behaviors and foster a sense of shared purpose. Through a combination of visible leadership, articulated expectations, and thoughtful encouragement, legal leaders can nurture a culture that supports both individual growth and collective excellence.

Defining the team's common purpose and collective success

What transforms a collection of individuals into a true team? It is not simply about bringing people together. The hallmark of an effective team lies in its ability to become something far greater than the mere sum of its parts. A genuine team cultivates a common purpose, a powerful sense of belonging, loyalty, and mutual responsibility among its members. This is not just an abstract concept. Your team becomes your professional 'tribe', a source of identity and shared purpose rather than just another organizational structure.

The benefits of such a team environment are multifaceted. Team members enjoy the collective intelligence and support of their colleagues, drawing not only on the security that comes with "safety in numbers", but also the wealth of experience and expertise that their peers bring to the table. In a strong team, individuals are never isolated. They know they can rely on each other for guidance, creative problem-solving, and encouragement. This support network is the defining difference between a truly cohesive team and a mere assembly of individuals. Like multiple chefs in a professional kitchen, team members realize that becoming a world-renowned restaurant with three Michelin stars is something that they can only accomplish as a team, which therefore defines their common purpose.

The notion of a common purpose is at the heart of what truly unites and motivates legal teams, yet defining it is far more nuanced than in other fields. In sports, the objective is immediately apparent – it is the pursuit of winning, not only this and the next game, but grand trophies of which every player has dreamt since a child. These bold ambitions ignite passion and drive among athletes, compelling them to push themselves every Monday morning out of bed and to give that extra effort. Crucially, it is quickly understood that victory is only possible through teamwork. Individual brilliance alone cannot secure a win. Scoring five goals matters little if your defense concedes ten. Winning as a collective not only achieves results but also forges strong bonds and a shared purpose – the singular goal of bringing home the cup.

In the world of business, the idea of "playing to win"[1] is also more straightforward to articulate. Success may take different forms – becoming the largest, most profitable, most sustainable, most admired, or most highly valued organization, or perhaps being recognized as the employer of choice. These clear metrics provide direction and unite teams under a shared ambition. However, for legal teams, the definition of common purpose is inherently more complex. The purpose must be intrinsically linked to the company and its business objectives as the *raison d'être* of any in-house legal department lies in its support of the wider organizational agenda. There is little value in building a world-class legal department with an exemplary compliance program if its impact never reaches the business or contributes meaningfully to ambitious growth targets.

Furthermore, the common purpose for legal teams cannot be measured by business metrics alone. Short-term commercial success is not always a reliable indicator of the quality of legal advice provided. The contribution of the legal team often extends beyond direct numbers but underpins the sustainable, long-term health of the organization. The story of the janitor at NASA is often cited in this context: when President John F. Kennedy visited the Space Centre in 1962, he asked a janitor leaning on a broomstick what he was doing, to which the janitor replied, "I'm helping put a man on the moon,

Mr President". While inspiring, a purpose that is overly grand or disconnected from day-to-day realities can lose its power to unite the team. A common purpose must be relatable. Proclaiming that your mission is to "change the world" may be noble, but it does little to inspire action or create cohesion on a Monday morning.

After much consideration and extensive discussions with my teams, I have come to the conclusion that the common purpose for legal teams is to bring to life the vision that we have defined together.[2] We strive to be the business advisors of choice, committed to both the growth and protection of the company. This is an ambitious aim – one that cannot be realized by any individual working in isolation. The legal team's value lies in our collective expertise and our shared commitment to serving not just one person, but a multitude of stakeholders, all working towards the ultimate goal of supporting the company's interests.

Working towards the shared vision, making tangible progress, unifies the team. By utilizing visual management tools and scoreboards, progress towards the goals can be tracked and made visible to all team members. This transparency fosters a real sense of achievement and pride, reinforcing the common purpose and ensuring that everyone understands how their individual contributions fit into the bigger picture. It is key that leaders recognize team member contributions formally and do not take performance for granted. A common purpose must be actively embodied and lived in corporate life, as is frequently illustrated by sports coaches who deliver motivational speeches that reinforce the team's collective goal of winning the championship. The shared journey towards fulfilling the vision is what truly binds legal teams together, transforming a group of professionals into a cohesive, high-performing unit.

Understanding the value of team cohesion is not just an academic exercise. It has tangible implications for organizational culture, structure, and recruitment. At headquarters or within regional hubs, lawyers typically operate in larger teams in close physical proximity to each other. Hence collaboration, knowledge-sharing, and swift escalation of issues happen almost organically. In these settings, team members are readily accessible for advice, support, or even a casual conversation, which fosters a sense of connection and shared responsibility.

Contrast this with the challenges faced by sole practitioners or those working alone in remote business units or countries. Without the immediate support of a larger team, it is much more difficult for individuals to access collective wisdom, seek a second opinion, or simply feel part of a broader community. Over the years, I have observed instances where such isolation led to system failures – lawyers making incorrect decisions, perhaps succumbing to pressure from business leaders, or simply lacking access to the right expertise at the right moment. These risks highlight the crucial responsibility of leaders to ensure robust checks and balances are in place, supporting those who may be working more independently and mitigating the dangers of professional isolation.

But how do we get there? How does one transform a group of individuals into a high-performing, interconnected team that consistently delivers outstanding results? The answer lies in a deliberate and ongoing process, one that requires persistent effort, open communication, and a commitment to continuous improvement. Teams do not spontaneously organize themselves. Unlike social events that might come together organically, building an effective team demands energy, intentional leadership, and dedication from legal leaders.

What motivates people to embrace change and become active, engaged team members? Drawing on the insights of the neo-liberal economist Ludwig von Mises, three key conditions must be present: first, a sense of dissatisfaction or discomfort with the current state of affairs; second, a clear vision of a better future; and third, the belief – and the capability – that this improved state is achievable through collective effort.[3]

For instance, consider a legal department where lawyers are frustrated by the lack of standard templates, resulting in every contract requiring labor-intensive drafting from scratch. Team members may feel isolated, struggling with complex problems without the budget for external counsel or the support of actively engaged colleagues. Senior staff may withhold their expertise, creating barriers to knowledge-sharing and contributing to disengagement and frustration. Such an environment inevitably leads to low morale and diminished performance.

Now, imagine a different scenario – templates are readily available and kept up to date by subject matter experts, lawyers collaborate frequently and share knowledge as a matter of course, and there is a tangible sense of commitment to supporting one another. Team members volunteer for additional responsibilities and legal leaders are visible, approachable, and actively involved in helping their teams succeed. The contrast is stark. This is not just a more pleasant environment, but a fundamentally more effective one.

The journey from the first scenario to the second is far from automatic. It requires leaders who are not only visionary but also hands-on in shaping the team's culture and processes. By fostering open dialogue, encouraging mutual support, and continually reinforcing shared goals, leaders can transform disparate individuals into a unified, high-performing team. The result is an environment where everyone feels valued, empowered, and capable of achieving more together than they ever could alone.

Overcoming the five dysfunctions of a team

When it comes to team building and culture, I have long admired the work of Patrick Lencioni. I had the privilege of meeting him in person during the Global Leadership Development Program in 2017 at Palm Desert, California. His 1982 book, *The Five Dysfunctions of a Team*, serves as an outstanding framework for embarking on the journey towards true teamwork and I have consistently drawn upon his principles – always tailoring them to suit the unique dynamics of each team I have led. This is especially true in the legal profession, where particular challenges and requirements must be addressed.

Lencioni outlines five core dysfunctions that can undermine a team's effectiveness:

1. Absence of trust.
2. Fear of conflict.
3. Lack of commitment.
4. Avoidance of accountability.
5. Inattention to results.

It is crucial to diagnose which specific dysfunctions are impeding your team's progress. The first step should be conducting a thorough assessment to pinpoint the exact issues affecting team performance. Following this, legal leaders ought to formulate a structured plan to tackle each dysfunction that has been identified. In my experience, the most effective outcomes occur when both the diagnosis and the development of an action plan are collaborative endeavors involving the entire leadership team. Initially, we would work together to carry out a diagnostic exercise, openly discussing and recognizing the areas that needed improvement. Subsequently, we would collectively devise an action plan to address these challenges, ensuring that everyone was invested in the process.

While legal leaders should guide and oversee both stages, it is equally important to empower team members by giving them the responsibility and autonomy to contribute their own ideas and solutions during the planning phase. This approach not only fosters a sense of ownership and engagement amongst team members but also taps into the diverse perspectives and expertise within the group, leading to more effective and sustainable solutions. By facilitating an environment where everyone's input is valued and encouraged, leaders can build stronger, more cohesive teams capable of overcoming dysfunctions and achieving shared objectives.

1. Trust

Trust is the basis for everything.[4] It is not solely about trusting the leader but extends to mutual trust among all team members. Trust is not automatically granted but must be cultivated and earned over time. Trust does not follow the rank or position of the leader – assuming the team's trust just because of a promotion or appointment to a leadership role is one of the biggest mistakes we can make. Genuine trust roots deep. It extends beyond merely believing in someone's competence – it encompasses confidence in their integrity and character as evidenced by actions.

Essential elements of trust

For trust to flourish, there are several key ingredients – credibility, reliability, and an additional component that triggers a psychological trust response in others.

- *Credibility.* Saying what is true and being honest in your communication.
- *Reliability.* Consistently ensuring your actions match your words. Trust is built when people do what they say they will do.
- *Vulnerability.* Willingly showing your authentic self, including your weaknesses and mistakes.

Credibility and reliability are evident conditions for trust. Bending the truth or failing to follow through on commitments rapidly eliminate trust. However, genuine and lasting trust within a team requires one further criterion – vulnerability shown by the leader and all team members.

The power of vulnerability

Lencioni emphasizes that trust is only truly established when team members are prepared to show vulnerability. This includes openly admitting mistakes and weaknesses and seeking help from one another. By doing so, they create an environment of psychological safety. When leaders take the first step, revealing their own vulnerabilities, they demonstrate humility and humanity. Admitting imperfections and trusting others not to exploit this openness fosters deep connections within the team.

I have experienced this in guided vulnerability sessions, where colleagues bravely shared personal stories that shaped who they are. One particularly inspiring account came from a Latin American colleague, who lost a parent in a road accident as a child and was raised by his grandmother. Her motto, "Life is for the brave," resonated powerfully within him and continues to inspire me. The emotional impact of these moments is lasting. As the saying goes, "People may forget what you said, but they will never forget how you made them feel when you said it".

Creating psychological safety

Vulnerability should be viewed in a wider context. Neuroscience shows that humans are wired for psychological safety. It is a survival mechanism inherited from our ancestors. We constantly scan our environment for reassurance, subconsciously assessing whether we are safe. In the workplace, this manifests as a fear of looking foolish, being criticized, or even ridiculed. When leaders succeed in creating a sense of safety, barriers fall away and team members can fully engage and contribute their best.

Michael Bungay Stanier's[5] TERA model highlights four psychological needs influencing how people experience their environment:

1. *Tribe:* Do I belong? Are you with me or against me?
2. *Expectation:* Do I know what is coming next?
3. *Rank:* Am I on equal footing with others? Is my status secure?
4. *Autonomy:* Am I in control of my situation?

To strengthen the sense of "tribe", leaders should break down barriers and foster belonging. Practical examples are sitting in meetings alongside the team (rather than claiming your usual chairperson seat), maintaining an open-door policy, or using inclusive language. Publicly recognizing achievements not only boosts the individual but also enhances the sense of team. Avoiding surprises is also crucial. Be clear and transparent about meeting purposes and expected outcomes, whether in person or via email.

Hierarchy can stifle honest discussion. Leaders should strive to be "first among equals", sharing roles and not dominating processes. Small gestures, like making coffee for the team or rotating meeting chairs, can disrupt perceptions of rank. Similarly, giving team members autonomy, like asking them to lead on topics or share their thoughts first, encourages ownership and engagement.

Nurturing and sustaining trust

Trust is delicate, much like a cautious deer. Easily startled and quick to vanish. Even after establishing a strong sense of unity, it can fade amid day-to-day pressures. To maintain trust, it's valuable to remind the team of past moments when they worked as a united, supportive group. Times when open discussions, shared challenges, and mutual sacrifices led to the collective success of the team. Naming these moments, such as "the spirit of *Malente*" – after the German football team's focused training camp ahead of its 1974 World Cup victory – provides a lasting symbol of what true teamwork and trust can achieve.[6] In this regard, I frequently reference the names of particular locations or landmark legal victories to evoke and reinforce the unique bonds or camaraderie we forged as a team during those pivotal moments. For example, I might say, "Remember what we accomplished in *Malente*?" or "Can you recall the spirit we shared in *Malente*? We need to recapture that energy now." Such references serve not only as reminders of our shared history, but also as powerful motivators, encouraging the team to reconnect with the determination, unity, and sense of purpose that defined our past successes. Drawing upon these collective memories helps foster a renewed sense of belonging and inspires us to approach current challenges with the same commitment and collaborative spirit that enabled us to triumph together before.

2. Open and constructive conflict

The second essential foundation for uniting a team is fostering an environment where open, healthy, and constructive conflict can take place. It is vital that, within the team, we cultivate a space in which genuine, unfiltered debates about ideas are not only permitted but actively encouraged. Artificial harmony where disagreements are swept under the carpet for the sake of peace ultimately harms the team and erodes trust. Instead, we must create a culture where team members feel both empowered and obligated to challenge one another, always focusing on critiquing the idea rather than the person presenting it. This is the key requirement for successful challenging of each other – always (make it about) the idea, never the person (unless personal behavior gives rise to the challenge, but this is another discussion).

Respect must be the golden rule for healthy conflict. Disagreements should be about advancing the team's goals, not about undermining individuals. In this way, every member has a voice and it is precisely through this process of constructive challenge that we grow stronger together as a team.

Circumstances are everything; timing and setting are crucial. Not every forum is appropriate for airing conflict. Heated debates do not belong in the weekly operating meeting or public town hall gatherings. Meaningful conflict requires a degree of intimacy and trust in the room, with the understanding that challenges come from a place of assuming good intentions and wanting the best for the team, rather than pursuing individual ambitions. As such, it is beneficial to deliberately schedule conflict sessions as part of the team's agenda, creating a safe space for robust discussion. As a leader, you have the responsibility to set the tone and depth of these sessions. Proactively invite dissent by asking questions like, "What is the strongest argument against this?" or "What are we overlooking?". When someone does voice an opposing view, acknowledge and thank them for their honesty and courage.

For deeper, more provocative sessions, encourage team members to arrive prepared to engage and challenge. The leader's role in these conversations is pivotal. Moderating the discussion, reminding everyone of the boundaries of respect, and ensuring that even when debates become heated, they never cross the line into personal attacks. Active listening is paramount – summarize what you hear to ensure clarity and keep the conversation on track.

It is also important to recognize that some individuals may naturally gravitate towards a critical stance, enjoying the reputation of being the team's chief sceptic or the most demanding member. While a critical perspective can be invaluable if it leads to improvement and action, it becomes counterproductive if it devolves into habitual negativity or overly cautious, pessimistic "black hat thinking". To address this, always require that criticism is accompanied by a constructive alternative: "What do you propose we could do instead that equally supports our plans and vision?" Simply rejecting ideas without offering solutions is not acceptable. Leaders are ultimately accountable for delivering results, not for solely airing concerns.

Every debate that embraces conflict must conclude with a clear, actionable outcome. Sometimes, further discussion may be necessary, but extended debate for its own sake, often seen in overly consensus-driven organizations, can cause frustration, especially among action-oriented team members. Nevertheless, in situations where total alignment is crucial for effective execution, it may be necessary to continue the dialogue until every team member is genuinely committed, even if the decision is unpopular: "We are not there yet. We need to discuss this further."

Equally vital, once the storm of debate has passed, the team must regroup and move forward with unity and clarity. Ongoing conflict without resolution quickly becomes corrosive, distracting from the team's mission and undermining its purpose. The ultimate aim is to create a culture where open challenge is balanced with decisive action and collective harmony – uniting diverse perspectives into a single, purpose-driven team, ready to deliver on its commitments.

3. Real and tangible commitment

The third element for sustainably successful teamwork is real and tangible commitment. At the conclusion of every debate, it is essential that the team reaches clear, actionable decisions. Success hinges not merely on the quality of the discussion, but on the unwavering commitment of each member to carry out the decisions collectively agreed upon. This is irrespective of whether these decisions are reached by consensus or, when necessary, determined by the leader. Without this absolute buy-in, the team's efforts are undermined and execution falters.

The principle at play here is "disagree but commit". Rather than settling for a lukewarm "let's agree to disagree", we must foster a culture where, even if individual team members hold reservations, they choose to put those aside and support the outcome wholeheartedly. I recall a time when, following a particularly intense debate, a colleague said to me, "I disagree, but I trust your instincts and judgment and will support the decision". This is precisely the spirit we must encourage. As leaders, it is our responsibility to summarize the conversation and communicate the final decision with clarity, ensuring everyone understands the path forward.

Few things are more demoralizing than concluding meetings without a definitive decision or course of action. Phrases like "let's take this offline" often serve as veiled attempts to avoid confronting disagreements in the open. Instead, the intention behind "offline" is to opt for informal or political maneuvering outside the official channels. Such practices erode trust and transparency, turning business into politics and devaluing the authority of the team. This is something legal leaders must resist. We must ensure every debate ends with a clear summary and a decisive outcome, requiring every team member to align fully and without hesitation.

In practice, however, securing this level of commitment is not always straightforward. Some colleagues will naturally embrace the decision, implementing it with the same conviction as if it had been their own idea. This could be motivated by trust in leadership, loyalty to the team (and its leader), or simply by virtue of having been included in the decision-making process. For others, the journey to full commitment might be more challenging.

Their reluctance may stem from experience, differing viewpoints, or personal pride. As leaders, it is vital not to overlook or dismiss these "pockets of resistance". Instead, we must address concerns directly, making it clear that everyone is expected to publicly endorse the decision and act as if it were their own initiative.

One practical approach is to ask each team member for a visible, verbal commitment – looking them in the eye and asking for their assurance that they will support the decision fully. This ritual, reminiscent of the African expression "I see you,"[7] is about more than words. It is a demonstration of sincerity and accountability. It signals that there is no room for hidden reservations or passive resistance.

If, after this process, you sense lingering doubts or lackluster commitment, do not simply move on. Persist in seeking genuine alignment and follow up with one-to-one conversations as needed, particularly with those who remain hesitant. Monitor their engagement closely and address any behaviors that do not align with the team's objective. Make expectations clear – the success of the team depends on the full commitment of each member. If someone continues to hold back, they risk undermining the entire group's efforts.

When things do not go to plan, conduct a thorough review of what occurred.[8] However, do not tolerate retrospective blame or "I told you so" attitudes from those who failed to propose viable alternatives during the debate. Remind the team that it is easy to criticize from the sidelines, but true leadership involves making decisions and standing by them. Ultimately, everyone on the team should be expected to demonstrate leadership qualities by supporting collective outcomes and working relentlessly towards shared success.

4. Accountability

The fourth element of successful teamwork is accountability. After a team has committed to a particular course of action, be it a new initiative, a comprehensive plan, or even a complete overhaul of strategy, the next crucial step is ensuring accountability to see it through to completion. While top-down accountability, such as performance evaluations or managerial oversight, may provide some level of discipline (and, as a leader, there is always the temptation to "even the score" during the next appraisal), this approach alone is insufficient for building a truly high-performing team. What truly matters is cultivating a deep-seated, intrinsic sense of accountability that is shared by every team member. Not just to the leader, but to the team as a whole, its shared purpose, collective goals, and to each individual within it.

Patrick Lencioni, a leading authority on teamwork, emphasizes that peer-to-peer accountability is the most significant driver of team effectiveness. It's about holding each other to the commitments made and being able to challenge one another constructively when standards slip. For example, a team member might say, "You promised to provide your expert input by Friday and it's already Tuesday". Such a challenge, delivered respectfully and with the appropriate tone, is not about confrontation but about maintaining clarity and decisiveness on what has been agreed. This sort of candid communication, grounded in mutual respect, is vital for delivering results with excellence.

In high-performing teams, every member feels a genuine responsibility not just to deliver their own work to the best of their abilities, but to go above and beyond for the sake of their colleagues. There is a strong desire not to let others down. Not merely by missing deadlines or submitting subpar work, but by failing to contribute fully to the team's collective success. It is much like an eight-person rowing crew – the only way to win is if each individual gives one hundred percent effort. Success is not just about individual achievement, but about every team member pulling together in perfect harmony towards a shared objective. This sense of accountability is owed to one's peers, not just the person at the helm.

As a leader, it's important to recognize that you cannot possibly observe or control every detail of your team's day-to-day work. You may receive reassuring status updates, but the true picture often resides in the collective experience and observations of the team itself. Sometimes, a leader might be told that all is progressing smoothly, while other team members quietly disagree. This is why establishing a culture of collective accountability is so important. Team members must understand that their commitment is not just to the boss, but to the group's mission and to each other. Everyone is both responsible for their own delivery and empowered to hold their colleagues accountable for theirs.

To foster this culture, leaders should encourage open dialogue about commitments and outcomes. Create regular opportunities for team members to check in with each other, raise concerns and celebrate successes. Make it clear that challenging each other is not a sign of hostility but a demonstration of trust and shared ownership. In doing so, you build an environment where accountability is not imposed from above but lived and breathed by everyone. The team not only makes promises but keeps them and ultimately delivers on its commitments.

5. Attention to results

The fifth element is attention to results. At the heart of every high-performing team lies the consistent achievement of outstanding results. This is the definitive measure of success – the scoreboard that truly counts. For legal teams, winning is not about pleasing business executives or personal recognition but best serving the client, who is the company.[9] It's about each team member aligning their efforts with the shared vision, putting aside personal ambition, ego, or sectional interests. Instead of seeking individual acclaim – such as being named "Lawyer of the Year", "Most Valuable Player", "Academy® Award Nominee" or "Ballon d'Or winner" – the focus is firmly on the "WE", securing victory as a united team, much like lifting the World Cup together.

Fostering this kind of unity requires the recognition that the legal team can only achieve its vision as a team, and this is the common purpose that stands above individual distinction.[10] Team members understand that their greatest achievements come not from standing out alone, but from working in concert with their colleagues towards a common goal. This spirit of collaboration and selflessness is what ultimately propels the entire team to greater heights.

Failure as necessary part of success

As discussed extensively throughout this book, failure is not merely an unavoidable aspect of professional development. It is an essential ingredient in the pursuit of growth and excellence. Embracing the reality that mistakes will occur should not be mistaken for tolerating inadequate preparation or a lack of diligence. However, even the most competent, well-trained and resourceful teams are susceptible to occasional errors or unexpected failures. The true measure of professionalism (and leadership) lies not in the absence of mistakes, but in the manner in which they are addressed and managed.

Accepting and addressing errors

When setbacks arise, it is imperative that issues are identified, reported, and escalated without delay. Swift and transparent communication ensures that corrective measures can be implemented promptly, mitigating potential damage and facilitating a comprehensive analysis of what went wrong. This proactive approach converts mistakes into invaluable learning experiences, highlighting precisely where systems or procedures may have failed and presenting opportunities for meaningful improvement.

There are two foundational principles to uphold when addressing errors. Firstly, organizations must cultivate an environment where mistakes are recognized as an inherent part of working life, rather than something to be concealed or feared. For instance, a team member may inadvertently overlook an important contractual clause, misinterpret its provisions, or encounter a shift in the factual circumstances that necessitates a reassessment of previously given advice. In these scenarios, the most constructive response is to act with openness and integrity – acknowledging the error, escalating the matter rapidly, and communicating clearly about the possible implications for business decisions – and their swift remediation. This stage should prioritize resolving the immediate challenge and securing the best possible outcome, rather than assigning blame or prematurely embarking on root cause analysis.

Once the immediate issue has been addressed and stability is restored, the true challenge of leadership begins. It is at this juncture that the experience should be harnessed as a springboard for collective progress. Leaders must conduct a thorough and honest post-mortem, delving into the underlying reasons for the mistake and identifying practical steps to prevent its recurrence. This process should be rigorous yet supportive, encouraging team members to reflect on their actions, share insights, and contribute to the refinement of internal processes.

Effective leadership in the face of adversity is defined by perseverance, resilience, and a commitment to continuous improvement. Rather than allowing failures to cast a shadow over individuals or teams, strong leaders inspire their colleagues to view these experiences as opportunities for personal and professional growth. By fostering a culture of learning, transparency, and mutual support, organizations can ensure that setbacks serve not as stumbling blocks, but as stepping stones towards greater capability, confidence, and success.

Black Box Thinking

Black Box Thinking represents a transformative approach to cultivating a culture where learning from mistakes is not only encouraged but systematized. Drawing inspiration from Matthew Syed's influential 2016 book, *Black Box Thinking*, I find the concept both motivational and directly applicable to our work in the legal profession. Syed's core premise is to explore why some industries, such as aviation, experience consistent year-on-year improvements, while others remain stagnant or repeat their errors.

An impressive example of applied Black Box Thinking is the "Vision Zero" philosophy, as recently applied by the city of Helsinki (the capital of Finland) to prevent traffic fatalities.[11] It worked and Helsinki recorded a period of 12 months without a single traffic fatality. Its underlying vision states that no traffic death is acceptable and that the transportation system should be designed to accommodate human error. The "Vision Zero" model shifts the focus from blaming the road user to identifying and fixing systemic failures in the transportation system. The city of Helsinki conducted in-depth investigations into every fatal traffic accident to understand the contributing factors and then made changes to prevent similar incidents. This has led to a multi-layered approach to road safety, rather than relying on a single solution – general speed limits of 30 km/h for the majority of the roads, redesigned streets prioritizing the safety of pedestrians and cyclists (narrower lanes, raised crosswalks, separate infrastructure), enhanced enforcement, and prioritizing public transport over individual automobility.

In aviation, the relentless drive towards safer skies has been achieved through the rigorous investigation of every single incident, no matter how minor. The use of "black box" flight recorders ensures that every mishap is meticulously dissected, with lessons extracted and processes adapted to prevent recurrence. This methodical analysis, free from blame and defensiveness, underpins a culture where failures are viewed as opportunities to enhance performance and prevent future errors.

Conversely, industries such as healthcare – and, regrettably, legal services – have often taken the opposite route. Rather than confronting mistakes head-on, there is a tendency to disguise or downplay them, with ambiguous phrases like "there were complications" serving as an all-purpose explanation. This reluctance to engage with failure is frequently driven by a culture of blame, fear of litigation, and the stigma attached to error. The result is a missed opportunity for critical reflection and meaningful change.

Syed argues convincingly that success is seldom the result of a single breakthrough or dramatic innovation. Instead, it emerges through a process of continuous trial and error, incremental improvements, and the willingness to learn from both major failures and minor "near misses". Near misses, which General Electric once referred to as "the gift of the near miss", are particularly valuable because they present an opportunity to learn and adapt before any real harm is done.

Embracing the power of failure, however, demands a high level of trust, psychological safety, and organizational maturity. Legal leaders must work to establish an environment where mistakes are acknowledged as inevitable and where they are treated not as grounds for punishment but as essential fuel for growth. To lay the foundations for this kind of learning culture, leaders should lead by example – candidly admitting their own mistakes and using storytelling as a tool to build trust and foster a sense of shared vulnerability. By focusing discussions on the underlying causes and impacts, rather than on the individuals involved, leaders can personalize the learning process and make it constructive rather than punitive.

On a practical level, Syed advocates for the adoption of formal systems, akin to those used in aviation, to embed Black Box Thinking within organizational processes. Such systems should provide structured mechanisms for collecting feedback, analyzing errors, and systematically integrating lessons learned into revised procedures or best practices. It is essential that these systems have clear ownership – within a legal team, the legal operations function is ideally positioned to manage and coordinate these processes.[12] While practicing lawyers generate the content and insights, legal operations can ensure that lessons are effectively shared, visualized, and translated into continuous improvement across the practice.

A further, proactive application of Black Box Thinking is the "pre-mortem" exercise. Unlike traditional post-mortems, which dissect failures after the event, a pre-mortem invites the team to imagine a scenario in which a project has failed spectacularly – before it has even begun. The team then works backwards to identify all the plausible causes of this hypothetical failure. This process of "prospective hindsight" helps to uncover hidden risks, overlooked dependencies, and potential biases that could jeopardize the project. By collaboratively developing mitigation strategies for each identified risk, the team can stress-test its assumptions, build resilience into its plans, and avoid the trap of blind optimism. In this way, proactive problem-solving is embedded in the planning stage, replacing the passive hope that everything will go according to plan.

In conclusion, Black Box Thinking champions a mindset of openness, curiosity, and relentless improvement. By systematically learning from both our mistakes and our near misses – and by institutionalizing these practices through robust systems and proactive exercises such as pre-mortems – legal teams can transform setbacks into valuable stepping stones towards greater excellence, capability, and client value.

References

1 *Playing to Win* is a 2013 HBR title written by former Procter & Gamble CEO, A.G. Lafley. He and co-author Roger Martin emphasize that strategy is about making clear, deliberate choices to win. They argue that many companies fail because they simply "play to play" or try to be everything to everyone, which leads to mediocrity. The central message is that a good strategy is a coordinated and integrated set of choices that create a sustainable competitive advantage.

2 See chapter ten, a vision for the legal team.

3 Ludwig von Mises, *Human Action: A Treatise on Economics*, Part One, Chapter One: Acting Man (1949).

4 In *Team of Teams* (Penguin, 2015), General Stanley McChrystal emphasises that the bonds of trust among team members are the essential building blocks of an effective organization. See chapter ten, The Next Level: Creating a Team of Teams.

5 Michael Bungay Stanier, *The Coaching Habit. Say Less, Ask More and Change the Way You Lead Forever* (Page Two, 2016).

6 In 2014, during the FIFA World Cup hosted in Brazil, the German national football team replicated this approach and stayed at a specially built sport and nature resort called Campo Bahia away from World Cup excitements. Campo Bahia became the team's (physical and mental) base camp and was considered a significant factor for the victory.

7 The phrase "I see you" is a profound African expression, particularly from the Zulu culture in South Africa, where it is a translation of the greeting "Sawubona". Its meaning is: "I see your soul. I see you for who you are, with all your strengths, weaknesses, pain and joy."

8 For more details see the section on Black Box Thinking in this chapter.

9 See chapter four, Who is the Client?

10 For details, see my thoughts on the definition of the common purpose that builds and unifies the team, in chapter two.

11 "How Helsinki Went an Entire Year Without a Single Traffic Death," published on 11 August 2025 at forbes.com.

12 See chapter eight on legal operations.

Part Two:

Purpose and direction – legal leaders as strategists and planners

For legal leaders, it is essential to provide their teams with a clear sense of purpose and a defined direction. The culture within the legal team acts as the foundational glue, fostering unity, harnessing diverse skills, and encouraging everyone to work collaboratively towards shared objectives. However, unity alone is not enough. It must be channeled towards meaningful goals. This is where strategy and planning come into play.

A well-crafted strategy sets out the course and direction for the team, grounded in a purpose-driven vision for the legal function. This vision serves as the north star, guiding the team's journey and offering clarity on the value it creates within the wider organization. Strategy is not simply about lofty ideals. It is about translating that vision into reality through practical, incremental steps, each articulated in well-considered plans.

Planning is the mechanism that transforms vision into actionable objectives. It makes the vision operational, providing a framework through which progress can be measured and achievements can be tracked. By breaking down the strategic vision into tangible actions, legal leaders enable their teams to see how their everyday work contributes to the bigger picture. This, in turn, reinforces a positive culture, as successes are celebrated and milestones achieved, leading to greater fulfilment and sustained motivation amongst team members.

Ultimately, when legal leaders combine a compelling vision with effective strategy and structured planning, they not only give their teams purpose and direction but also create an environment where people are inspired to excel and continuously improve. This integrated approach ensures that the legal department is not just operationally effective but also strategically aligned with the organization's long-term goals.

Chapter 3:
Creating a vision for the legal team

The function of the vision

Effective leaders are able to articulate a clear vision for their teams or organizations. The vision plays a dual role that is essential to organizational success. First, it is the north star that illuminates the direction of travel that has been chosen. This overarching direction brings the team together, instilling a shared sense of purpose and belonging. It prompts crucial questions: Why do we exist as a team, and in what ways do we generate meaningful value for our company? The vision provides answers.

Second, the vision operates as an aspirational blueprint, articulating the desired future state of the team. It is not merely a reflection of the current status quo, but a bold declaration of what excellence could look like within a specific domain. By encouraging ambition and daring to look beyond the immediate, the vision challenges individuals and the collective to surpass the ordinary and strive for outstanding achievements.

At its core, the vision functions as the ultimate reference point for strategic decision making. It forms the bedrock upon which leaders devise cohesive strategies and actionable plans. Every decision made by a team member can be measured against the vision, ensuring alignment with the organization's overarching goals. This clarity empowers people to prioritize tasks effectively, recognizing that those contributing directly to the fulfilment of the vision are, by definition, strategic priorities.

Perhaps most significantly, the vision offers team members a sense of purpose and clarity in expressing their unique contribution to organizational success. This is embodied in the mission statement. The mission statement is a personalized, yet abstract, declaration that captures how each individual brings the vision to life through their work. The mission statement bridges the gap between the collective ambition of the vision and the tangible actions of each team member, reinforcing both personal accountability and collective progress.

Famously, and often feared, Steve Jobs, co-founder and then CEO of Apple, was known for engaging employees regularly in the elevator on his morning routine and asked them, directly and without warning, what they do in the organization. Shellshocked and caught off-guard, many were only able to produce generic answers like "I work in marketing". Apparently, Jobs was not impressed. "Marketing? I got plenty of those, I don't need you. You are fired!"

When he returned to a struggling Apple in 1997, Steve Jobs was on a mission to refocus the company on its core values. Jobs created a novel vision for Apple with an internal and external component. Internally, he demanded the team to think differently. He didn't see Apple as a computer company but, as impressively illustrated in the 1997 Apple commercial "Think Different", as a brand for "the crazy ones, the misfits, the rebels, the troublemakers ... because the people who are crazy enough to think that they can change the world are the ones who do".[1]

It was not about selling computers on technical specifications but about selling a lifestyle and philosophy, creating an emotional connection with the company and its products. Externally, Jobs' vision was about creating "insanely great products". Jobs put the consumer in the center of his vision. Innovative but intuitive and easy-to-operate products with a beautiful design. Not ugly machines but pieces of art to which consumers build an emotional connection.

Back to the elevator encounter. Jobs, already a Silicon Valley legend, was known for his hands-on approach and uncompromising pursuit of excellence. Wherever possible, he cut through corporate hierarchy and bureaucracy and engaged with employees directly. The purpose of the elevator encounter was for Jobs to understand whether the person's role was essential to Apple's new strategy and contributing to his vision. At the same time, Jobs wanted to assess whether the employee was able to articulate their purpose and value to the company in a clear, concise, and passionate way. A weak or confused answer could be (and often was) a career-ending move.

And this is where the mission statement comes into play. Rather than saying "I work in marketing", employees who understood and embraced Apple's vision would respond: "At Apple, we do things differently. My mission is to learn and evaluate consumer demands and apply them to design, product utility, and communication, for a unique consumer experience."

When it comes to living the mission statement, nobody was better at it than my former Israeli colleagues. Maybe it was because they all spent time in the military together or because they heavily promoted (and highly appreciated) behaviors like accountability, initiative, and efficiency. As a team, they developed a vision for their business based on the corporate vision. Every team member then defined an individual mission statement in clear and concise terms as to how they contribute to the jointly developed vision. It not only became their elevator speech but was their flight path with concrete objectives and milestones. "If we get this right, nobody needs a boss", they famously said. The mission statement was purpose and value creation lever. And, in case challenged by Steve Jobs, their job guarantee.

Purpose as the basis for the vision

The vision is more than a simple, forward-looking statement. It is something that is deeply rooted in the organization and its values. It is more than a pathway to profit maximization and shareholder value. Purpose-driven visions provide answers to core existential questions of the team, its *raison d`être*. With intellectual honesty and sincerity, not using simple "brands with purpose" labels.

The concept of purpose-driven vision goes back to Jim Collins and Jerry Porras.[2] Collins and Porras conducted a six-year study exploring what makes companies truly "visionary" and why some companies thrive for decades while others fade away. The central thesis of Collins and Porras is that great and lasting companies are not a result of a single brilliant idea, a groundbreaking innovation, or charismatic leaders. Truly visionary companies have a purpose that consistently and continuously creates value for society beyond short-term financial gains and profit maximization. Visionary companies understand this purpose, putting it in the center of their strategy and are able to articulate a purpose-driven vision internally and externally. This purpose-rooted vision stands the test of time and continues to be relevant as it is intertwined with the mere reason of the organization's existence. This allows companies to adapt to a changing world while staying true to their value.

Here are examples of companies that commit to a purpose-driven vision, which they bring to life as follows:

Table 1: Purpose-built companies.

	Apple	Tesla	Nike	IKEA	Patagonia
Purpose	We do things differently	We accelerate the world's transition to sustain-able energy	We bring inspiration and innovation to every athlete in the world	We create a better everyday life for many people	We save our home planet
How	We are consumer-centric, innovative and focus on beau-tiful designs	We make EVs superior in perform-ance, tech-nology, consumer-utility, and design	We put athletes and perform-ance at the heart of the company and deliver emotional connection through (sports) marketing	We provide functional, well-designed home products at low prices. simplicity as authentic scandina-vian lifestyle	We use sustain-able materials, promote repair over replace-ment, and donate parts of our profits to environ-mental causes
What	We are a computer company	We are a car company	We are a sporting goods company	We are a furniture company	We are an outdoor clothing company

Key considerations for the vision statement

It is one of the key responsibilities of legal leaders to give the team an inspirational, relevant, and compelling vision. Something that speaks to the head and to the heart. Something intelligent and accurate but also short enough to be remembered (the power of repetition) and emotionally connecting. Something that gets you out of bed on a Monday morning.

Few of us are chosen and able to define the vision alone. Leaders are responsible for the process of outcome but are best advised if they use the collective intelligence of the team when defining the vision. Besides, I truly believe that you only own what you helped to build. Therefore, early involvement of the team is a key success factor for later alignment and passionate execution. But in light of its fundamental importance, leaders should not make the definition of the vision a popularity contest. There are certain non-negotiables like purpose and excellence. Leaders need to set ambitious expectations, continuously challenge the team, be practical and relevant at the same time. For the vision to work, alignment is as necessary as relevance and communication. The vision must be something that the team can remember easily – get rid of legal jargon and legal drafting. The easier the better. And yet delivering on its core.

In summary, successful business visions should embody the following elements in order to deliver its intended purpose:

- The vision is *purpose-driven* and articulates the specific *value-creation proposition* of the team. It answers why we are here and of key importance for the organization. The vision should also highlight what is the "core work product" of the team, what is it that drives the highest value and has the highest impact.
- The vision is the *flight path* and *compass* of the organization. It should define the general direction of travel grounded in core values. Where do we see the team and ourselves in three years from now? What does excellence in collaboration and on substance look like? Where are role models that we inspire to be like and overtake? The vision does not have to answer this in detail. This is for the strategy and the plan. Like a compass, the vision should capture and point towards the general direction of travel.
- The vision is *future-oriented* and *ambitious*. It is not simply a description of the status quo but should lead the way to a better state. It has to be ambitious as only ambition drives excellence and inspiration. The vision should instill pride in team members and motivate them to take part.

- The vision should emphasize that it can only be accomplished as a team. It should define the *common purpose*, why we act as a team rather than as a group of loosely connected individuals.
- The vision must be *relevant, meaningful*, and *practical*. It has to be easily remembered, concise, and clear. It should be a simple statement that all team members can articulate and internalize. Use the power of repetition – the more often it is repeated the more prominent the vision is in any decision-making process.
- The vision must capture the *hearts and minds* of the team. That is why Apple's "Think Different" was so impactful. It gives people freedom and encourages them to break free from corporate straitjackets. It awakens curiosity and fosters a spirit of challenge and experimenting. The vision has to deliver this inspirational part that motivates the team to change and develop.

References

1 Steve Jobs: Back to basics – great products, great marketing, great distribution. Video "Steve Jobs unveils the Think Different campaign", 1997.
2 Collins and Porras, *Successful Habits of Visionary Companies* (1994).

Chapter 4: Case study – a vision for the legal team

Over the last 20+ years, I have devoted significant effort to crafting a meaningful and effective vision for legal teams. While each organization and team possess their own characteristics, the underlying principles that shape a successful vision for legal teams have been remarkably consistent, even as the details may differ. The vision must always be tailored to the unique circumstances and strategic objectives of the business. Drawing upon the principles and concepts discussed earlier, there are, nonetheless, some foundational elements that consistently emerge as vital components.

The most effective starting point in this process is to articulate the fundamental purpose of the legal team, identifying its distinct value proposition within the company. With the availability of alternatives such as outsourcing legal services, it becomes essential to clarify why the in-house legal team is indispensable. This means focusing on the specific advantages and contributions that only an internal legal function can deliver – such as deep organizational knowledge, proactive risk management, and seamless integration with business operations. It is also helpful to reflect on the unique "work product" generated by in-house legal teams, which goes beyond merely providing a legal service. It encompasses strategic counsel, commercial acumen, and the ability to facilitate and protect business growth while ensuring compliance and ethical standards.

By anchoring the vision on these building blocks, the legal team can clearly communicate its purpose, align its efforts with strategic business objectives, and inspire collective commitment to excellence. Such a vision not only motivates the team internally but also enhances its standing and influence across the organization, providing clarity, direction, and a shared sense of pride in its vital role. A business vision for the legal team should be built upon three key pillars, each representing a core aspect of the team's role and impact:

1. *Protecting the business and its stakeholders.* At its heart, the legal team is entrusted with safeguarding the organization, its people, and its assets. This includes defending against external threats, enforcing

rights, ensuring compliance, and managing crises – always with the integrity and resilience required to uphold the company's reputation and values.

2. *Driving growth*. The team should actively enable and support the company's ambitions for growth, whether by opening up new markets, negotiating robust contracts, protecting intellectual property, or removing barriers to innovation. Legal professionals should be regarded as key contributors to the company's success and expansion.
3. *Business advisors of choice*. The legal team should strive to be the preferred partner for business leaders, offering insightful, pragmatic advice and facilitating sound decision-making. This means being approachable, commercially minded, and proactive in identifying opportunities and risks.

By anchoring the vision on these three building blocks, the legal team can clearly communicate its purpose, align its efforts with strategic business objectives, and inspire collective commitment to excellence. Such a vision not only motivates the team internally but also enhances its standing and influence across the organization, providing clarity, direction, and a shared sense of pride in its vital role.

Protecting the business

From the very beginning, the fundamental responsibility of the legal team is to act as the vigilant guardian of the company. This role encompasses a wide array of essential activities designed to safeguard the organization from threats both internal and external. The legal team is entrusted with protecting the company's rights and interests, especially when the business faces legal action or regulatory investigations. Its duties include mounting defenses in litigation, pursuing legal remedies when others violate contracts or laws, and enforcing intellectual property rights when its innovations and assets are at risk of misappropriation. The team is instrumental in designing and implementing robust compliance programs that not only detect and mitigate potential risks but also foster a culture of integrity throughout the organization. Furthermore, the legal team ensures that whistleblowers are given a safe channel to voice concerns and are protected from retaliation. The legal team is also at the forefront during times of crisis, managing and orchestrating response procedures to navigate both anticipated and unforeseen challenges. In essence, its function is to protect the company, its people, brands, assets, and stakeholders – an enduring mission that underpins the organization's resilience and reputation. Delivering on this protective mandate is not just important – it is central to the value corporate counsel provide.

Growing the business

Simultaneously, the legal team is an indispensable partner in driving the business forward. Its involvement is pivotal in opening and facilitating access to critical markets or by providing legal frameworks and contracts that safeguard performance. By leveraging intellectual property rights, it helps transform innovative ideas and creative output into valuable business assets. The legal team works collaboratively to identify, capture, and maximize business opportunities while diligently removing obstacles that hinder progress. Its advocacy extends to ensuring fair competition by demanding a level playing field and addressing unfair practices that may disadvantage the business. As problem solvers, the team deploys the full spectrum of legal and compliance tools to devise solutions and when conventional legal mechanisms fall short, it develops advocacy strategies to overcome unique challenges. All these efforts reflect the "growth" side of its value proposition.

While protection is an inherent legal mandate, the role of enabling growth operates in close alignment with the business' vision and direction. The business defines its objectives, strategies, and priorities – deciding where and how to compete – while the legal team acts as a proactive enabler, making those ambitions a reality without overriding commercial prerogatives. It is essential that the legal team is deeply integrated into the business, providing advice and support from the earliest stages and contributing meaningfully to the decision-making process. This approach fosters a collaborative environment, where legal and business functions work towards shared goals, rather than operating in isolation or opposition. Ultimately, while the business sets the course, the legal team champions and facilitates its execution – always with a proactive, solutions-oriented mindset.

In matters of protection, however, the legal team's authority and expertise are paramount. While strategies and action plans must be developed in concert with business leaders, it is poor governance to allow commercial interests to override identified material risks. The legal team must maintain its independence and uphold the standards of integrity to ensure the long-term health and sustainability of the organization.

Business partner of choice

The third pillar of a compelling legal team vision centers on the manner in which legal services are delivered. For in-house counsel, the aspiration must be to operate as true business partners rather than simply as technical experts or back-office functionaries. Unlike external lawyers, who are often remunerated based on time invested rather than outcomes achieved, in-house legal teams must consistently demonstrate tangible value for the business. This is achieved through a partnership approach grounded in trust, expertise, and shared experience.

Having a seat at the table is crucial – legal must be present and engaged where key business decisions are made, ensuring that its guidance shapes and informs strategic direction. While some progressive business leaders instinctively value legal input – particularly in highly regulated or litigious environments, or in emerging markets where the legal landscape is complex – others may be less inclined to seek legal participation. In such cases, building trust and credibility becomes the first order of business and nothing accelerates this process more effectively than standing shoulder-to-shoulder with business leaders during high-stakes situations such as major litigation or crises. Through these shared experiences, the legal team can tangibly demonstrate its problem-solving abilities and contribute meaningfully to value creation.

Governance provides another avenue to forge close relationships with business leadership. Taking on roles such as company secretary or facilitating board and committee meetings brings legal professionals into direct contact with decision-makers, affording opportunities to influence, advise, and build mutual respect. In addition, accompanying business leaders on their business travels can foster valuable informal interactions – airport lounges and long journeys provide the perfect setting for deeper, more strategic conversations. As always, preparation is key – legal leaders should research the markets they are visiting, review current business challenges, and be ready to discuss substantive issues that matter, ensuring these moments are memorable and impactful rather than superficial.

To be the business partner of choice means legal is the first port of call for sound, pragmatic advice. Not by competing with other corporate functions such as finance, marketing, operations, or HR, but by contributing a unique, complementary perspective. In high-functioning teams, the principle of comparative advantage ensures that legal's voice is not only heard but actively sought out in the decision-making process. The "of choice" element signifies that the legal team consistently delivers advice that is insightful, best-in-class, and tailored to the needs of the business, striking the right balance between caution and commercial ambition, always striving for accuracy, reliability, and practical impact.

Advice as most valuable work product

Building upon this, the concept of being a "business advisor of choice" goes hand in hand with clearly articulating the primary value that legal services bring to the organization. Legal support can manifest in a variety of forms, each with its own merit and significance. However, it can be challenging to pinpoint a singular "work product" that stands above all others in terms of importance.

One particularly illuminating example comes from a conversation with a fellow general counsel. In the wake of a significant government investigation, the company in question asked why its legal team had not foreseen or prevented the misconduct that had occurred. Upon review, it became apparent that the lawyers had been predominantly occupied with contractual matters, especially procurement contracts, and were somewhat detached from the core business operations. Their focus was on the administrative side, rather than being embedded in the decision-making process or proactively identifying potential risks. As a result, the company decided to shift its approach – the legal team would no longer prioritize standard contracts. Instead, the procurement team was provided with a comprehensive set of contract templates and received training to handle common amendments, with the expectation that only exceptional issues would require escalation to the legal team. This strategic adjustment allowed lawyers to step away from routine paperwork and focus on adding value where it truly matters.

The key lesson from this experience is that the core contribution of the legal team is not simply the production of documents or the management of contracts. Rather, it is the provision of expert advice – the insight, judgement, and foresight that only skilled legal professionals can offer. While contracts remain a fundamental aspect of value creation, especially when they are meticulously drafted to define obligations and allocate risks clearly, the routine elements of contract work can often be delegated or automated, particularly as technology continues to evolve.[1] By doing so, lawyers are freed up to engage with higher impact, business-critical issues that require nuanced understanding and strategic thinking.

In summary, while standard contracts are necessary for operational efficiency and risk management, they are not the central pillar of a modern legal team's value proposition. Instead, the ability to provide timely, pragmatic, and strategic advice is what distinguishes an in-house legal team as a true business partner. Leveraging technology and alternative solutions for routine tasks ensures that lawyers can devote their expertise to those matters that have the greatest potential to influence the success and resilience of the organization.

Point of reference – the client

Being the business advisor of choice is not just about providing exceptional service to those in need. It is about understanding the broader context and responsibilities that come with representing the interests of the entire organization. By doing so, the legal team becomes an indispensable partner, guiding the business with insight, prudence, and a steadfast commitment to ethical conduct. But this raises an essential question – who, in fact, is the client that the legal team is committed to supporting?

Who is the client?

For in-house lawyers, the client is not the individual requesting legal support, but rather the organization itself. Technically, the client is the corporate entity overseeing the business or, in some jurisdictions, the corporate entity that employs the in-house lawyer. This is a core tenet of legal ethics, as reflected in frameworks such as the US ABA Model Rules of Professional Conduct.[2] In practice, this means a lawyer's duty is to the organization, which acts through its authorized representatives – directors, officers, employees, members, or shareholders.[3] This principle applies to all varieties of organizations, whether private, public, or governmental.

Consequently, lawyers must consider what is in the "best interest of the organization", rather than simply advancing the interests of any one individual or business unit. A business leader's willingness to take a particular risk does not, and should not, override sound legal advice. This approach should be ingrained in the legal team's culture, ensuring that advice consistently reflects the company's broader interests.

Fiduciary escalation duties

In-house attorneys owe a duty of loyalty to their corporate client and must avoid conflicts of interest. For example, if a lawyer learns of a breach of law, especially when an individual has authorized and is prepared to accept that risk, professional obligations may require the lawyer to escalate the issue internally.[4] Typically, such matters should be reported ultimately to the general counsel, audit committee, or the board of directors, depending on the seriousness of the issue.[5] Although rules differ in detail across jurisdictions, broadly similar obligations exist in Europe[6] and Asia.[7] While the "reporting up" requirements may not be as explicit as the ABA rules, whistleblowing laws, internal codes, and professional expectations may lead to similar outcomes. Lawyers may have at least the right – and in some situations the duty – to raise concerns at the appropriate level of authority. This could be a fiduciary duty to prevent wrongdoing, such as serious criminal acts[8] or breaches under anti-money laundering legislation,[9] which may even require lawyers to alert authorities.

Every lawyer should be clear about this obligation – pursuing the best interests of the company is fundamental to professional conduct and integrity. It is essential that team members instinctively escalate matters up to the general counsel when they sense that individuals are prepared to take risks out of step with company policies or the law.

Practical considerations – risk-taking and authority

The main takeaway is that, when providing legal advice, lawyers must always act in the company's best interests, including its reputation and public standing. Business leaders cannot simply override legal or ethical restraints in pursuit of high-risk strategies.

It is interesting to note that companies almost always have clear capital expenditure approval processes, with internal decision rights and financial thresholds determined by rank or seniority. Major investments require sign-off from various leaders to ensure they are financially sound, aligned with strategy, properly justified, legally reviewed, and within budgetary and policy limits.

However, equivalent systems for approving risk-taking are rare to non-existent. Bold statements such as "We are a risk-taking company" often substitute for careful analysis of financial, legal, or reputational risks. Ideally, risk-taking authority should be matched to expenditure authorization levels. For example, if the only risk associated with an initiative is loss of inventory and the value is within a business leader's decision-making rights, then, presuming no other legal issues exist, the legal team does not need to intervene. However, if the risk exceeds established authorization thresholds, a thorough discussion with the project owner is essential.

Client-centric legal advice and communication

A distinct but separate commitment is a deep understanding of business requirements and delivering legal advice in a manner that creates genuine value. It is not simply about providing information but ensuring that guidance is both practical and actionable. Pragmatism is key. Advice should be straightforward, devoid of unnecessary legal jargon, and should present compelling arguments that resonate with the intended audience. In legal practice, whether external or in-house, there is always someone to persuade – be it the client, an opposing party, or the judiciary. For in-house lawyers, it is essential that legal recommendations are not only convincing for the immediate client, but also for the broader range of stakeholders across the organization. This wider perspective ensures that advice is robust and stands up to internal scrutiny.

Backing up recommendations with clear explanations and sound reasoning is crucial. The depth of detail required may vary depending on the level of trust and familiarity established with the client – sometimes a concise sentence suffices, while at other times a thorough legal memo is warranted. Ultimately, advice is most persuasive when the underlying logic is transparent, it is consistent with previous practice, and the rationale for the conclusion is clear.

To maximize the effectiveness of the guidance, it is beneficial to present clients with a range of options. By outlining the merits and drawbacks of each alternative, the audience is empowered to make informed decisions. This openness about the team's thought process fosters trust and strengthens the credibility of its advice. Where applicable, it is advisable to express a clear preference for a particular course of action, unless new facts emerge during discussions that warrant reconsideration.

Client-centricity also demands that the team selects the most suitable mode of communication for the situation. While face-to-face interactions are generally preferable for complex or sensitive matters, sometimes a succinct email or text message can be more impactful and efficient. Whatever the medium, it is best practice to begin with a concise executive summary and to clarify the purpose of the correspondence – whether it is simply for information ("For your information only, no action required") or a request for approval ("I am seeking your approval to proceed with…").

It is important to be mindful of the limitations surrounding legal privilege, particularly for in-house lawyers. Legal privilege may be limited in scope, but advice from external counsel typically carries the protection of privilege, provided it is not widely disseminated within the organization. Therefore, when briefing clients, be explicit about what you expect from the audience and clear about the intended level of confidentiality. This approach not only protects sensitive information but also ensures that advice remains fit for its intended purpose and audience.

In summary, placing the client's needs at the center of a team's legal service means tailoring its advice, its communication, and its processes to build trust, foster collaboration, and support effective decision-making throughout the organization. This approach aligns with the broader professional obligation to act in the company's best interests, as emphasized in the surrounding context regarding fiduciary duties and risk management and ensures that legal advice is both relevant and impactful within the corporate setting.

References

1 See Part 4: Legal Leaders Fit for the Future – the Artificial Intelligence Challenge.

2 American Bar Association, Model Rules of Professional Conduct 1983, www.americanbar.org, Rule 1.13.

3 Section 13.1 (a): A lawyer employed or retained by an organization represents the organization acting through its duly authorized constituents.

4 The Sarbanes-Oxley Act of 2002 and related SEC rules impose a similar "reporting up" duty. An attorney who provides legal services to an issuer and has an attorney–client relationship must report evidence of a material violation of securities law or breach of fiduciary duty to the company's chief legal counsel or chief executive officer.

5 Under Model Rule 1.13(b), if a lawyer knows or reasonably should know that a constituent is acting, intends to act, or refuses to act in a way that violates a legal duty to the organization or the law, and this could cause significant harm to the company, the lawyer must take action. Unless the lawyer reasonably believes that escalation is unnecessary for the company's lawful best interests, they must refer the issue to a higher authority within the organization, up to and including the board of directors if warranted.

6 See Section 6 of *The Role of the In-House Solicitor*, 14 May 2025, The Law Society of England and Wales, www.lawsociety.co.uk.

7 See for instance Japan Federation of Bar Associations, www.nichibenren.or.jp/en and Singapore Corporate Counsel Association, www.scca.org.sg.

8 See Section 138 of the German Criminal Code.

9 Section 43 German AML act in conjunction with lawyers' regulation BRAO, Sections 330 and 331 of the UK Proceeds of Crime Act, French Law No. 71-1130 of 31 December 1971, which also contains a reporting obligation for lawyers.

Chapter 5: **Strategy**

The strategy is the platform that delivers the vision. Strategy is the high-level concept to achieve the long-term goals as defined in the business vision. The strategy outlines the specific approach as to how to get there in general terms – it will become operational through the plan, which breaks down the journey into objectives, milestones, and targets. While plans follow the business cycle and are developed annually, the strategy is the frame that lasts for several years. It might need adjustments from time to time but as a concept it provides a constant in the planning process.

The concept of strategy as a formal discipline has a long history with roots in military thinking. The word strategy itself derives from the ancient Greek word "strategos", which means "general". Sun Tzu's *Art of War* (500 BC) highlights strategic warfare through reconnaissance and intelligence ("knowing your enemy and yourself, you win every battle"), avoiding direct conflict and deception. Von Clausewitz (*Vom Kriege*, 1833) developed strategic thinking as a concept for military planning and decision making ("tactics is the art of using troops in battle, strategy is the art of using battles to win the war"). These concepts were quickly adopted in business. Alfred Chandler defined strategy in his 1962 book, *Strategy and Structure*, as "the determination of the basic long-term goals of an enterprise and the adaptation of courses of action and the allocation of resources necessary for carrying out these goals". Peter Drucker (*The Practice of Management*, 1954) saw the definition of a company's strategy as essential for management to define the company's business, its purpose, and its future. It was the thinking process that was essential for strategic planning, asking the right questions, and providing meaningful answers that guide the organization in practical terms.

The foundation of legal strategy is intrinsically linked to the overarching business vision, with the dual objectives of "Growth" and "Protection" serving as its cornerstone. These two elements are not merely functional aims, but integral components that drive the overall direction of the legal function within the organization. To truly embody the vision of becoming the "business partner of choice", it is fundamental that both growth and protection are seamlessly integrated into every aspect of operations. This concept acts as the unifying third element, ensuring the strategy is both comprehensive and aligned with broader organizational ambitions.

When conceptualizing the legal strategy framework – often referred to as the "strategy house" – see Figure 1 overleaf – five key pillars provide the essential structure:

1. *Growth*. This pillar reflects the commitment to advancing the company's ambitions by actively enabling, supporting, and driving business expansion. The legal team plays a central role in identifying opportunities, facilitating market entry, and ensuring contractual and regulatory frameworks are robust enough to support sustained growth.
2. *Protection*. Equally important is the role of safeguarding the business and its interests. This encompasses risk management, regulatory compliance, the protection of intellectual property and assets, and the anticipation and mitigation of potential legal threats. The legal function ensures the company remains resilient and well-defended against challenges.
3. *Integrity and ethical conduct*. Given its fundamental importance, integrity and ethical behavior stand as a distinct pillar. This commitment underpins all legal advice and interactions, reinforcing the organization's reputation as a trustworthy and principled partner. Upholding the highest standards of ethics ensures that every action taken supports the company's credibility and stakeholder trust.
4. *Governance excellence*. Excellence in governance is vital for the smooth functioning of both administrative and operational processes. The legal team is responsible for setting and maintaining rigorous standards in compliance, reporting, and oversight. By doing so, it ensures that business practices not only meet regulatory requirements but also exemplify industry best practice.
5. *People strategy*. People are the bedrock of success. Investing in talent development, fostering a collaborative and inclusive culture, and prioritizing continuous professional growth empowers the legal team to deliver exceptional outcomes. Recognizing and nurturing the team's capabilities ensures long-term value and adaptability.

Supporting these pillars is a "winning culture", which comprises five core elements – empathy and care, legal excellence, initiative, accountability and ownership, and transparency.[1] Integrity and ethical conduct, forming the

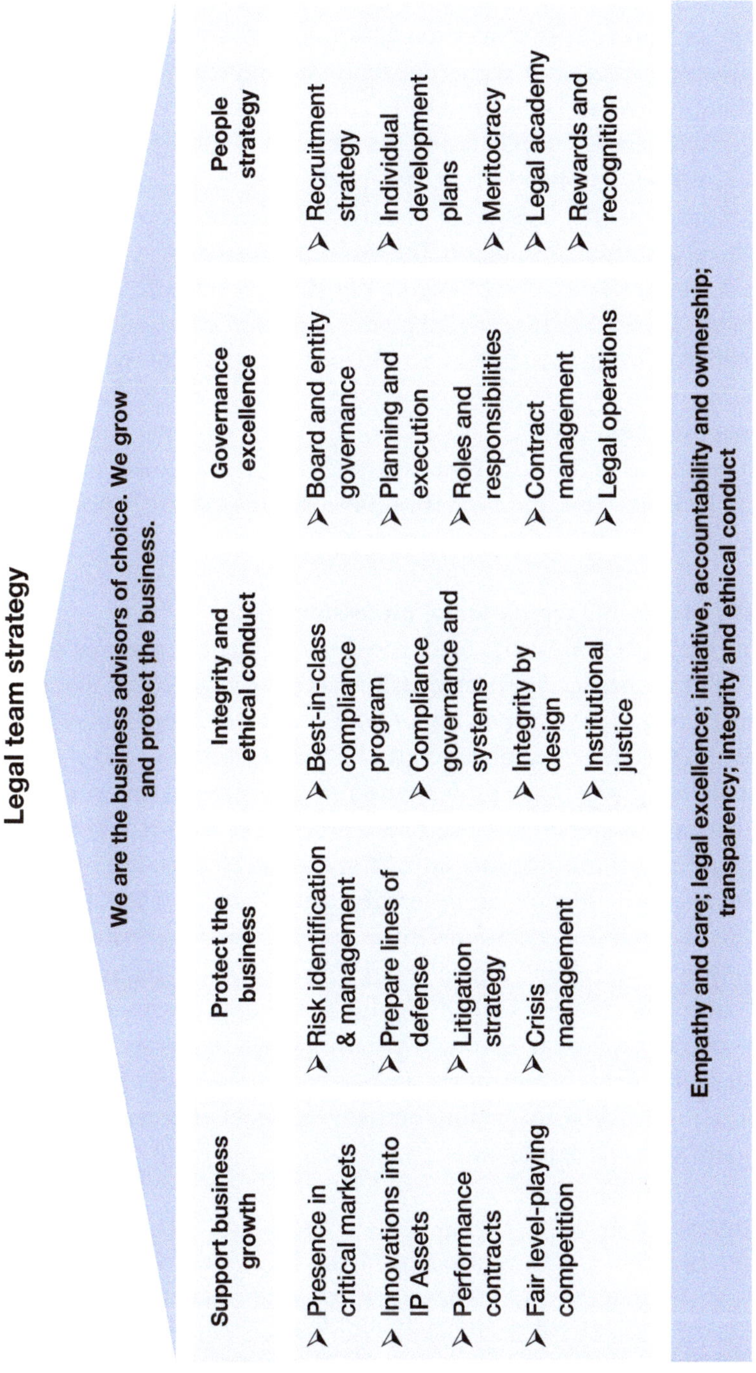

Figure 1: A strategy for the legal team.

fifth element, are woven throughout, emphasizing their relevance beyond a single pillar. This culture shapes the approach to every stakeholder interaction, drives collaboration across departments and ensures legal service is both client-centric and impactful.

Collectively, these five pillars and the underlying culture form a resilient, future-ready legal strategy that not only aligns with the company's vision but also positions the legal team as a trusted adviser, growth enabler, and guardian of corporate reputation. The example below illustrates the presentation of a legal strategy, emphasizing key strategic initiatives aligned with each pillar. The overarching vision guides these initiatives, all of which are anchored in a strong foundation of a collaborative and winning culture.

Support business growth

The strategic goal of "Growth" encompasses all activities initiated by the legal team to actively drive and underpin the company's growth ambitions, as outlined by the broader business strategy.

Integrity profile and reputation of professionalism

A prime example of this support is the establishment of a robust presence in key markets, especially those classified as emerging economies. In such regions, having a lawyer physically present is often indispensable – not just for ensuring seamless expansion but also for pre-empting and mitigating potential disruptions. Legal professionals are instrumental in overseeing all essential administrative and governance procedures required for setting up new operations. If these foundational steps are inadequately executed, the business may face ongoing obstacles, disruptions, and setbacks. Conversely, constructing a top-tier operational infrastructure fosters a reputation for the company as a serious and reliable market participant (often referred to as "good corporate citizen"). Cultivating this image of corporate integrity and professionalism serves as a protective buffer. When unforeseen issues arise, regulatory bodies and government agencies are more likely to extend goodwill and leniency, recognizing the company's diligent efforts to comply with all relevant laws and regulations.

Performance contracts

Another significant contribution from the legal team towards strategic growth is the creation and management of performance-based contracts. These contracts serve two fundamental purposes. Firstly, they clearly articulate each party's roles, responsibilities, and deliverables. Secondly, they provide a framework for the fair allocation of risks. While statutory laws often address risk allocation, certain jurisdictions or business circumstances may necessitate bespoke solutions tailored to unique requirements. The precise definition of deliverables is particularly crucial in service agreements. If a contract lacks specific quantitative and qualitative service benchmarks, it becomes ineffective and unenforceable. By thoroughly understanding business objectives and embedding these requirements into performance contracts, the legal team ensures that the agreements genuinely drive growth and operational excellence.

When drafting such contracts, the focus is on promoting sustainable growth aligned with predetermined criteria, which then informs the partners' remuneration structure. In the context of distribution, for instance, the goal is to encourage partners to cultivate markets in a manner that is both qualitative and enduring, rather than seeking short-term gains at the expense of brand reputation. Accordingly, performance contracts must address not only overall revenue growth but also targeted expansion in strategically important markets or cities. This demands the inclusion of well-defined key performance indicators and deliverables. License partners should be incentivized to nurture and protect brands as if they were their own, recognizing that brand protection investments are just as vital as marketing spend. These provisions should be embedded in contracts to guarantee effective enforcement if actual outcomes diverge from expectations. Although the aim is to foster long-term relationships, performance contracts are inherently time-bound, with clear processes for renewal specified within the agreement.

Intellectual property rights as driver of growth

In addition, the legal team plays an essential role in shaping the intellectual property (IP) strategy to fuel and sustain business growth. IP rights transform innovations and creative outputs into valuable business assets, making them critical to the company's expansion efforts. However, not all IP rights deliver tangible value or fully support growth objectives. The IP strategy must therefore define the scope of protection – both in terms of products and geographic markets. For example, it is not merely about securing a single trademark in one jurisdiction, but potentially hundreds, each with varying degrees of distinctiveness. In cases where trademarks may not provide adequate protection – such as for products with less distinctive features –

design rights or trade dress protections become crucial. The approach to IP protection must be highly selective, as it is neither practical nor cost-effective to pursue it universally. The starting point should be the business' strategic plans, focusing on priority markets and forecasting the direction of marketing communications. Integrating IP protection into marketing initiatives can be particularly effective, for instance, by enhancing trademark rights through "acquired distinctiveness".

A further challenge lies in the time-bound nature of IP rights. Simply securing rights and leaving them dormant is ineffective, as they may lapse, become vulnerable to cancellation for non-use, or lose distinctiveness due to the introduction of generic competitors. The true value of an IP strategy, much like that of performance contracts, is measured by its capacity for enforcement – investments in IP should be made with future enforcement in mind. Reputation is paramount – companies renowned for their rigorous IP strategies tend to adopt a zero-tolerance stance concerning their core assets, deterring infringement and safeguarding competitive advantage. There is a notable correlation between the creation of IP rights and subsequent enforcement activities. Key considerations include identifying the optimal ratio between rights filed and those enforced, determining the return on investment for IP protection and distinguishing which IP assets are genuinely strategic – those that provide a real business advantage, either through enforceability or by underpinning critical business claims.

In summary, the legal team's strategic objectives are intricately linked to the company's growth trajectory. By ensuring meticulous market entry, crafting robust performance contracts, and implementing a targeted, enforceable IP strategy, the legal function not only supports but actively accelerates business expansion and resilience.

Illustration through value-creation flywheel

An alternative and compelling approach to demonstrate how the legal team contributes to business growth is to map out the value creation flywheel and highlight the specific legal interventions and value-add at each stage of the process. By systematically identifying where and how the legal function supports value creation, it becomes clear that their role is interwoven with every phase of the company's expansion journey.

For instance, at the initial stage of innovation and product creation, the legal team is instrumental in generating intellectual property (IP) that transforms creative work into valuable business assets, all while ensuring that third-party rights are not infringed. This process involves thorough due diligence to confirm originality, strategic filing of patents, trademarks, or design rights, and the establishment of clear ownership structures, thereby laying the groundwork for future commercialization and enforcement. In addition, the legal department's vigilance during this stage prevents costly disputes and bolsters the company's reputation for integrity and innovation.

At the procurement stage, the legal team ensures that buyers are equipped with a toolkit comprising best-in-class contracts that clearly articulate expectations, deliverables, and risk allocation. These meticulously drafted agreements safeguard the company's interests, facilitate seamless transactions, and foster productive relationships with suppliers and partners. The legal team's involvement extends to negotiating favorable terms, embedding compliance clauses, and providing guidance on regulatory requirements, thereby mitigating risks and optimizing value throughout the supply chain.

Regarding production, lawyers offer critical support by advising on regulatory compliance, employment law, and permitting requirements. Their expertise enables the business to navigate complex legal frameworks, secure necessary licenses and approvals, and implement robust workplace practices. This proactive approach minimizes operational disruptions, ensures adherence to health and safety standards, and promotes a culture of accountability and excellence within the production environment.

At the distribution stage, the legal team deploys sophisticated tools and contractual frameworks to drive qualitative market expansion and build a resilient marketplace. They negotiate and structure distribution agreements that incentivize partners to uphold brand standards, protect the company's reputation, and pursue sustainable growth in strategically important regions. By embedding key performance indicators and enforceable obligations, the legal function ensures that distribution activities align with long-term business objectives and foster enduring relationships with market participants.

Within the retail arena, the legal team plays a pivotal role in keeping the marketplace clean and secure by negotiating and maintaining best-in-class leases. Their involvement ensures that retail operations are underpinned by clear terms, robust protections, and compliance with local regulations. This vigilance not only safeguards physical assets but also enhances the customer experience and strengthens the company's brand presence.

Marketing claims are rigorously reviewed and substantiated by the legal department to prevent misleading representations and ensure compliance

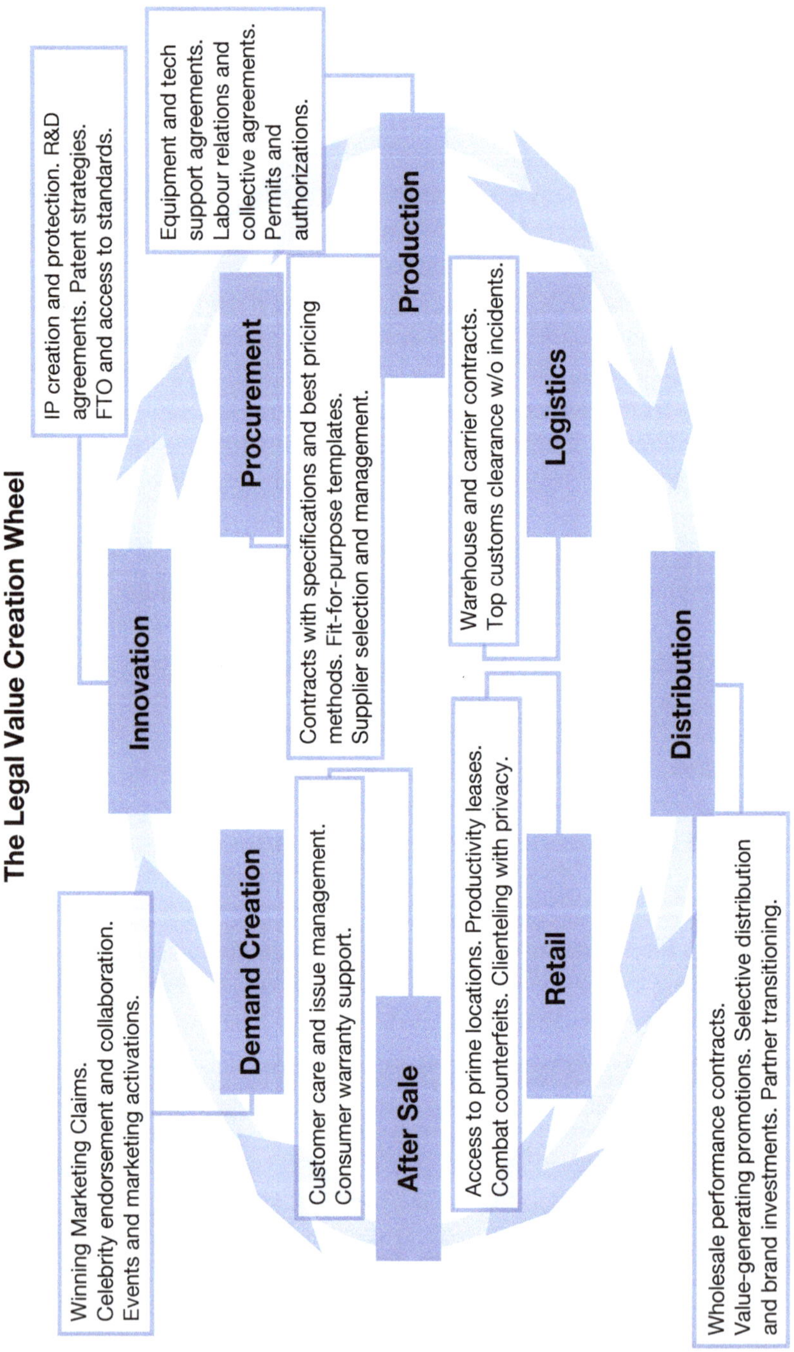

Figure 2: The legal value creation wheel.

with advertising standards. Every brand activation and marketing campaign undergoes thorough legal scrutiny to confirm that creative concepts are both compelling and compliant. This process protects the company from reputational harm, regulatory penalties, and potential litigation, while also reinforcing consumer trust and loyalty.

In summary, the legal team's value-add is evident at every stage of the value creation flywheel (see Figure 2) – from innovation and procurement through production, distribution, retail, and marketing. Their proactive interventions and strategic guidance safeguard assets, promote operational excellence, and underpin the company's growth and resilience in an increasingly complex marketplace.

Protecting the business

The second principal strategic imperative for the legal team centers on safeguarding the business. This objective can be divided into two distinct yet complementary components. The first component focuses on shielding the company from external threats – situations that necessitate a robust and coordinated exercise of the company's right to defense, whether in criminal, administrative, or civil matters. Effective protection against such risks demands proactive strategic planning, beginning with thorough preparation. Here, the corporate risk management process plays a pivotal role, as it forms the foundation upon which resilient and responsive defense mechanisms are built. This includes establishing clear protocols for responding to investigations, litigation, or regulatory scrutiny and ensuring that the business is ready to escalate and address external challenges promptly and systematically.

The second component is internally oriented, concerning the creation, implementation, and continual refinement of comprehensive compliance programs. These programs serve as critical instruments for both detecting and preventing misconduct within the organization. By fostering a culture of integrity and embedding rigorous compliance procedures across all business operations, the legal team not only mitigates the risk of internal wrongdoing but also reinforces the company's reputation and long-term sustainability. A detailed discussion on the design and practical operation of these compliance frameworks will be addressed in the following section.[2]

Framework for exercising the right of defense

With regard to external safeguarding, the legal department's foremost strategic focus lies in constructing robust defense mechanisms that facilitate prompt escalation and ensure the organization is poised for an effective and timely response. This entails the development and dissemination of guidelines specifically tailored to situations where criminal proceedings are initiated against the company or its personnel. Fundamentally, such guidelines function as an alert protocol, incorporating a detailed checklist that enables the legal team to swiftly assess the legitimacy of any investigation and to gain clarity regarding its precise nature and scope. This preparatory step is crucial in informing subsequent decisions – whether, to what extent, and under what conditions the company should engage and cooperate with the authorities.

In cases of complex regulatory scrutiny, such as antitrust investigations (which are commonly referred to as "dawn raids" as they rely on the element of surprise), the process must be more sophisticated. These situations demand readiness for both traditional investigative measures and advanced digital forensic examinations. The overarching objective is to comprehend the substance of the allegations and to implement a meticulously organized procedure that ensures the legal defense team can accurately monitor every document and piece of information disclosed to regulators. This enables the defense to retain strategic options – the team might choose to fully cooperate, furnishing supplementary documentation that adds value to the inquiry, or alternatively, contextualize and clarify the documents that have been seized, offering background details and explanations that could potentially dispel initial suspicions. At the same time the company must adhere to the procedural rules of the investigation. Removing seals or deleting correspondence is likely to result in additional, substantial fines. It is critical that these actions adhere strictly to a predefined protocol, ideally developed in collaboration with external legal counsel, to preserve the highest level of legal privilege and confidentiality throughout the process.

For broader criminal investigations, several key principles must be observed to safeguard the company's interests. First, the team must rigorously verify the credentials and authorization of any investigators before any action is taken. It is also imperative to instruct all employees to refrain from responding or providing any documentation prior to obtaining legal advice. In particular, staff should be cautioned against signing any documents presented by investigators, as these may carry significant legal implications. By instilling these protocols and fostering a culture of vigilance, the legal function ensures that the company is consistently prepared to respond decisively and in accordance with best practice, regardless of the nature of the external threat.

Brand protection

Brand protection has become an increasingly complex and critical area for businesses, particularly in the face of ever more sophisticated counterfeiters. Today, the challenge posed by counterfeiting far surpasses the issue of so-called "lookalike" brands, where competitors merely adopt similar design cues or features without directly claiming to be the original. Modern counterfeit operations are so advanced that some even boast their own in-house legal departments, making them serious adversaries. The scope of the problem is highlighted by research – according to the US Government Accountability Office, cited by McKinsey,[3] 43 percent of items purchased online in the United States from third-party resellers were found to be counterfeit. Further, McKinsey reports that a third of American consumers have knowingly or unknowingly bought low-cost imitations of luxury goods. Valued at around $500 bn a year globally, counterfeiting generates more than 60 percent of that value from fashion and luxury goods.[4]

The issue is pervasive on social media as well. Ghost Data's research indicates that up to 20 percent of Instagram content related to luxury fashion brands is generated by counterfeiters.[5] Certain Chinese actors are increasingly using platforms like TikTok or Instagram to market (sometimes even made-on-demand) dupes of luxury products directly to consumers. These trends have made it nearly impossible for even savvy shoppers to distinguish genuine products from sophisticated imitations, posing a significant threat to the value and integrity of established brands.[6]

A primary driver behind the explosive growth of counterfeit goods in the last decade has been the rapid expansion of e-commerce. Where once counterfeit goods were primarily found in bazaars or flea markets, they are now readily available through a multitude of online channels, including social media platforms. Although most e-commerce partners have developed their own anti-counterfeiting initiatives, these efforts often fall short of what is required to stem the tide. As such, for brand owners, a robust collaboration with social media companies and e-commerce platforms is essential, as is close cooperation with customs authorities to tackle traditional distribution routes.[7] Such partnerships are vital for swift detection and removal of questionable goods from the market. Moreover, since many counterfeiting operations are tied to organized crime, there is a broader public enforcement interest, which can be leveraged to encourage government agencies and law enforcement to allocate the necessary resources to combat this issue effectively.

For a brand protection strategy to be truly effective, companies must also invest in building strong brand protection intelligence capabilities. This involves developing a deep understanding of how counterfeiters operate, from their manufacturing processes to their methods of distribution and marketing. Implementing advanced brand protection tools with cross-referencing and data analysis features enables organizations to establish comprehensive in-house databases, facilitating the identification of patterns and emerging threats. In addition, collaboration with other companies that have been targeted by counterfeiters, while always remaining mindful of antitrust regulations, can provide valuable insights and intelligence, strengthening the overall defensive posture of all parties involved.

Ultimately, an effective brand protection program must be multifaceted. It should combine technological tools, legal enforcement, and strategic partnerships with both private and public sector stakeholders. Regular training for employees, clear internal reporting channels for suspected counterfeiting activity, and ongoing engagement with consumers to educate them about the risks and signs of counterfeit products are all essential components. By adopting a proactive, intelligence-led approach and fostering a culture of vigilance, companies can better safeguard their brand equity and maintain the trust of their customers in an increasingly challenging global marketplace.

Litigation strategy

Establishing a comprehensive litigation strategy is another fundamental aspect of the broader mandate to protect the company. Significant legal disputes, particularly in jurisdictions known for aggressive litigation and the potential for punitive damages, can pose existential risks to a business. When a company becomes a prime target for plaintiff lawyers – often due to its industry profile or perceived deep pockets – a robust and well-considered defense strategy is essential for safeguarding corporate interests.

As with all strategic planning, a clear understanding of the specific nature of the legal threat and the ultimate objectives is vital. For instance, where the litigation arises from alleged harmful effects associated with substances in a company's products, the risk may be systemic, potentially affecting a wide population and generating substantial legal exposure. In such situations, the response must be multifaceted and may require a combination of scientific research to refute or mitigate claims, operational measures such as divestitures or restructuring, and consideration of alternative dispute resolution frameworks to manage claims efficiently. In extreme cases, it may even be appropriate to implement a "good company/bad company" restructuring, whereby liabilities are isolated within a separate legal entity, which can then be declared insolvent. This approach can trigger an automatic stay on legal proceedings against the wider group, providing breathing space to manage the crisis and restructure liabilities. Proactive measures, such as developing a litigation risk prevention system, are also essential – particularly in light of new research that may reveal adverse impacts associated with the company's products or services on individuals or the environment.

Conversely, when the threat is potentially significant but has not escalated to the level of a mass claim, a more discreet and targeted approach may be preferable. This might involve negotiating settlements on a case-by-case basis, thereby containing reputational fallout and avoiding the escalation of claims into a broader crisis. Confidential settlements can be an effective tool for resolving disputes efficiently while minimizing public attention.

Effective litigation management also hinges on setting and managing expectations, both internally and externally. Unanticipated developments in court proceedings, particularly jury trials, can introduce considerable uncertainty and early resolution may sometimes offer a valuable degree of certainty and control. Settling cases at an early stage can also help the company avoid the substantial time and financial costs associated with protracted litigation, reduce the risk of senior executives being called as witnesses, and mitigate potential reputational damage. However, legal leaders must be cautious not to create the impression that the company is inclined to settle at any cost, as this could encourage further opportunistic claims. Instead, the company should project a balanced stance, demonstrating a willingness to defend itself robustly when justified, while also being open to pragmatic resolution where appropriate.

In essence, a successful litigation strategy should be dynamic and tailored to the specific risks the company faces. It must blend rigorous risk assessment, preventive measures, and flexible response options, always mindful of the broader business objectives and the need to protect both tangible and intangible corporate assets.

Integrity and compliance strategy

Compliance programs are designed to proactively prevent and detect instances of misconduct, ensuring that all business activities are carried out in accordance with applicable laws and regulations. Many law enforcement bodies actively encourage organizations to adopt such self-regulatory measures, including the voluntary disclosure to authorities of any wrongdoing uncovered internally. While the mere existence of a compliance program does not necessarily shield a company from prosecution, it is a significant mitigating factor considered during investigations. The quality and effectiveness of a compliance program, alongside remedial actions taken and the overall corporate culture, are weighed in determining potential penalties and sentencing.

At its core, the fundamental objective of a compliance program is to embed integrity and ethical standards into the daily operations of the organization. This involves making ethical conduct a practical reality by integrating compliance and control mechanisms into every level of decision-making and corporate behavior. A robust compliance program also serves to protect senior management and executives from personal liability by demonstrating that the company has established adequate procedures to prevent and address individual misconduct.

It is important to acknowledge that even the most thoroughly designed compliance systems cannot eliminate the risk of isolated rogue behavior or instances where individuals may attempt to bypass established protocols for personal gain or convenience. The true measure of an effective compliance environment lies in its ability to detect and address such issues swiftly and efficiently. This is achieved through a culture of compliance that is pervasive throughout the organization, reinforced by regular training, clear policies, accessible reporting tools, and decisive action when breaches occur.

Ultimately, the success of a compliance program depends on its integration into the company's culture, ongoing communication, and commitment from leadership. By fostering an environment where ethical conduct is the norm and employees are empowered to raise concerns without fear of reprisal, organizations can minimize the risk of misconduct, safeguard their reputation, and strengthen their resilience against both internal and external threats:

> *"While the Department recognizes that no compliance program can ever prevent all criminal activity by a corporation's employees, the critical factors in evaluating any program are whether the program is adequately*

designed for maximum effectiveness in preventing and detecting wrongdoing by employees and whether corporate management is enforcing the program or is tacitly encouraging or permitting employees to engage in misconduct to achieve business objectives. The Department has no formulaic requirements regarding corporate compliance programs. The fundamental questions any prosecutor should ask are: (1) Is the corporation's compliance program well designed? (2) Is the program being applied earnestly and in good faith? In other words, is the program adequately resourced and empowered to function effectively? And (3) Does the corporation's compliance program work in practice?"[8]

Adequate design of the compliance program

A compliance program should be carefully customized to fit the specific needs of the business. Rather than adopting a generic or off-the-shelf solution, the compliance framework should be bespoke, specifically devised to identify, assess, and address the particular risk profile facing the organization. This customization is essential because risk exposure varies considerably between companies, depending on factors such as location of the company's operations, the industry sector, the competitiveness of the market, the regulatory landscape, clients and business partners, transactions with foreign governments, payments to foreign officials, use of third parties, gifts, travel and entertainment expenses, and charitable and political donations.[9]

For instance, the systematic tracking and identification of government interaction, either through the company, its representatives, or third-party service providers, is important to understand a company's exposure to corruption. Even where the company is not doing business with the government, there are a variety of government processes that require careful review, such as customs and tax declarations, permits and authorization, certifications or licenses.

In the realm of competition law, understanding exposure to antitrust risks requires a close look at interactions with competitors – whether through formal consortia, joint ventures, collaborative projects, or membership in trade associations. The analysis should also extend to the movement of goods and services across borders, intra-EU trade flows, pricing differentials, and the potential for arbitrage. When products are distributed via third parties rather than sold directly to end users, practices such as resale price maintenance and other forms of price control warrant particular attention.

On data privacy and information security, the collection, processing, and storage of personal data is subject to stringent regulatory oversight. Failure to comply with data protection laws, such as the EU GDPR,[10] can have significant legal and reputational consequences. Accordingly, the compliance program must provide clear guidance on data handling procedures, data retention schedules, consent management, employee training, and the regular review of policies and practices to ensure continued adherence to evolving legal standards.

All identified risks should be systematically documented in a centralized risk management platform or register. This register ought to be reviewed at least annually, with input from all relevant business leaders, to ensure it reflects the latest developments in both the internal business environment and the broader regulatory landscape. Regular legal and regulatory horizon scanning is also essential to anticipate new risks and learn from external enforcement actions or regulatory changes.

Once key risks have been identified and evaluated, the next step is to design compliance systems to mitigate and ideally eliminate the risk of overstepping the line. Best practice is to appoint business leaders in the most exposed areas as compliance system owner. For antitrust, a logical conclusion is to appoint the head of sales as system owner. The appointment of the business leader as system owner ensures that the compliance system is deeply embedded in the business, which ensures credibility and relevance. For anticorruption, the head of logistics is a good choice as owner of the compliance system. For data privacy, leaders of HR and consumer marketing are the most suitable compliance system owners. The compliance system is designed and run in close cooperation and partnership with the respective subject matter expert, who is a lawyer specialized in the respective field.

Compliance systems typically consist of several components, including training and workshops. It should also include a clear "tone from the top" from the compliance system owner and other business leaders. Senior management needs to articulate the company's position on integrity and misconduct in its own words, unambiguously and regularly. The organization must understand that integrity is not outsourced to a specialized function but at the heart of doing business in the right and only sustainable way. Bespoke audits and internal process benchmarks are equally important components of the compliance system.

A compliance system is not a static process but requires regular adaptation and revisions. Actual case studies prepared by the subject matter expert and shared with a wide audience are an effective tool to illustrate potential vulnerabilities and showcase expected behavior.

A well-designed compliance program utilizes clear and accessible policies and procedures at the heart of its mission control. Policies are not guidelines or suggestions but are mandatory rules that address fundamental questions about how the company conducts its business and achieves its objectives. Policies must be written in plain, audience-friendly language, avoiding unnecessary legal jargon. Policies should include practical examples of expected behavior. Each policy should have an identifiable owner, ideally the relevant compliance system owner, and be subject to regular review and revision to reflect changes in the business or regulatory environment. All policies should be consolidated in a single, well-structured digital repository, ensuring that employees can readily access them as needed. Mechanisms should be in place for employees to seek clarification or additional guidance, with responses captured and shared, for example, through FAQs or internal guidelines.

Regular monitoring and enforcement of compliance with these policies are essential. Where breaches occur, appropriate remedial action must be taken, both to address the immediate issue and to deter future violations. Compliance reviews and audits should be scheduled periodically to ensure adherence, identify gaps, and drive continuous improvement.

Another indispensable element of an effective compliance program is the provision of confidential and accessible misconduct reporting channels, such as whistleblower hotlines. Many jurisdictions now require such channels, which must be easy to use and available in the employee's preferred language. It is imperative that employees feel secure in raising concerns without fear of retaliation. The protection of whistleblowers is fundamental to the integrity of the system. All reports should be investigated promptly and discreetly and where allegations are substantiated, decisive remedial action must follow. The complainant should be kept informed of the investigation's outcome. The compliance function should regularly analyse data from these reporting mechanisms, looking for trends and using the insights gained to strengthen the program.

It is important to interpret whistleblowing reporting trends with care. An increase in the number of reports, especially when a new reporting tool is introduced, is not necessarily a negative sign. It may rather reflect growing trust in the system. A higher proportion of named (as opposed to anonymous) reports is a positive indicator, as is an increase in the share of substantiated complaints. Both demonstrate that employees have confidence in the process and that the compliance program is operating effectively.

Furthermore, managing third-party relationships is a critical aspect of compliance. An effective program incorporates thorough, risk-based, due diligence processes for business partners, agents, other intermediaries, suppliers, or customers. This is often not only best practice but a legal requirement under anti-money laundering and know-your-customer regulations. Enhanced scrutiny should be applied to those third parties presenting the greatest risk exposure – such as those empowered to act on the company's behalf in high-risk jurisdictions. Cutting-edge technological solutions, including self-learning platforms and real-time transaction monitoring tools, can enhance the effectiveness and efficiency of third-party due diligence processes.[11]

In summary, a well-designed compliance program is not a static or tick-box exercise, but a living, evolving framework deeply embedded in the business' day-to-day operations. It reflects an ongoing commitment to integrity, ethical conduct, legal compliance, and corporate integrity – safeguarding the company's reputation, protecting its people, and enabling sustainable success.

Effective compliance program as part of corporate culture

Compliance programs must work in practice. For this, it is essential that the compliance program goes far beyond being a mere "paper exercise" and is demonstrably well-resourced, robustly funded, and effectively implemented throughout the organization.[12] A credible compliance function must operate with a degree of independence from senior management to avoid conflicts of interest and ensure objective oversight. Ideally, this independence is evidenced by compliance leaders reporting directly to the audit committee or a similarly autonomous board-level body. This structure strengthens the perception and reality of impartiality in compliance operations.

Crucially, compliance personnel must possess the necessary expertise, qualifications, and practical experience to identify, assess, and mitigate risks effectively. Their work should be fully supported and championed by senior management, not merely tolerated. The tone set at the top is critical – senior leaders must consistently and authentically articulate their expectations regarding integrity and compliance, using clear, relatable language. It is particularly powerful when leaders share real-life examples that demonstrate the principle that no business results are worth pursuing if they compromise the organization's unwavering commitment to ethical conduct and integrity.

Integrity should be framed as an ongoing journey with all employees encouraged to participate actively by speaking up and engaging in open dialogue. While many employees may value integrity, this does not automatically translate into ethical behavior in every situation. Taking shortcuts, such as bypassing seemingly redundant procedures or circumventing bureaucratic hurdles, may appear tempting but can easily result in unintended consequences and deviations from the highest ethical standards. It is essential for the collective – supported by vigilant colleagues and an open culture – to assist in and constructively challenge individual decision making. Senior leaders must also demonstrate humility, recognizing their own fallibility and limitations.

The more frequently and sincerely senior management discusses integrity and the importance of compliance, the more deeply these values become embedded in the company culture. Conversely, if senior leaders undermine the compliance program by trivializing it, making jokes about its necessity, or portraying it as mere bureaucracy or a "necessary evil", the effectiveness of the program is severely compromised. Legal leaders have a special responsibility to set the tone, not only by modelling exemplary behavior themselves but also by actively encouraging senior management to foster an environment where challenges are welcomed and employees feel empowered to speak up without fear of reprisal.

A further hallmark of a truly effective compliance program is its integration into the company's remuneration and performance management systems.[13] Business leaders, especially those overseeing areas with elevated compliance risks, should have compliance-related KPIs embedded within their performance objectives. This approach should extend beyond compliance and control functions to include all senior leaders, right up to the executive team. Regular benchmarking of compliance system owners – who, as previously discussed, should be business leaders – against their peers can be a powerful motivator, highlighting best practices and driving greater engagement across the organization.

Equally important is the establishment of clear and consistently applied "consequence management" processes.[14] Compliance or policy violations must be addressed promptly and transparently through disciplinary measures, which may include formal warnings, denial of bonuses, termination of employment, or, in the most severe cases, the recoupment of previously awarded compensation. Where appropriate, the outcomes of disciplinary actions may be communicated internally to reinforce a culture of accountability and serve as a deterrent to others. The unambiguous enforcement of these measures provides tangible proof of the compliance program's effectiveness and demonstrates the company's commitment to maintaining the highest standards of ethical conduct.

In summary, a compliance defense is only credible when the company's program is genuinely operational, embedded in daily practice, and actively supported at all levels of the organization. It must be dynamic, evolving in response to new risks, lessons learned, and changes in the regulatory landscape. When senior leaders visibly champion integrity, align incentives with ethical behavior, and enforce consequences for misconduct, the compliance program becomes a living framework that protects the company's reputation, people, and long-term success.

Governance and administrative excellence

The fourth pillar of the legal strategy encompasses robust governance and the effective administration of statutory processes. At its core, it prioritizes the management of the board, legal entities, and subsidiaries, recognizing these as critical elements for achieving sound governance. Central to this endeavor is the indispensable contribution of the company secretary, whose responsibilities underpin the entire governance framework.

The company secretary plays an essential role in ensuring the organization's full compliance with statutory obligations, governance legislation, and best practice standards. This includes not only the punctual submission of annual reports, financial statements, and notifications of director changes, but also the careful handling of any other corporate filings required by regulatory bodies. Beyond these administrative tasks, the company secretary serves as a trusted adviser to the board, offering guidance on directors' legal duties and responsibilities and helping to maintain the highest standards of boardroom conduct.

Operational effectiveness at board level is also significantly enhanced by the company secretary's stewardship. The role involves overseeing meeting procedures, managing the flow of information and communication between management and the board, and ensuring that the board's agenda is both strategically aligned and compliant with legal requirements. The company secretary is the custodian of the company's official records – including statutory books, registers of members and directors, as well as invitations, agendas, and precise minutes of meetings. By safeguarding these documents, the company secretary ensures that the decision-making process is transparent, that resolutions are adopted in accordance with legal and quorum requirements, and that all actions are properly documented and communicated.

It is important to recognize that governance obligations extend far beyond the central, often listed, parent entity. Subsidiary governance, which has historically received less attention, is now increasingly scrutinized by regulators in various jurisdictions. The legal team is responsible for maintaining rigorous governance standards across all subsidiaries, as lapses can expose subsidiary directors or board members to personal liability. Like the parent entity, each subsidiary must conduct regular board meetings, maintain accurate minutes, pass resolutions, and fulfil statutory filing obligations.

Operational excellence within the legal function also encompasses contract management. Contracts are not just legal instruments but crucial business records. The legal team is ideally positioned to implement systems that facilitate efficient contract creation and full life-cycle management, ensuring that contractual obligations are met, risks are minimized, and organizational knowledge is retained. This area presents significant opportunities for innovation, particularly through the adoption of technology such as AI-supported business self-service tools, which can streamline processes and empower business units to operate more autonomously while maintaining compliance.[15]

As a further strategic priority, effective legal budget management should not be overlooked. With legal budgets representing a substantial cost – especially in organizations managing large intellectual property portfolios – prudent financial stewardship is essential. A well-managed legal budget not only contributes to a leaner cost base but also drives superior outcomes by enabling investment in quality resources and technology. Cost efficiency, therefore, becomes a genuine source of competitive advantage for the business, supporting both operational excellence and sustainable growth.

Excellence in governance and administrative processes is foundational to the legal team's ability to safeguard the organization and support its long-term objectives. By embedding best practices, leveraging technology, and maintaining rigorous oversight across both the central entity and its subsidiaries, the legal function reinforces the company's integrity, resilience, and capacity to adapt in an ever-changing regulatory landscape.

People strategy

Running the risk of stating the obvious, (the right) people are the essence of any high-performing legal team. A truly effective legal strategy must place the development, engagement, and wellbeing of its people at its very heart. This commitment must go far beyond a focus solely on qualified lawyers. It should embrace all individuals who contribute to the legal function, including paralegals, administrative professionals, and other vital support staff. Each role, regardless of its official designation, plays a significant part in ensuring the seamless operation of the legal and governance framework, and the cumulative impact of these efforts is what ultimately defines the strength of the legal department.

To build a resilient and dynamic legal function, it is essential to foster an inclusive culture where the value of every team member is both recognized and nurtured. Rather than placing all emphasis on star performers, the focus should be on developing collective capability, encouraging collaboration, and promoting the continuous growth of every individual within the team. This approach ensures that the department is not only robust and adaptable but also able to sustain high standards even in the face of change or challenge. Indeed, the old adage holds true – a team is only as strong as its weakest link. By actively supporting and developing all roles, the legal team can ensure consistency, resilience, and excellence across the board.

An effective people strategy for the legal function must, therefore, be comprehensive and multifaceted. It should consist of several interdependent elements, including:

- *Strategic talent acquisition.* Attracting and selecting individuals who not only possess the requisite technical expertise but also demonstrate the behaviors and values that align with the team's culture and long-term objectives.
- *Ongoing talent management.* Proactively managing and nurturing existing talent through structured development plans, career progression pathways, and succession planning to ensure the team remains agile and future-ready.
- *Team experience and engagement.* Creating an environment where every member feels valued, empowered, and motivated. This includes fostering open communication, recognizing contributions, and supporting wellbeing initiatives that enhance job satisfaction and team cohesion.
- *Targeted learning and development.* Investing in continuous learning

opportunities tailored to the diverse needs of the team, covering not only technical legal skills but also essential enabling skills such as organization, project management, communication, and leadership.
- *Ambitious and fair performance management.* Implementing clear and transparent performance review processes that set expectations, provide constructive feedback, and reward both individual progress and collective achievement.

By systematically integrating these components into the legal strategy, the department can foster a world-class team that is highly skilled, resilient, and equipped to deliver excellent outcomes for the company. Ultimately, investing in people is not just a human imperative but a source of lasting competitive advantage, ensuring the legal function remains adaptable, effective, and positioned for long-term success.

Talent acquisition strategy

The recruitment process serves as a fundamental pillar of an effective people strategy within the legal function. Its significance cannot be overstated, warranting detailed consideration and the establishment of robust best practices.[16] Appointing the right individuals is about much more than simply addressing an immediate staffing gap. It requires a discerning approach to attract candidates who not only bring the necessary technical skills but also embody the values, attitudes, and behaviors that resonate with the team's culture and strategic vision.

It is essential to treat each recruitment opportunity as a valuable investment in the team's future, rather than a routine administrative task. Settling for a candidate who only meets the bare minimum requirements, or making hasty decisions to fill vacancies quickly, risks squandering the potential for long-term growth and undermining the team's cohesion. This is especially critical when filling leadership positions, where the impact of an ill-suited appointment can reverberate across the entire department, affecting both performance and morale. Seasoned leaders recognize that the quality and suitability of new hires are directly linked to the team's trajectory and overall success. Conversely, leaders who do not prioritize excellence in recruitment may inadvertently set a lower standard, leading to a cycle of mediocrity that stifles collective achievement.

To avoid these pitfalls, the recruitment process must be rigorous, structured, and forward-thinking. It should involve a thorough assessment of each candidate's technical proficiency, interpersonal skills, and alignment with the organizational culture. A clear, transparent selection framework helps to eliminate unconscious bias and ensures that all candidates are evaluated consistently and fairly. Moreover, involving a diverse panel in the selection process can further strengthen objectivity and reinforce the organization's commitment to inclusion and diversity.

Beyond addressing current vacancies, a strategic recruitment approach anticipates the evolving needs of the legal department. This involves identifying talent with the capacity for growth, adaptability, and the willingness to take on new challenges as the organization changes. Succession planning should be woven into the recruitment strategy, ensuring that the team remains agile and that future leadership pipelines are proactively developed. By seeking out individuals who are not only capable in their current roles but also demonstrate long-term potential, the legal team can remain dynamic, resilient, and prepared for whatever the future may hold.

In essence, a comprehensive and methodical recruitment strategy is a key enabler in building a high-performing legal function. It fosters an environment in which every team member is empowered to contribute, collaborate, and develop their full potential. Such an approach underpins the team's collective resilience, promotes sustained excellence, and equips the department to navigate both anticipated and unforeseen challenges with confidence.

People development initiatives

A strategic approach to individual development is just as essential as focusing on the collective progress of the team. The starting point should be a comprehensive mapping of the key roles within the legal department, aligning each position with the necessary skillsets. This alignment must go beyond mere technical expertise to encompass crucial enabling skills – such as organization, project management, effective communication, and people skills. In particular, the latter deserves special attention, as the practice of law, at its core, is fundamentally a people-centric profession.

Table 2 outlines principal roles within the legal function in conjunction with the evolution and progression of the required skills and competencies over time.

This chart is of importance for both organizational design (determining the number and scope of key roles in the legal team), as well as for strategic people development initiatives. The latter should be guided by this roadmap, emphasizing the ongoing progression and refinement of skills rather than imposing a rigid or one-size-fits-all approach.

Table 2: Roles, skills, progression, and succession.

Title	Function	Key technical skills	Key enabling skills	Summary of ideal candidate
Paralegal	Expert in ***specific areas of focus with routine tasks*** like corporate governance, IP operations, and claims review.	Knows this area of law and business processes. Keeps apprised of developments in this field.	Diligent, transparent, and reliable. Strong work ethics and ***organizational skills.***	***Pro in position***. A real expert in this field. Gets job satisfaction from being in control of this area and being recognized as expert by the team.
Junior Counsel	Counsel with 1-5 PQE typically working closely with a Lead Counsel or above.	Masters ***standard queries*** and tasks but elevates regularly more complex cases to supervisor for review. Develops ***communication*** and ***drafting skills***.	Curious and ***eager to learn***. Spends at least 20 percent of the time querying and ***learning***. Ambition with care. ***A humble team player*** with drive.	Junior and smart. Stands out volunteering for work or through other initiatives. Too early for top talent classification but ***potential stands out***.

continued on next page

Title	**Function**	**Key technical skills**	**Key enabling skills**	**Summary of ideal candidate**
Senior Counsel	Counsel with 5+ PQE typically working in a team or as sole contributor.	Masters the legal fundamentals and develops expertise in a specific area of law (building her/his own brand). More experienced in standard advice and takes on more ***complex matters*** but elevates when in doubt. Clear progression in development of ***communication skills***.	Still learning but has a good level of ***experience*** to build on. More ***pragmatic*** and ***impactful*** than junior counsel. Responds well to ***feedback*** and implements accordingly. Good degree of ***self-awareness***.	Mature and is noticed for taking ***initiatives*** and making constructive proposals for improvement. ***Development trajectory*** stands out. Early sign for ***top talent*** classification.

continued on next page

Title	Function	Key technical skills	Key enabling skills	Summary of ideal candidate
Head Counsel	Counsel with 8+ PQE supporting a smaller business unit, country or brand. Mostly sole practitioner but could have one or two reports.	In process of becoming trusted advisor to business leaders. Building ***advisory and influencing skills***. Shows ability and willingness to ***train and coach*** junior colleagues on the job.	Stands out with strong ***problem-solving skills***. Understands a business holistically. Not only reacting but engaging ***proactively*** with the business. ***Confident*** and ***convincing***.	Grown further in strong position, already established as senior counsel. In addition, shows strong ***project management skills*** as base for leadership.
Lead Counsel	Counsel with 10+ PQE supporting a larger business unit, country, brand or function. Typically a team leader with one to three reports.	Now trusted advisor to a more complex and wider-spread business. Not afraid to tackle the unknown but ***sheds light with expert legal and problem-solving skills***.	Accepts ***leadership*** as new challenges and focuses on both ***organizational*** and ***people skills***. Develops a plan for the team and drives execution.	***Continues development trajectory*** and is viewed as a potential ***candidate*** for the legal leadership team.

continued on next page

Title	Function	Key technical skills	Key enabling skills	Summary of ideal candidate
Chief Counsel	Counsel with 15+ PQE supporting a division, region, or central function including IP. Leads typically a team of five to ten lawyers. Member of the legal leadership team.	Solid expertise at all relevant laws applicable to business. Masters even very complicated matters and works constructively with peers and the team.	Is able to handle ***senior business leaders***. Strong ***leadership*** skills with a focus on planning and short-term deliverables. Accepts ***strategic thinking*** as next challenge. Spends 50 percent of time on leadership, 50 percent on legal matters. Builds strong network through the organization. Does not fold under pressure.	Has what it takes to become the next GC and progresses in position. Puts her/himself in the shoes of the GC and comes with constructive ideas as to how to continuously improve. Is widely considered an ***inspirational energy-giver with humility and genuine care*** for the team.

continued on next page

Title	Function	Key technical skills	Key enabling skills	Summary of ideal candidate
General Counsel	Counsel with 20+ PQE. Leading the ***global*** law department and representing the legal function at executive/board level. Head of the ***legal leadership team***, which encompasses all chief counsel and potentially other heads.	Based on experience, a good understanding of all relevant laws around the globe. Is able to ask the ***right questions*** and ***challenges constructively*** when briefed by local counsel. Takes the lead on elevated matters as ***primus in pares***. Enjoys trust as established advisor of choice to the executive team and board.	Strong ***executive presence*** and leadership skills. 80 percent of time dedicated to leadership (people and planning). 20 percent on elevated legal matters. Does ***not panic*** and holds their nerve, not afraid of the unknown. ***Active listeners***. Empathetic and takes ***care*** of the team. Fosters a ***culture of engagement*** and ***constructive challenge***.	Leads the department with humility and drive. Uses their GC position and authority ***wisely*** in representing the function externally and rewarding internally. Spends fair amount of time planning for the future. Starts realistic ***succession planning*** early.

Individual development is as unique as the individuals themselves. Every team member brings their own strengths and weaknesses to the table. Some people may possess a natural talent for planning and organizational tasks and naturally excel at project management. Others are natural people-persons and might thrive in connecting with people and communicating effectively.

The foundation of effective people development lies in understanding what motivates each member of your team. Some individuals may candidly express their ambitions, perhaps even aspiring to take on your own role someday. Others might be less forthcoming, but their goals and aspirations can be uncovered through thoughtful, in-depth career conversations led by legal leaders who invest genuine quality time in their people. Such discussions are invaluable for uncovering hidden talents and helping individuals clarify their professional objectives.

Responsibility for crafting and overseeing individual development plans falls to line managers. Strategically, however, the team as a whole should collaborate to devise a set of core development modules, ensuring a consistent and comprehensive approach to upskilling. It is crucial to establish a strong, collaborative partnership with human resources, as their expertise and experience are indispensable. Legal teams often have unique requirements and while HR brings invaluable subject matter knowledge, flexibility and tailored solutions are necessary to address specific challenges. Reinventing established HR processes is unnecessary while leveraging HR expertise accelerates success.

Individual development plans serve as a vital instrument for both personal advancement and broader team progress. These plans not only track each member's growth in their identified areas for improvement but also shed light on their ability to collaborate with others, respond constructively to feedback, and demonstrate a willingness to invest in their own development. Progression in these domains is essential for qualifying as talent within the team. It is important to recognize that initial talent varies – some individuals may start with a higher aptitude than others, but isolated talent is of limited value unless it is continuously nurtured and expanded upon through sustained development efforts.

Ultimately, a robust and dynamic approach to individual development ensures that every member of the legal function is empowered to reach their full potential. When combined with a centralized learning strategy and a commitment to collective excellence, this creates a resilient, agile, and world-class legal team capable of exceeding expectations and navigating future challenges with confidence.

Top talents

Talent development stands out in any forward-thinking people strategy. However, when weighing the relative importance of nurturing the team as a whole versus focusing on individual star performers, my preference is firmly for prioritizing the collective. The analogy with football management is illuminating – a manager might be tempted to invest heavily in outstanding players such as Lionel Messi or Cristiano Ronaldo, banking on their brilliance to deliver results. Alternatively, the manager could choose to invest in the broader squad, deliberately forgoing the notion of the superstar and placing the group at the heart of their tactical philosophy. I align with the latter approach.

This philosophy mirrors the principles of "total football" – a concept championed by the Ajax, Barcelona, and Dutch national team football coach Rinus Michels and his captain Johan Cruyff during the 1970s. At its core, total football is about engaging the collective with agility and adaptability for the entirety of the game.

In conventional football, the game operates within a fixed formation comprising a goalkeeper, defenders, midfielders, and forwards. Each player's position essentially defines their role and identity. For example, a "right back" refers to a defender stationed on the right flank, tasked specifically with protecting that zone and marking designated opponents. Under this traditional approach, it was deemed tactically irresponsible for a defender to venture forward all the way to the opposing goal, as this would leave their defensive position exposed and unattended. Similarly, defensive duties were not expected of attackers, who were meant to remain advanced, ready to receive passes from midfielders. It was considered improper for forwards to drop back, as this would leave crucial attacking roles unfilled, jeopardizing the team's ability to counterattack.

Total football broke with this rigid assignment of roles and responsibilities. Every player shares responsibility for both attacking and defending. Roles are now fluid, enabling individuals to take initiative and to seize opportunities as and wherever they arise. Proactively thinking teammates are stepping in seamlessly to cover vacated positions.

The system depends on collective intelligence, versatility, and mutual trust. The entire team is working in concert to expand the pitch during attacks and compress space defensively to restrict the opposition. Players accept responsibility for the entire play and not only for their assigned position. This requires players not only to be agile in their physical play but also in their way of thinking. As opportunities arise, players must not only anticipate how to capture them swiftly but also the ripple-effect on the game as positions rotate during the play. This results in a collective sense of responsibility. The ultimate objective is to deliver (and win) the game, not only to play brilliantly on their assigned position. Total football has limited space for superstars. Success in this model is only possible through a shared commitment to the collective, where individual brilliance is channeled for the benefit of the whole.

Translating these lessons to the development of legal teams, the emphasis should not be on identifying and grooming solitary stars at the expense of the wider group. Talent development is not a quest to select and groom the next general counsel. Instead, the focus must be on fostering an environment where the collective effort is recognized, nurtured, and celebrated. The aim is to build a team in which everyone is empowered to contribute, adapt, and support one another, amplifying overall performance.

Those who truly grasp and embody the principles of collective success, becoming informal "ring leaders" on the field, should indeed be encouraged and offered further development opportunities. However, these opportunities should be designed not to set them apart as individual luminaries, but to reinforce their role within the team dynamic. By doing so, their growth and learning serve as catalysts for wider team development, ensuring that advancements benefit everyone. This approach creates a virtuous cycle, where individual progression and team evolution go hand in hand, ultimately resulting in a high-performing, agile and cohesive legal team.

Central learning capabilities

A further element of a winning people strategy is the establishment of a centralized learning and development platform, often realized through a dedicated "legal academy". This initiative is charged with curating and delivering a comprehensive learning curriculum, tailored to the needs of the legal team. The emphasis must be on a systematic and thoughtful approach, ensuring that the curriculum not only addresses immediate skill gaps but also prepares the team for future challenges in a rapidly evolving legal landscape.

Crucially, the success of such a legal academy hinges on the relevance and practicality of its content. It is counterproductive to focus on highly specialized areas of law that have limited applicability to the majority of the team. Instead, the curriculum should center on universally valuable capabilities that underpin high performance across the board. For example, cultivating advanced problem-solving skills provides a solid foundation for all legal professionals, regardless of their area of expertise. Developing and advancing leadership skills is also of high importance and a subject on the platform. Firstly, because developing leadership skills has an amplified impact on the team as it affects more people. Secondly, it takes away the mystique of leadership but shows everybody how to progress their career through committed learning and hard work. Drawing inspiration from recognized experts – whether through masterclasses, interactive workshops, or compelling storytelling – can spark creative thinking, encourage resilience, and foster a culture of continuous learning throughout the team.

The legal academy should leverage both external inspiration and internal expertise. Inviting distinguished guest speakers can inject fresh perspectives and provoke new ways of thinking. Harnessing the skills and experiences already present within the team allows for practical, context-specific learning. Active participation and active learning are encouraged. Team members are empowered to develop and present their own, actively acquired content, showcasing how innovative approaches and acquired knowledge are being translated into tangible improvements in team performance.

To ensure ongoing effectiveness, it is essential that the learning curriculum is meticulously structured and thoughtfully planned in advance. Recognizing the realities of heavy workloads and competing priorities, the legal academy must offer flexibility and accessibility, enabling team members to seize learning opportunities without feeling overburdened. Its governance model should embody a "by the people, for the people" ethos, with team members actively involved in shaping both the direction and content of the academy. This participatory approach ensures that the learning agenda remains closely aligned with the evolving needs and aspirations of the group, ultimately fostering a sense of ownership, engagement, and shared purpose across the legal function.

References

1 See chapter one on cultural building blocks – essential values and behaviors.
2 See Integrity and Compliance Strategy in this chapter.
3 McKinsey & Company, "Can e-commerce help customs agencies fix old problems," 24 August 2022.
4 McKinsey & Company, "The State of Fashion 2022", www.mckinsey.com.

5 Ghost Data, "Instagram and counterfeiting in 2019". See also 2016 report "Social media and luxury goods counterfeit".
6 "Buying Fakes", letter from Alexander Booth to *The Economist*, published on 17 May 2025.
7 See AI in IP Enforcement and Brand Protection in chapter 15.
8 US DoJ, "Justice Manual 9-28.800 - Corporate Compliance Programs"; US DoJ Criminal Division, "Evaluation of Corporate Compliance Programs" (ECCP, updated September 2024).
9 DoJ, ECCP, page 2.
10 Regulation 2016/679 of 27 April 2016, https://eur-lex.europa.eu/eli/reg/2016/679/oj.
11 See AI in Internal Audit and Risk Assessment in chapter 15.
12 DoJ, ECCP, page 10.
13 DoJ, ECCP, page 14.
14 DoJ, ECCP, page 14.
15 See Corporate Governance in chapter 15.
16 See also chapter 12 on leadership in successful talent acquisition.

Chapter 6:
Plans and deliverables

Operating plans serve as the practical bridge between overarching strategy and day-to-day execution, converting high-level ambitions into specific, actionable steps. These plans are consistently shaped and anchored by the legal vision, acting as a north star to ensure every tactical initiative remains aligned with broader strategic goals. It is crucial, particularly during the intricate process of finalizing operating plans, to periodically step back and ask: are our actions still steering us towards the intended vision, or have we veered off course into less valuable territory? If the latter, we need to go back to the drawing board until we are convinced that the plans are 100 percent aligned with and are delivering the legal vision.

Results-oriented operating plans

By nature, operating plans are tactical documents. They are detailed, short-term action guides that set out exactly what must be achieved, by whom, and by when. They translate strategic objectives into tangible operational targets, breaking them down into manageable components that can be tracked and delivered within clear timeframes. To maximize effectiveness, these operational objectives should be formulated using the "SMART" criteria – they must be Specific, Measurable, Ambitious, Relevant, and Time-bound, providing clarity and accountability for everyone involved.

When developing operating plans, it is generally preferable to focus on results-oriented objectives rather than simply committing to processes or support activities. This results-driven approach encourages teams to pursue real-world outcomes rather than just ticking procedural boxes. However, in the legal function, crafting meaningful results-based objectives presents unique challenges. For example, if the legal M&A team sets a goal to complete a specific number of transactions before the end of the year, this target might inadvertently prioritize speed over substance, potentially incentivizing the wrong behaviors if linked to performance metrics or rewards.

In legal matters, the company itself is the client and its best interests must remain paramount. The priority should not merely be to close a deal quickly, but to ensure the deal is structured in a way that appropriately balances risk and delivers the company's strategic objectives without incurring undue liabilities. In other words, success is not defined by getting the deal done, but by getting the deal right. Thoughtfully constructed operating plans in the legal discipline will therefore emphasize quality, due diligence, and alignment with the company's risk profile, ensuring that every legal initiative supports sustainable, long-term growth, and governance excellence.

In Table 3 overleaf is a comprehensive template designed to guide the development of annual operating plans in four strategic areas – growth, compliance, governance, and team. This template serves as a practical framework, facilitating the translation of strategic objectives into detailed, actionable steps that can be tracked and delivered over the course of the year. It encompasses sections for defining overarching goals, specifying measurable targets, outlining key deliverables, and assigning responsibilities to individual team members. In addition, the template incorporates timelines for each activity, ensuring that progress can be monitored and milestones met in a timely fashion.

Purposefully defining objectives and KPIs

Defining meaningful strategic objectives is one of the most difficult tasks for every legal leader. These objectives must eventually be cascaded down into individual and team key performance indicators (KPIs), serving as the foundation for both personal and collective achievements and performance assessments. Unlike in sales, where targets can be easily quantified – such as increasing overall revenue or expanding within key strategic accounts and geographies – the legal function often lacks readily available, quantifiable metrics. This makes the task of defining robust performance criteria inherently more challenging.

In some legal domains, the most pragmatic approach is to set an objective to formulate a comprehensive plan at the start of the year, followed by diligent execution of each step outlined within that plan. For example, where the objective is to enhance the company's anti-corruption framework, it is insufficient to merely commit to obvious or superficial measures. One example would be to prohibit all business dinners or entertainment with government officials. It is easily formulated and simple to track, but fails to address the fundamental areas of risk if corporate entertainment is not the core of the problem. Easily implemented solutions may create the appearance, even the illusion, of progress but often miss the point. Instead, real

Table 3: Template for annual operating plans.

Pillar	**Objective**	**Measures**	**Timing (completed by)**	**Owner**	**Resource needs**
Growth	Win all five dragon cities in KSA (Project Lead: Carol Winter)	1. All key customers under performance contract (V2.5.1) 2. Certifications for all new products within three months 3. Advocacy support of key biz initiatives a. Map gov officials b. Top-to-top meetings c. Working group follow-up (position papers and meetings) 4. Address counterfeits in Riyadh and Jeddah a. Build brand protection intelligence b. Build network at customs c. Combat counterfeits in public markets d. Address E-Com issues	1. Q4 2. Q1 3. Q2 a. By Jan b. In Mar c. In Mar 4. Q3 a. By Mar b. By Mar c. By Sept d. By Sept	1. Peter Smith 2. Sue Spring 3. Joel Miller 4. Franz Webber	CoE Support Templates and Contracts (update of V2.5.1) Gov Affairs expertise (plan by Q1) Brand Protection expertise (plan by Q1) Support from CEO for top-to-top Saudi Counsel with 50k budget

continued on next page

Pillar	Objective	Measures	Timing (completed by)	Owner	Resource needs
Compliance	Roll-out new antitrust compliance system (Project Lead: Peter Townsend)	1. Classroom training for all sales personnel 2. Update of selective distribution policy and implementation 3. Tone-from-Top a. CEO message (four p.a.) b. Toolkit for all business leaders c. Quarterly AT briefings 4. Update AT defence kit a. Dawn raid procedures b. Trade association guidelines c. Buying/ selling competitors d. Joint R&D projects	1. Q3 (80%) 2. Q3 3. Q4 (overall) a. By Q4 b. By Q1 c. By Q4 4. Q3 a. By Mar b. By Mar c. By Sept d. By Sept	1. Peter Smith 2. Peter Smith 3. Joe Kelly 4. Caroline Zic	CoE Support AT subject matter expert Templates and Contracts GC connect to CEO and other Execs Facilities and IT

continued on next page

Pillar	Objective	Measures	Timing (completed by)	Owner	Resource needs
Governance	Implementation of new matter management, reporting and budgeting tool (Project Lead: Will Wine)	1. Go live date confirmed 2. Training all personnel of legal team 3. Problem-Solving Workshops (min four) a. Update user interface recording matters b. Update reports creation functionalities c. Update invoicing and AP d. Kaizan (all input) 4. Reports a. Automated GC reports b. Automated litigation reports c. Automated budget reports 5. User rate of 80 percent by year-end with a minimum of 500 matters recorded	1. Q4 2. Q1 3. Q2 a. By Jan b. In Mar c. In Mar 4. Q3 a. By Mar b. By Mar c. By Sept d. By Sept	1. Will Wine 2. Will Wine 3. Will Wine 4. Caro Supper 5. Will Wine GC and leadership team: tone from the top	GC office and Lit CoE IT project team (committed) Finance project team (committed) Implement-ation costs: 110k (budgeted)

continued on next page

Pillar	Objective	Measures	Timing (completed by)	Owner	Resource needs
Team	Deliver leadership develop-ment program (Project Lead: Luigi Capos)	1. Leadership development plan for all L2 and above team member a. External training course b. 360 assessment and guided feedback session c. Mentor initiative d. Detailed plan with individual focus area 2. Communication plan about leadership development initiative a. GC message (regular updates) b. Testimonies 3. Leadership workshops a. Guest speakers b. Small session problem solving c. Pairing participants	1. Q3 a. Q4 b. Q4 c. Q2 d. Q4 2. Q4 3. Q4	1. All L1 Leaders 2. Chantal Wise (with GC) 3. Mary Muffin	HR Business Partner Funds of 100k as budgeted

exposure might stem from the fact that the company has outsourced all its government interactions to a large number of unvetted and unmonitored third-party intermediaries. Examples could include customs brokers, product certification bureaus, or planning and construction permit intermediaries. Tackling this more complex challenge is likely to yield far greater improvements in risk mitigation than simply banning hospitality, which may not have been the primary source of exposure in the first place.

A far more effective performance objective would therefore be to conduct a thorough, holistic assessment of corruption risks, identifying vulnerabilities through a comprehensive risk-mapping process. The next step is to develop and implement targeted actions to address the most significant threats with urgency and precision. This approach ensures that efforts are directed towards the areas of highest impact and that the legal function is genuinely strengthening the organization's compliance posture.

Alignment with the business

When defining strategic deliverables within the growth pillar,[1] significant time should be dedicated to collaborating with the team to review upcoming business plans and to strategize on how best to support the company's growth agenda. Following initial internal deliberations, the team engages with business leaders and their respective management teams to present its proposed objectives for the forthcoming year. Such discussions are always productive, generating new ideas and surfacing additional ways in which the legal function can contribute to business success. Parallel to this, compliance strategies can be designed during these sessions – scrutinizing each business unit's compliance risk profile using established checklists and making adjustments where necessary to ensure alignment with current realities.

To gain further insight, make a point of seeking out direct conversations with key business leaders. In these exchanges, encourage them to set aside the granular analysis and instead take a step back to consider, from a high-level vantage point, what the true non-negotiables are – the "must-dos" to ensure a successful business year. These strategic conversations help to prioritize efforts and allocate resources where they will have the greatest impact.

Planning for impact – the Pareto Principle

When crafting a strategic plan and its key deliverables, it is essential for legal leaders to prioritize and focus on those initiatives that will deliver the greatest value and impact. One of the most effective frameworks for this purpose is the pareto principle – commonly known as the 80/20 rule. This principle helps leaders to prioritize by identifying a small number of key factors that drive the majority of outcomes. Typically, it is observed that 80 percent of results stem from just 20 percent of causes. For instance, if a company's revenue is largely generated by 20 percent of its customers, concentrating efforts on nurturing and retaining these high-value customers is likely to be far more productive than expending significant resources on acquiring new, untested ones. Similarly, if 20 percent of safety risks are responsible for 80 percent of workplace incidents, targeting and mitigating those specific hazards will yield the greatest improvement in safety performance.

Applying the pareto principle within the legal function enables leaders to pinpoint the "vital few" issues that are responsible for the bulk of inefficiencies, errors, or compliance risks. For example, an excessive workload can lead to lapses in attention, resulting in misapplication of legal standards or missed deadlines. Uncontrolled email traffic may cause crucial messages to be overlooked, which in turn means that legal input is absent when business decisions are made. Similarly, reliance on outdated contract templates can lead to systemic errors across the organization. By identifying and addressing these recurring patterns, legal teams can resolve the root causes of multiple negative outcomes, delivering significant improvements with targeted interventions.

The pareto approach is also highly effective in refining internal processes that frequently give rise to mistakes or delays. If analysis reveals that 80 percent of missed deadlines or process bottlenecks stem from just 20 percent of internal workflows, such as approval or document-signing procedures, then streamlining or automating these steps can have a transformative effect. One practical solution is to introduce pre-approved work products. For instance, our team developed a repository of pre-approved marketing claims for certain products, dubbed "The Fridge", which was made accessible to the entire marketing department. Approvals were valid for a defined period and users were required to adhere to a strict submission and usage protocol. This not only expedited processes and boosted efficiency but also deepened the marketing team's understanding of legal requirements, as they engaged directly with the self-service framework.

Moreover, the pareto principle is invaluable when targeting corrective actions. If it is found that 80 percent of incorrect legal advice originates from newcomers (who might only represent 20 percent of the legal team) it becomes clear that enhanced supervision, training, or support mechanisms are needed for these individuals. In some cases, newcomers are assigned tasks without sufficient context or briefing, which can result in superficial contract reviews that overlook critical details. To address this, implement contract review guidelines that explain the business rationale behind key contractual clauses and provide a tiered system of "gold", "silver", and "bronze" clauses for reference. The integration of generative AI is poised to further revolutionize this area, as current technologies are already capable of conducting initial contract screenings and flagging potential concerns for further review.[2]

Equally, it is crucial to establish a clear understanding of the business objectives and expected outcomes before commencing any legal review. A contract may appear standard and well-balanced on the surface, but if the underlying business purpose or intended use of the product or service is unclear, the agreement may fail to offer adequate protection. For example, it is impossible to pursue an "unfit for purpose" claim if the intended purpose is not explicitly defined in the contract, or to enforce a warranty if the product is sold "as is". Addressing these seemingly minor but critical causes – the true "vital few" – can have a profound and positive impact on the quality, effectiveness, and risk mitigation capacity of the legal function.

Finalization of the plan

Once all objectives and priorities have been clarified, typically in late autumn, ahead of the new business year commencing in January, I would typically convene an offsite meeting with my leadership team. The focus here is to ensure full alignment, especially where collaboration between central and regional teams is essential for executing shared objectives. Recognizing the unpredictability of today's business environment, we also incorporate flexibility into our plans, building in contingencies and identifying early which objectives might need to be deprioritized or adjusted, should business circumstances change.[3] In this respect, I adopt a principle akin to military strategy – maintaining reserves at the central level to provide agility, while requiring each team to specify their needs precisely and avoid inflating requests for resources. This discipline prevents the emergence of opaque, politically-driven demands and ensures transparency and fairness in resource allocation.

Ultimately, the true value lies not in the plan as a static document, but in the dynamic, adaptive capability that the planning process itself engenders.

Setting clear, well-defined objectives and systematically tracking progress is essential. Without reliable, measurable data, it becomes impossible to determine whether the team is achieving its goals, where improvements are required, or if the broader strategy is having the desired effect. Embracing this adaptive planning approach ensures that the legal function remains agile, accountable, and fully aligned with the evolving needs of the business, capable of responding effectively in an increasingly complex and unpredictable environment.

Visual management

Visual management serves as a powerful mechanism for keeping teams consistently aligned with the team's broader strategic direction and ensuring sustained focus on critical deliverables. By transforming data and progress metrics into clear, easily digestible formats, such as dashboards, scorecards, or visual timelines, visual management enables team members to quickly assimilate information, recognize current status, and identify any obstacles that might hinder progress. This approach moves away from micromanaging individual contributions. Instead, it centers attention on collective achievements and shared challenges, promoting a culture of joint responsibility and cohesion.

One of the principal strengths of visual management is its capacity to simplify intricate information, making it immediately accessible and understandable.

Like a scorecard in a football match: if you are 1:2 behind and have ten minutes to play during the final, everybody knows what to do. This level of real-time transparency not only heightens accountability but also supports more informed, timely decision making, allowing teams to address issues before they escalate into larger problems.

Moreover, visual management brings greater clarity to project and initiative ownership. Assigning clear accountability for each project or initiative ensures ongoing monitoring of progress, proactive anticipation of risks, and routine updates on developments. This structured approach guarantees that all initiatives remain on track and encourages open, constructive dialogue regarding successes and aspects in need of adjustment. It also enhances cross-functional collaboration, as status and progression is accessible to everyone with the underlying request to help out where the team appears to be falling behind.

Scorecards should be prepared with intellectual honesty and full transparency. Their purpose is to reflect and virtualize reality – not to assign blame or protect reputations. Unfortunately, in some organizations, a red mark on a project is perceived as a career-limiting event. This mindset is counterproductive. Marking an initiative as red simply indicates that we are behind expectations – whether due to internal challenges, external factors, or unforeseen circumstances. It is not a judgment of failure, but a signal that attention and support are needed. A red status should be seen as a call to action for the entire team, nothing else.

Expanding further, visual management can be integrated with other operational tools, such as matter management or resource tracking systems, to provide a holistic picture of team activities.[4] Linking visual boards to underlying data sources – such as budget utilization, investment tracking, or even legal operations metrics – enables teams to correlate their efforts with strategic outcomes. For example, a dashboard can combine case progress, resource allocation, and financial impact, allowing teams to quickly assess whether their activities are delivering the intended value to the organization.

Eventually, visual management not only improves team engagement and streamlines communication but also acts as a catalyst for driving collective performance towards strategic goals. By fostering transparency, reinforcing shared accountability, and facilitating timely intervention, it equips teams to navigate complex tasks with confidence, adapt to changing priorities, and consistently deliver high-quality results that align with the organization's ambitions.

References

1 See Support Business Growth in chapter five.

2 See Contract Management and Generation in chapter 15.

3 See VUCA Strategies for Legal Leaders: Embracing Agility and Adaptability in chapter 13.

4 See Process Ownership, Reporting and Analytics in chapter eight.

Chapter 7: Organizational design

Before delving into the topic of organizational design, I'd like to recount a personal reflection that has shaped my thinking. I frequently ask myself the question: if I were embarking on a start-up venture as entrepreneur, when would be the ideal moment to bring a lawyer on board as in-house counsel and begin building internal legal capabilities? External legal support is available in most jurisdictions, so when is the right moment, in light of the growth and expansion of the venture, to make this investment? Outsourcing legal support could remain the preferred model. Corporations such as Rolex and (historically) Mars, for example, continue to place substantial emphasis on external legal expertise. In contrast, functions like finance, sales, demand creation, and operations are typically viewed as central pillars of the enterprise, and external consultants for these areas, especially for short-term or ad hoc assignments, are less commonly accessible compared to legal professionals within our sector.

There's a compelling anecdote from Nike's formative years that serves to illustrate the strategic value of early in-house legal expertise. Phil Knight, co-founder of Nike, had a background in accounting and valued technical proficiency in his executive leadership team to ensure effective company operations. Rather than relying solely on external counsel, Knight chose to invest early in establishing legal capabilities internally, recognizing that legal insight would be fundamental to the company's long-term success.

Phil Knight launched Blue Ribbon Sports in 1974 alongside his running coach, Bill Bowerman, a company that would eventually evolve into Nike.[1] Their initial business concept centered on importing Japanese running shoes from Onitsuka Tiger (now known as Asics) into the United States. The relationship between Knight's venture and its Japanese partner had its challenges, especially around the crucial distribution agreement that Knight described as the company's "lifeline". Knight had sought exclusive distribution rights for the US, but Onitsuka Tiger was reluctant to grant such terms, prompting ongoing friction. Simultaneously, Knight was determined to harness Bill Bowerman's creative genius to develop his own footwear designs, much to the consternation of their Japanese partners. The resulting innovation, the iconic waffle sole, would go on to redefine the running shoe market. However, these disputes and ongoing frictions underscored the necessity for robust legal support from the very beginning.

Recognizing the critical importance of the distribution agreement and the legal challenges it presented, Knight made a conscious decision to build legal expertise in-house from an early start. After Blue Ribbon Sports secured a pivotal victory before the US courts for breach of contract and trademark infringement, Knight extended an offer to his legal advisor, Rob Strasser, inviting him to become the company's very first in-house counsel.[2] Strasser accepted, joining the core leadership team. At that time, it was comprised of the two founders, two salespeople, one finance lead, a lawyer, and an administrator – demonstrating that legal expertise was considered integral from day one, with legal counsel having a seat at the leadership table.

This narrative illustrates the strategic benefit of embedding legal capabilities within an organization at an early stage. It reinforces the notion that legal expertise is not merely a support function, but a vital contributor to shaping business strategy, safeguarding critical relationships, and enabling innovation. As such, when considering organizational design for the legal function, it's imperative to recognize the value of having legal professionals involved in core decision-making processes from the outset, ensuring the legal team is fully integrated and positioned to drive business success.

Design principles

At its core, the organizational design of the legal team should closely reflect the structure of the business. If this alignment is lacking, the legal function risks becoming disconnected from the organization's decision-making processes, making it challenging to fulfil its value proposition as the business partner of choice as highlighted earlier.[3] When the legal team's configuration strays too far from the business's operational reality, it can become isolated from the key forums where strategic decisions are made, ultimately undermining its effectiveness and influence.

Equally critical is the need to define a clear purpose for each role within the legal team. Simply increasing the number of staff to manage routine tasks is not a sustainable solution. Positions created without a specific, well-defined purpose are vulnerable to being deemed superfluous and may not withstand future organizational restructures. As legal leaders, we have a responsibility to ensure the team's long-term viability by growing it purposefully and thoughtfully. This means that every job description – especially for newly created roles – should begin with a concise and compelling "mission statement". This mission statement should be directly derived from the overarching legal vision and should clearly articulate how the role will contribute to achieving that vision and making it a practical reality within the organization.

Another valuable approach is to define each position through comprehensive roles, responsibilities, and expectations (RREs).[4] Unlike traditional job descriptions, which often focus on general tasks and duties, RR&Es emphasize the unique value that each role brings to the team and the business by considering the comparative advantages and opportunities for growth. RR&Es set out the specific domains of accountability and responsibility, granting employees the necessary authority and decision-making rights to fulfil their roles effectively.

It is important to recognize that a role extends far beyond a mere job title. A role is a well-defined position within the team, encompassing the functions and contributions of the individual occupying it. The variety and number of roles required will depend on several factors, including the nature of the business, its geographical reach, the complexity of its operations, and the strategic objectives it seeks to achieve. Each role should be associated with clearly outlined areas of responsibility, which collectively help to shape and reinforce its core purpose.

Finally, setting clear expectations for each role is vital. These expectations provide a concrete definition of what success looks like in each position, specifying the outcomes and results that the organization requires in order to realize its objectives. By establishing and communicating these expectations, legal leaders can ensure that every team member understands how their individual contributions support the broader business strategy, fostering a sense of engagement and shared purpose across the legal function.

Fully integrated legal team

The legal team delivers the greatest value when it operates as a truly cohesive and fully integrated unit. In this context, intellectual property (IP) should not be viewed as a standalone discipline, but rather as a fundamental component woven into the fabric of legal service delivery. My experience has shown that significant advantages are gained by pairing commercial lawyers with their IP counterparts and situating them in close proximity, ideally within the same office environment. This arrangement, particularly effective at senior level, fosters a dynamic exchange of information and insights. Both commercial and IP lawyers frequently encounter overlapping business challenges, albeit from different perspectives – the commercial lawyer addresses contractual and transactional matters, while the IP specialist focuses on protecting and leveraging intangible assets. By collaborating closely, they are able to formulate comprehensive, strategic legal solutions for the business, drawing on the full breadth of legal expertise and ensuring that all available legal mechanisms are considered and utilized.

A similar principle applies to the compliance function. While it is prudent for good governance to ensure the independence of the compliance role, such as having the chief compliance officer report directly to the audit committee, this structural separation should not lead to operational isolation. For the organization to function smoothly and avoid unnecessary friction, it is imperative that the compliance team's services are deeply integrated into the ongoing work and strategic planning of the legal department. When compliance operates in a silo, separate from legal, it almost inevitably results in misunderstandings, misaligned priorities, and operational disruption. Conversely, a fully integrated approach ensures that compliance considerations are woven into the business' legal strategy from the outset, supporting better risk management, consistent communication, and a unified direction across governance, legal, and business objectives.

Ultimately, the most effective legal teams are those that foster a culture of collaboration, encourage the sharing of expertise across different legal disciplines, and break down barriers between related functions such as IP, commercial law, and compliance. This holistic approach not only enhances the team's ability to address complex business challenges but also strengthens its contribution to organizational success by delivering more robust, well-rounded legal solutions.

Efficiency by design – the comparative advantage model

The principles of absolute and comparative advantage serve as foundational frameworks for designing the structure of high-performing legal teams. By applying these economic concepts, legal leaders are better equipped to determine not only who possesses the highest proficiency for a specific task (absolute advantage), but also who can undertake it at the lowest opportunity cost (comparative advantage). This nuanced perspective guides the allocation of work in a way that maximizes team productivity and ensures that each member operates where they add the greatest value.

In practical terms, incorporating these models during the organizational design phase enables legal teams to achieve greater efficiency and effectiveness. Rather than defaulting to assigning tasks solely based on seniority or expertise, leaders can strategically delegate responsibilities so that routine or lower-value matters are handled by those whose opportunity costs are lowest (typically more junior staff), while reserving complex or high-stakes work for senior lawyers. This approach not only optimizes resource deployment but also reduces costs and enhances the agility and competitiveness of the legal function.

Moreover, embedding the principles of comparative advantage within the legal team's structure fosters a culture of purposeful collaboration and professional growth. Team members are empowered to take on meaningful responsibilities aligned with their strengths and developmental goals, while senior lawyers can focus on leadership and complex issues where their expertise is most impactful. Ultimately, this results in a legal team that is not only more productive and cost-effective, but also better positioned to deliver superior advice to the business.

The comparative advantage model explained

Originating as a theory in international trade,[5] the principle of comparative advantage has since gained significant traction in management and organizational theory.[6] The model posits that individuals, teams, or organizations will achieve greater collective benefit by concentrating efforts on activities where they have the lowest opportunity cost, rather than trying to excel at everything themselves. Opportunity cost is the key metric here, as it represents the value of what is sacrificed in order to pursue a particular activity.

To illustrate, imagine a senior partner in a law firm who is not only an exceptional lawyer but also possesses a remarkable talent for designing visually compelling presentation slides. While this senior partner may be the best in the firm at both legal work and slide design (holding the absolute advantage in both), the time spent on designing slides comes at a steep opportunity cost – namely, the loss of billable hours that could be devoted to high-value legal matters. By comparison, an assistant, whose primary role is administrative support, incurs a much lower opportunity cost in preparing slides. Therefore, even if the assistant is less skilled at slide design, the comparative advantage lies with him or her and it is more efficient for the senior partner to delegate this task and focus on core responsibilities. Realizing this cost advantage, the senior partner is best advised to train the assistant in slide design, transferring this knowledge and expertise rather than continue what he or she is doing.

Practical considerations

Several important lessons emerge from applying these economic models to legal team design. Firstly, as legal leaders, our greatest value is realized when we concentrate on guiding and developing our teams, rather than becoming involved in every operational detail ourselves. Taking on tasks that can be efficiently managed by others with lower opportunity costs detracts from our ability to lead effectively. Secondly, the structure of the legal team should be designed to maximize these efficiency gains. Senior lawyers, whose expertise is most valuable in complex or high-stakes matters, should be reserved for such cases, while more routine or standard matters should be handled by junior lawyers, paralegals, or technology. This approach ensures that all team members are engaged according to their strengths and the relative value of their time.

It is also critical to recognize that client-facing responsibilities should not rest exclusively with legal leaders. Instead, junior lawyers and paralegals should be empowered to interact with clients and manage new matters, fostering their development and distributing workload more evenly. This mirrors the structure of a surgical team – junior colleagues and assistants handle standard procedures, but when complications arise, they call upon senior surgeons whose expertise is required for the most challenging aspects. Once the critical intervention is completed, responsibility returns to the original team for ongoing care. Ultimately, the goal is to build a team that operates with lower overall opportunity costs than competitors. Achieving this requires a culture of open collaboration, transparency, and the intelligent allocation of resources and tools to support effective teamwork in practice.

Another consideration is where to deploy your most experienced and senior legal professionals. Logically, one might be tempted to assign top talent to the most visible or profitable areas. However, if these areas are legally straightforward, well-controlled, and carry minimal risk, it may be more impactful to place your legal "superstars" where they can prevent business disruption, mitigate significant risks, or protect the organization's reputation. In other words, legal resources should be allocated where they can make the greatest difference, not just where the business is most lucrative.

While organizational structure is essential, flexibility must also be built into the design to allow for dynamic allocation of work. For example, should all transactional work automatically go to a specialized M&A legal team, or should business-facing lawyers handle smaller transactions such as the acquisition of a single asset or a minor supplier? Often, a comparative advantage analysis reveals that it is more efficient and rewarding for business lawyers to manage straightforward transactions, reserving the M&A team for larger, more complex deals. This not only optimizes resource allocation but also provides valuable growth opportunities for less specialized lawyers.

The principle of comparative advantage extends to complex, cross-jurisdictional matters as well. Consider a partner dispute in the Middle East: should the case be led by the central business lead lawyer, who is regularly advising the leadership team of this business at HQ, is deeply familiar with the company's strategy but inexperienced in local law, or by a regional lawyer, who knows the legal landscape but less about the business' broader objectives? The answer lies in teamwork – a collaborative approach allows both sets of expertise to be leveraged, with the lead role determined by organizational skills and the ability to coordinate a successful outcome.

Similarly, when it comes to routine compliance training, does it make sense to have your highly specialized antitrust counsel deliver every session, or should general business lawyers take the lead? From a comparative advantage perspective, business lawyers are well-suited to provide standard training, while the specialist's time is best reserved for advanced topics or particularly complex situations.

In summary, applying the principles of absolute and comparative advantage to legal team design promotes a more efficient, flexible, and collaborative working environment. It ensures that everyone, from senior legal leaders to junior staff, focuses their efforts where they can contribute the most value, both for the team and the wider organization. In this dimension, the principle of comparative advantage goes far beyond organizational design. It is a very valuable tool when considering assigning projects to the team or deploying personnel resources to the most critical areas. This approach not only enhances individual job satisfaction and professional growth but also significantly strengthens the legal team's overall effectiveness and impact.

Roles, skills, progression, and succession

As legal leaders, our responsibility extends beyond assigning tasks or delineating roles within our teams. We must thoughtfully define not only the specific responsibilities attached to each role but also the critical skills required for success and how these skills should evolve as team members progress in their careers. This process is more than a paperwork exercise. It is a foundational element in building a high-performing, resilient legal function. The Eisenhower principle is particularly instructive here – it reminds us that while planning is indispensable, the details of any plan may quickly become outmoded if the business environment or team composition shifts unexpectedly.[7] However, it is the act of planning itself – carefully considering what is necessary to succeed in each role and to foster meaningful career progression – that is truly valuable. By rigorously identifying the fundamental building blocks of each position, you create a flexible framework that can be readily adapted when roles, titles, or team structures inevitably change.

Titles, though sometimes underestimated, play a significant role in team dynamics and individual motivation. While some may not be particularly concerned with titles, for many colleagues they serve as an important marker of professional progress and recognition. If you fail to establish a clear structure, team members may invent their own titles, which can lead to confusion and potentially misrepresent the nature of their responsibilities. Moreover, fairness dictates that individuals performing substantially the same role should share the same title.

By sharing a well-considered role chart[8] and explaining the rationale behind it, legal leaders demonstrate genuine care for the team's aspirations and provide transparency around advancement opportunities. This approach not only builds trust but also boosts engagement, as team members see a clear pathway to achieving their career ambitions. For each role, it is essential to outline the main functions and the required level of experience. Furthermore, detail the essential technical and enabling skills necessary for success in each position, as well as those needed for career progression. This chart serves as both a practical guide for current team members and a strategic tool for leaders to manage succession planning, talent development, and resource allocation. By regularly reviewing and updating this framework, you ensure that the team remains agile and well-equipped to meet evolving organizational needs and external challenges.

Technical skills represent the core legal competencies that every team member must possess. These skills are grounded in a robust academic foundation and a genuine enthusiasm for the law. However, technical skills extend beyond an understanding of legal theory – they encompass the ability to communicate complex ideas clearly, draft precise and effective documents, and apply legal knowledge practically to achieve business objectives. As lawyers progress into more senior roles, it becomes increasingly important to acknowledge that no one can be an expert in every legal domain. Senior legal professionals must be comfortable stepping outside their personal areas of expertise and be prepared to consult with subject matter experts, whether within the organization or externally, when necessary. The most critical technical ability, therefore, is not only mastering the law itself, but also knowing how to structure a comprehensive briefing, ask incisive questions, and critically evaluate the advice received. Accepting recommendations at face value is risky. Senior lawyers should ensure they understand the rationale behind advice so they are prepared to respond confidently to challenges and queries. Developing this competency requires both intellectual curiosity and the courage to venture into unfamiliar territory, gradually building expertise to deliver sound, well-informed legal counsel to the business.

Enabling skills are often referred to as "soft skills", but this term does not do justice to their significance. These are the essential non-technical abilities that underpin high performance and career progression within the legal function. Enabling skills include, but are not limited to, emotional intelligence, adaptability, teamwork, leadership, influencing stakeholders, effective communication, and strategic thinking. At the earlier stages of a legal career, the primary focus should be on learning and developing both technical and enabling skills, approaching each task with humility, curiosity, and a willingness to improve. Ideal new team members are those who are humble (valuing teamwork and demonstrating empathy and a sense of belonging), hungry (driven by ambition and curiosity without sacrificing their commitment to collaboration and humility), and smart (constantly honing their abilities, seeking constructive feedback, and striving for personal and professional growth).[9] These characteristics together define the enabling skills that legal professionals need to succeed. The relative importance of specific enabling skills may shift as the business evolves or as team requirements change, so it is crucial for leaders to regularly reassess and update the skill set needed to thrive.

Leadership in the legal team involves not just identifying and nurturing these skills but also committing to a regular review and refresh of skill requirements as the organization and its environment change. This ongoing process ensures that the team remains agile, competitive, and prepared to meet new challenges.

Ideally, legal leaders should focus on developing talent internally, promoting from within to build a strong, cohesive team culture and to reward commitment and growth. However, there are occasions when external recruitment is necessary. For instance, this is the case when a specific skill set needs to be developed quickly, an unexpected vacancy arises, or when injecting new perspectives and energy could benefit the team. Bringing in external candidates can invigorate the team, introducing fresh ideas and approaches. Nonetheless, this decision must be made thoughtfully, as external hires may face a longer integration period and could be perceived as outsiders, especially if there is only a modest cultural fit. Furthermore, internal team members may feel disappointed or frustrated if senior roles are filled externally despite robust succession planning. It is therefore essential that the rationale for external appointments is communicated transparently, ensuring the team understands the decision and remains engaged in the company's direction.

Big roles and layers of management

Another factor to consider in organizational design is the determination of how many significant or "big roles" should exist within the legal team's hierarchy. These big roles are typically senior positions that oversee a greater number of direct reports, thereby contributing to a streamlined and more efficient management structure. Creating an optimal number of such roles helps maintain a flatter organization, ensuring that decision-making channels remain clear and that leaders are close enough to the business to respond swiftly to challenges and opportunities. A well-calibrated leadership layer prevents unnecessary bureaucracy and supports open lines of communication, which ensures that material matters or developments are reported swiftly to the general counsel. But it is important to strike the right balance – too few big roles may overburden senior leaders, while too many could reintroduce hierarchy and slow down processes.

Key considerations for big roles

When structuring the legal team, careful thought should be given not only to how many of these substantial positions are needed, but also to the specific scope and remit of each. Ideally, these big roles should be aligned with key business areas, major functions, or significant geographies, with each leader taking responsibility for a broad part of the legal function's activities. This approach allows for both operational efficiency and the flexibility to adapt as organizational needs evolve. The precise number of big roles will depend on factors such as the size and complexity of the business, the volume and variety of legal work, and the level of experience among team members. Ultimately, the goal is to create a leadership structure that empowers legal leaders, fosters collaboration, and delivers consistent, high-quality legal advice across the business.

Should the hierarchy of the team end with all members of the legal team reporting directly into these senior "big roles" or is there a case for introducing further layers of management? Determining the right number of managerial tiers and reporting lines is essential for building an effective legal organization. The depth of the team's structure, how many hierarchical levels exist, and the number of direct reports each legal leader oversees will have a significant impact on team dynamics, effectiveness, and overall business outcomes.

As a fundamental guideline, increasing the number of management layers tends to slow down the flow of information in both ways from the center to the operating teams and vice versa. It makes the decision-making processes more laborious. Each additional tier can limit transparency and create additional barriers, potentially resulting in diluted messages or miscommunication. Excessively fragmented legal teams into very small, atomized groups, where each manager has only one or two direct reports, can foster silos. In such scenarios, collaboration and knowledge sharing across the wider organization may suffer, as isolated pockets of expertise become less connected to the broader legal function and its business objectives. In addition, too many layers of middle management give rise to the risk of unproductive bureaucracy and less focus on the task at hand. Mark Zuckerberg has been outspoken about the fact that he sees little value in a "managers managing managers" structure.[10]

Conversely, adopting a flatter organizational structure with fewer layers encourages direct engagement between legal leaders and frontline lawyers, helping to ensure that strategic priorities are well understood throughout the legal team and developments are elevated early. Flatter structures also tend to foster a culture of greater agility, enabling faster and more responsive decision-making and empowering team members to take ownership of their work.

However, it is important to strike a careful balance. Too few layers can overwhelm senior leaders, stretching their capacity to provide meaningful guidance, oversight, and support to their teams. The optimal approach will depend on several factors, including the size and complexity of the business, the experience and capability within the legal team, and the specific nature of the legal work being undertaken. A well-considered structure will provide enough managerial support to ensure effective oversight and talent development, while retaining sufficient flexibility and connectivity to support the organization's strategic objectives.

Ideal span of control

The ideal "span of control" – the technical term for the number of direct reports – is not set in stone. As noted by Bartleby, a columnist for *The Economist*, the answer resembles the usual lawyer's response: it depends.[11] There is no compelling reason to settle on a specific number – some suggest an optimum around seven, while others argue for ten plus. Exceptional leaders, such as Jensen Huang from Nvidia, may manage up to 50 direct reports.[12] However, as Bartleby notes, using such outliers as a benchmark for the average leader is as unrealistic as comparing a weekend park runner to Usain Bolt.

In central legal leadership teams, it is not uncommon for the number of direct reports to be higher than ten. This is largely because members of the central leadership team are generally seasoned professionals and leaders in their own right. Like experienced players on a national football team, they possess a deep understanding of both their area of expertise and leadership skills and therefore require less hands-on supervision compared to more junior colleagues in operating teams.

For other teams within the legal function, the optimal span of control is shaped by the nature of the roles and the complexity of the tasks involved. Where a manager is responsible for overseeing routine, well-defined operations, they can typically manage a broader span of control, supervising more direct reports. In contrast, where work is more complex or requires higher levels of judgement and oversight, a narrower span of control, with fewer direct reports, may be preferable, though this naturally results in a more hierarchical team structure. The experience level of the legal leader is also a key variable. More seasoned leaders may be comfortable managing larger teams while less experienced leaders may benefit from a more manageable number of direct reports.

As a general rule, I advocate for a lean leadership structure with a relatively wide span of control, allowing for greater efficiency, a reduction in hierarchical barriers, and more dynamic engagement across the team. There are, of course, exceptions to this principle. In certain circumstances like a standalone business unit, for instance, or a temporary arrangement designed to help a legal leader gain early managerial experience, a smaller team with just one or two direct reports may be entirely appropriate. Nevertheless, it is important to acknowledge that teams with fewer than five members often struggle to build the critical mass necessary for effective operation. Such small teams may also find that the time they must devote to internal collaboration, both within their core group and the larger divisional or regional team, becomes disproportionate. This extra layer of meetings and coordination can detract from their primary purpose – providing timely, high-quality legal advice to the business.

It is also worth recognizing the role of technology in facilitating larger spans of control. Modern communication and collaboration tools can help leaders stay connected with their teams, streamline knowledge sharing, and maintain standards and best practices, even when managing more people directly.

Ultimately, the organizational design of the legal team should provide a clear and robust structural framework, while retaining enough flexibility and agility to allow legal leaders to regularly assess and adapt to the evolving needs of the team, the business environment, and the demands of individual roles and projects. This should be reflected in the allocation of managerial responsibilities for key positions within the team.

The matrix organization and its challenges

Another imperative in organization design is that every core business unit, brand, or geographical region is supported by at least one dedicated lawyer. For larger units or regions, there arises a strategic decision – should a dedicated lawyer be centrally appointed for each brand or category within the region, or should the responsibility be delegated to the region itself, with the understanding that the regional lead lawyer acts as the principal contact for all queries channeled from the center? This decision will often be influenced by the size, complexity, and specific needs of the business area in question.

In practice, larger legal departments frequently operate within a matrix structure. This means lawyers are not only positioned according to their alignment with the business, functionally reporting to the head of legal and organizationally to the business leaders they support, but also within the legal team itself. This can lead to additional complexity. Within the legal department, teams may be organized either by specialist function (such as intellectual property or employment law) or by business unit, brand, or geography. Each approach has its merits – functional structures foster deep subject matter expertise and consistency of advice, while divisional structures ensure close integration with the business and a nuanced understanding of its operations.

To harness the benefits of both, many organizations combine these models within a matrix arrangement. For example, an employment lawyer based in Mexico might report locally to the lead lawyer for Mexico (divisional reporting) while also maintaining a functional reporting line to the global head of employment law. This dual-reporting structure enables the lawyer to remain closely connected to their local business clients and colleagues while also facilitating collaboration, knowledge sharing, and the maintenance of global standards within their area of expertise.

However, as is often the case with matrix organizations, the challenge lies in determining where ultimate responsibility and decision-making authority should reside – with the division (organization, unit, or geography) or the function. Prioritizing the divisional line can foster strong collaboration within a brand or business, ensuring alignment with business priorities and deliverables. Conversely, if functional (within the team of specialized lawyers) alignment is too rigid, it can stifle the agility and flexibility of smaller regional teams, making it more difficult for local legal leaders to allocate resources quickly in response to urgent or important matters. An overly prescriptive structure can become a straitjacket, inhibiting the team's ability to respond effectively to the needs of the business.

The most effective solution lies in striking a balance. Assigning responsibility for specific brands, business units, or regions to individual lawyers within the team promotes engagement and accountability, with each lawyer taking ownership of their client relationships and ensuring their needs are met. However, this does not mean exclusivity. Lawyers should continue to support other clients and remain integrated with the wider team – whether at a regional hub, within a divisional team, or at headquarters. It is important for every lawyer to develop their own area of expertise, but equally vital that they remain part of the collective whole. Clear communication is critical to prevent confusion and reinforce the principle that while lawyers may have areas of focus, they all contribute to the shared goals of the legal team.

Ultimately, this is as much about mindset as it is about structure. The concern that one cannot serve two masters – summed up by the phrase "nemo potest duobus dominis servire" or, as put by my former Brazilian colleagues, "a dog with two owners dies of hunger"[13] – need not hold true if the team adopts a collaborative, team-first mentality. If approached with the right mindset, a matrix structure can thrive, provided everyone remains focused on the team's vision and its agreed priorities. Regular communication and a strong sense of shared purpose are essential to making this model work in practice.[14]

As a legal leader, it is vital to foster a culture where office politics and divisive games are not tolerated. Team members must understand that, regardless of their specialization or client focus, they are all part of the same legal team, working towards common objectives. One way to achieve this is to define at least 50 percent of performance objective as common goals. Performance objectives determine the bonus so commonality in objectives guarantees collaboration. There should be no room for "first team issues" or internal rivalries. First team issues occur where team members prioritize the team they lead and do not collaborate in leadership teams. Instead, the emphasis should be on mutual support, shared success, and delivering high-quality legal advice that advances the organization's goals. By maintaining this approach, legal teams can combine the benefits of specialization and local integration while preserving unity and agility across the function.

Centers of excellence

Certain responsibilities are most efficiently executed or overseen when managed centrally, a principle grounded in the concept of comparative advantage.[15] Tasks that demand a high level of specialization and share significant commonalities across the organization are particularly well suited to centralization, as this approach minimizes opportunity costs and maximizes the quality and consistency of outcomes. The Centre of Excellence (CoE) model exemplifies this philosophy, offering a structured platform for delivering uniform standards, streamlined processes, and direct lines of communication as often CoE report directly to the general counsel.

Litigation is a prime example within large, international legal teams of where a CoE adds substantial value. Litigation inherently carries significant risk, with the potential for disruption and reputational damage to the business. Handling major litigation cases is outside the daily remit of most in-house lawyers and requires both a depth of expertise and practical experience. Here, CoE specialists play a pivotal role notably in defining a litigation strategy, providing essential subject-matter expertise, guidance, and support to frontline lawyers facing complex or high-stakes disputes. A similar rationale applies to merger and acquisition (M&A) activities, where transactions typically are both highly specialized and relatively uniform in nature. Centralizing M&A expertise ensures that the organization benefits from accumulated knowledge, best-in class templates for transactional documents, creative problem-solving, experienced project management (particularly outside deal counsel and costs), and a consistent approach to managing highly strategic projects which includes reporting up and stakeholder management.

However, it is equally important to recognize that a CoE cannot function effectively in isolation. Close collaboration with business-facing lawyers is essential, as their knowledge of the operational context and client relationships enriches the CoE's understanding and enhances the quality of its involvement and output. This partnership ensures that central expertise is effectively tailored and applied to the unique circumstances of each business unit or region.

Another critical function of the CoE is to serve as a central repository for best practices, precedents, and templates. Through ongoing exposure to complex matters and continuous professional development, CoE lawyers become genuine subject matter experts, maintaining up-to-date insight into the latest legal developments. This positions them to form early, informed views on emerging issues – much like a medical specialist who, while perhaps unfamiliar with the individual patient, can quickly assess whether symptoms are indicative of a serious condition that warrants further investigation.

A centralized approach can also be successful for a business partnership with other support functions like human resources or real estate. Whilst projects may be managed regionally, the oversight and collaborative input of the CoE helps ensure alignment with organizational objectives and drives successful outcomes. Close cooperation with the leaders of these support functions is crucial, fostering a culture of cross-functional partnership and shared accountability.

In addition, there is considerable merit in centralizing knowledge and skills in specialized legal domains such as intellectual property (IP), data privacy, and antitrust law. By appointing a subject matter expert to lead each CoE, with a remit that spans international or even global operations, organizations can unlock substantial value for their legal teams. The leaders of these centers are responsible for monitoring regulatory developments, interpreting new legal frameworks and advising on best practices, ensuring the organization remains compliant and competitive worldwide. Their international perspective allows them to identify trends, anticipate risks, and standardize approaches across different regions, promoting both efficiency and consistency.

Furthermore, having a recognized expert at the helm of each CoE fosters confidence among business stakeholders and frontline lawyers, who can rely on their guidance for complex or high-stakes matters. This structure encourages cross-border collaboration, enables rapid responses to emerging legal challenges, and supports the development of robust templates and precedents, all of which drive continuous improvement within the legal function.

The creation and development of CoEs provide significant career development opportunities for legal talent. Lawyers within the CoE have the chance to demonstrate both leadership and collaboration skills. First, leadership, through driving the success of the CoE while maintaining efficiency and cost-effectiveness. Second, collaboration, by working closely with a diverse range of operating lawyers from across the globe, thereby building a broad and influential professional network. This environment not only supports the delivery of high-quality legal services but also nurtures the next generation of legal leaders within the organization.

Ultimately, grouping specialized expertise within CoEs, led by subject matter experts with broad oversight, strengthens the overall capability of the legal department, supports strategic initiatives, and enhances the organization's ability to manage risk and deliver value at scale.

Shared service centers

When considering organizational design, another key question arises: should certain routine legal operations be outsourced to a shared service center, particularly one located in a lower-cost jurisdiction? This outsourcing can be managed either internally within the organization or externally via third-party providers. Typical candidates for such outsourcing include tasks like corporate governance administration, the drafting and review of standard contracts, procurement processes, and claims management.

There are both benefits and notable drawbacks to this approach. On the one hand, consolidating or outsourcing standardized activities to a shared service center is attractive not only from a cost-saving perspective but also because it can foster the development of centers of excellence (CoEs), as previously discussed. By concentrating expertise and focus in one area, organizations can reduce both absolute and opportunity costs, drive consistency and improve efficiency through specialization. Such centers can leverage their experience and scale to refine processes, produce high-quality output, and ensure compliance with organizational standards.

However, this model is not without its challenges. Shared service centers are often somewhat removed from the day-to-day realities of the business units they support. As a result, their advice and outputs can be based on incomplete or second-hand information, leading to potential misalignment with business needs. Furthermore, legal professionals working within these centers may feel undervalued, relegated to handling repetitive or less interesting work that others in the organization prefer to avoid. This perception can erode morale, leading to low engagement and high turnover rates at shared service centers.

Looking to the future, it is likely that technology will increasingly assume many of the standardized tasks currently performed by low-cost shared service centers.[16] The adoption of advanced legal technology – such as automated document generation, contract review tools, and AI-powered workflow management – will not only drive further cost reductions but also enable more seamless collaboration and oversight. These tools empower operating lawyers by placing sophisticated resources directly at their fingertips, minimizing delays and the risk of miscommunication caused by incomplete or inaccurate briefings. In turn, this enables the delivery of faster, more accurate, and business-aligned outcomes, reducing the reliance on shared service centers for routine tasks and allowing legal teams to focus on higher-value, strategic work.

In conclusion, while outsourcing routine legal operations to shared service centers can offer clear financial and efficiency benefits, organizations must carefully manage the associated risks of disengagement and misalignment. The ongoing evolution of legal technology promises to reshape this landscape, offering new opportunities to enhance both the efficiency and effectiveness of legal service delivery.

References

1 Phil Knight, *Shoe Dog* (2016). When Nike was suggested as new name for the company, Knight commented: "I don't like the name but it will grow on me."

2 *Shoe Dog* (2016), page 250: "You are one of us."

3 See Business Partner of Choice in chapter four.

4 Charles G. Koch, *The Science of Success* (2007), page 128.

5 David Ricardo, *On the Principles of Political Economy and Taxation* (1817).

6 About the importance of the comparative advantage model in business and management: Charles Koch, *The Science of Success* (2007), page 35.

7 See chapter six.

8 An example can be found in Table 2, in chapter five.

9 See The Ideal Team Player in chapter 12.

10 "I don't think you want a management structure that's just managers managing managers, managing managers, managing managers, managing the people who are doing the work." Mark Zuckerberg, quoted on Forbes.com in 2023.

11 Bartleby: "How many reports should a manager have?", *The Economist*, 18 September 2025, page 55.

12 The New York Times DealBook Summit 2023: Jensen Huang explains why he has 50 direct reports, available on YouTube.

13 "Cachorro com dois donos morre de fome." Also known as tragedy of the commons. Without clear rules and ownership, one person will assume that the other person will take care of feeding the dog which, as a result, does not get fed at all.

14 These are key requirements to work as a team of teams; see The Next Level: Creating a Team of Teams, in chapter ten.

15 See Efficiency by Design – the Comparative Advantage Model, in chapter seven.

16 See Part 4: Legal Leaders Fit for the Future – the Artificial Intelligence Challenge.

Chapter 8: Legal Operations

Legal Operations (Legal Ops) are the backbone of high-performing legal teams. This dedicated discipline is responsible for shaping and driving operational excellence of the legal function, ensuring that both efficiency and the value delivered by legal services are continually enhanced. Legal Ops achieves this by designing and embedding best-in-class processes, introducing innovative technological solutions, and fostering a culture of continuous improvement. In doing so, it provides essential support to the general counsel, the legal leadership team, and all practicing lawyers, equipping them to deliver high-quality, commercially attuned legal advice with greater speed, accuracy, and reliability.

Legal Ops offers expertise in process design and implementation – an area where lawyers often lack passion and proficiency. While the discipline is still emerging, more and more general counsels recognize the substantial value Legal Ops delivers to the team. The role presents both a demanding and rewarding opportunity, particularly for young professionals eager to work alongside the general counsel and gain insight into legal leadership. As Legal Ops is integral to the department's core functions, it is crucial that the GC provides ongoing support and guidance. To ensure Legal Ops has the influence and resources needed to succeed, it should be embedded within the general counsel's office and report directly to the GC. Failing to establish this direct reporting relationship could result in Legal Ops being marginalized, thereby hindering its capacity to drive long-term value and meaningful transformation throughout the legal team.

Crucially, Legal Ops acts as the organizational backbone for a multitude of vital activities, such as process ownership, reporting and analytics, matter management, budgetary control, and knowledge management. By seamlessly integrating and optimizing these core functions, Legal Ops empowers legal leaders to steer the department in line with the organization's strategic priorities. One of its most significant contributions is providing frontline lawyers with direct access to the collective wisdom, experience, and innovative thinking of the wider team. The principle of "think as thousands, act as one" is only possible through the behind-the-scenes yet highly effective coordination, alignment, and process design championed by Legal Ops.

A further fundamental strength of Legal Ops lies in its ability to bring transparency and clarity to resource allocation. Leveraging advanced tracking, reporting, and analytics tools, Legal Ops maintains a real-time overview of how critical resources – such as time, budget, and personnel – are being deployed. This visibility ensures that efforts remain focused on the initiatives and matters that deliver the highest value to the business, whilst helping to mitigate waste and prevent the duplication of work. Such data-driven oversight enables more strategic and informed decisions regarding investments in legal work, technology adoption, and the allocation of team capacity.

Process ownership, reporting, and analytics

Legal Ops plays a pivotal role in the establishment, oversight, and continual refinement of all central processes relating to legal strategy and planning. While the ultimate responsibility for formulating the legal department's strategic direction remains firmly with the GC and other senior legal leaders, Legal Ops ensures that the machinery supporting these efforts operates seamlessly and efficiently.

Legal Ops takes ownership of designing, implementing, and managing the processes required to draft, prepare, discuss, and finalize all strategic plans and submissions. This includes setting clear timelines, coordinating input from relevant stakeholders, and guaranteeing that necessary documentation is both complete and accurate. Rather than attempting to create entirely new methodologies from scratch, Legal Ops leverages established best practices and proven process frameworks, particularly those already in use within the organization's finance and supply chain community.[1] By doing so, the legal team benefits from robust, tried-and-tested process designs that have already demonstrated their value elsewhere in the business.

Stewards of the technology agenda

In partnership with the GC, Legal Ops is responsible for shaping both the immediate and medium-term technology strategy for the legal department. Technology acts as a critical enabler for seamless collaboration and its influence will only grow with the advent of innovative, AI-powered solutions.[2] Taking a stewardship role, Legal Ops establishes the technology needs of operating lawyers, as well as governance requirements, and develops priorities for investments. The team continually explores emerging technologies, evaluating their relevance and compatibility within the organization's broader IT framework.

Legal Ops leads on setting objectives, developing project plans, and allocating budgets, effectively managing technology planning for the entire legal function. This centralized stewardship guarantees that all legal systems and platforms remain interconnected and in harmony with the wider organization's IT infrastructure.

Such an approach necessitates centralized oversight of all legal department systems, including those used for compliance. In my experience, compliance leaders are usually very good at designing procedures and routines specific to compliance, so it is not always motivational asking Legal Ops to oversee compliance processes directly. Typically, the compliance team has the expertise required to develop processes such as risk assessments, compliance systems, reviews, and audits. However, close cooperation and alignment between Legal Ops and compliance ensures that the department operates as a unified team. It is vital that the technology agenda remains fully integrated, comprising systems that are entirely interoperable. Without this, there's a risk of fragmentation – multiple matter management and payment platforms may result in confusion and inefficiency. Therefore, Legal Ops should be entrusted with ownership of the technology strategy, with decision-making authority to safeguard consistency and interoperability across all legal systems.

Matter, document, and knowledge management

Matter, document, and knowledge management are all essential deliverables of the Legal Operations team, each requiring a robust and user-friendly system to maximize effectiveness.

Practical considerations for matter management

For matter management, the process begins with operating lawyers initiating new matters in the system, ideally via a streamlined intake form. This form should enable straightforward categorization by business area and end-product type. The work product could be legal advice, a draft contract, cease and desist letters, or litigation. Without structured intake, there is a risk of accumulating a vast repository of unorganized, never-seen-again data. At the same time, the intake process must be intuitive and swift, allowing lawyers to submit new matters in just a few clicks and minutes, thereby encouraging consistent use and minimizing administrative burden.

After a matter has been created, all members of the legal team can upload any documents generated in relation to that matter. Advice provided to the business is stored and emails can be assigned to the case via a straightforward drag-and-drop process. While business-facing advice comprises the majority of content, strategic planning documents and other Legal Ops records should also be systematically added to ensure team-wide access in an organized and easily navigable format. For significant litigation matters that may extend over several years, such a centralized filing system is vital as the authoritative repository for all case-related materials. Ideally, external (litigation) counsel should also be granted access, facilitating seamless collaboration and ensuring all parties work from a unified system rather than maintaining separate document archives.[3]

In addition, the system should empower lawyers to flag when external counsel might be required and to record anticipated budget accruals. When a matter surpasses predefined thresholds as to their impact on the business, be it financial, reputational, or overall, it should automatically escalate to the relevant team leader or, if necessary, to more senior legal leadership. This escalation mechanism is invaluable for general counsel, as it provides near real-time visibility into strategic and high-stakes matters. The same technology proves particularly beneficial for litigation management, generating timely reports for finance teams and accounting departments on the latest developments that may impact provisions or require amendments. By centralizing these processes, Legal Ops creates a single source of truth, eliminating reliance on fragmented email threads and reducing the risk of inconsistent information.

Practical considerations for knowledge management

Turning to knowledge management, it is imperative that frontline lawyers can effortlessly and swiftly locate the most current and updated contract templates, tested and battle-hardened clauses, or advice given on specific legal questions. While AI-powered search engines are a significant asset, the utility of the knowledge repository is amplified when lawyers upload documents and add concise annotations – explaining why a particular resource is especially valuable to the wider team and how it has been effective in practice. Experimenting with simple rating systems, such as five-star reviews accompanied by relevant keywords, allows AI agents to organize and surface high-impact know-how assets with ease.

Despite its transformative potential, knowledge management is too often sidelined in operational planning. When the day-to-day routine takes over and clients are constantly knocking at the door, the inverted process of recording knowledge in a transferable form becomes less of a priority. Legal leaders must recognize the strategic value of managing the team's acquired expertise and actively encourage better documentation and administration of know-how. Once the knowledge repository is populated with easily identifiable and well-annotated resources, adoption becomes almost automatic, as frontline lawyers quickly see the benefits and efficiencies gained for their day-to-day work. This fosters a culture of collaboration, continuous improvement, and shared expertise, positioning Legal Ops as a key enabler of legal team success.

Budgeting and budget management

Legal Ops assumes responsibility for developing the annual legal budget, overseeing its administration, and forecasting and tracking actual expenditure throughout the year. This is a very important task as nobody likes (negative) surprises, particularly as they relate to the budget.

Zero-based budgeting

I have worked extensively with zero-based budgeting principles (ZBB)[4] and, despite early resistance, became an enthusiastic advocate of it. Even in organizations where ZBB is not mandated, it proves to be an exceptionally effective mechanism for allocating financial resources precisely according to the strategic plans and anticipated needs.

ZBB fundamentally reorients the budgeting process, compelling legal leaders at every level to focus on future initiatives and resource requirements, rather than simply relying on historical allocations. This approach discourages the notion that previous budgets should be viewed as entitlements or a baseline, instead promoting a culture of forward planning and accountability. Each team is expected to formulate a detailed plan, identifying the resources needed for delivering on their initiatives. Budget allocation is determined by the projected impact, value to the business, and strategic priority of each initiative, rather than precedent or tradition. Past expenditure is only referenced to learn from historical missteps, not as justification for present or future resourcing. This ensures that funding is channeled towards teams with clear, ambitious, and actionable plans, while those unable to define their objectives are encouraged to improve their strategic focus, rather than receiving automatic allocations that may be wasted.

Of course, even the most meticulous planning cannot account for every eventuality. The legal function is inherently distinct from other corporate departments, frequently encountering unforeseen events, induced internally or externally. While budget constraints must be respected, they should not impede the delivery of high-quality legal advice to the business. Nevertheless, additional funding must be sourced purposefully, unless the legal department is fortunate enough to have access to a generous credit facility from the CFO.

In this context, earned trust between the legal function and the finance team is paramount. In my experience, CFOs recognize and appreciate the unique challenges faced by the legal team but they also expect that company resources are managed with the same prudence and discipline as by any other function. A transparent and collaborative approach is essential to striking this balance.

Controllable vs uncontrollable spend

A practical framework that I have found valuable is to clearly distinguish between controllable and uncontrollable spending. Controllable expenditure encompasses costs that can be planned and specified in advance, such as those for scheduled projects, compliance and regulatory obligations, intellectual property investments, or travel. Uncontrollable spending, on the other hand, covers unpredictable events such as new litigation, ad hoc M&A work, government investigations, disputes, or crisis-related support. However, it is important not to use a lack of detail as an excuse for categorizing planned expenditure as uncontrollable. This often signals inadequate planning and teams should be encouraged to improve their budgeting accuracy.

For genuinely uncontrollable costs, I recommend establishing a central contingency budget at a central level of the legal department. This central fund is dedicated to managing unexpected or extraordinary legal expenses and the engagement of external counsel. Centralizing this reserve prevents individual budget holders from inflating their requests with "safety margins", which can distort the overall picture. Statistically, it is more likely that unforeseen events requiring additional resources will arise somewhere in the global organization, rather than uniformly across all countries or teams. Central management of these funds therefore enhances forecast accuracy and ensures more efficient allocation of resources.

Budget transparency and investment tracking

A crucial aspect of Legal Ops' remit is to deliver transparency and insight into the effectiveness of legal spending and investments. The team is responsible for designing and producing regular reports that track adherence to budget plans, ensuring that resources are directed towards strategic priorities rather than dissipating without measurable impact. Such reporting supports ongoing dialogue with finance and senior leadership and facilitates data-driven decision making.

Investment tracking is particularly significant in intellectual property (IP) management. It is neither practical nor cost-effective to protect every conceivable brand, innovation, or creative work globally. Instead, the team must make informed decisions to maximize protection within the constraints of the available budget. This involves a targeted investment strategy, prioritizing IP registrations and enforcement actions that offer the greatest deterrent effect, serve as placeholders for future activity, or support real enforcement when necessary. Legal Ops plays a vital role in identifying redundant or dormant registrations within the IP portfolio – those that have not been leveraged commercially for years and, as such, offer limited value to the organization. By pruning these assets, the legal department can ensure that resources are focused on IP investments that contribute tangible commercial benefit.

Legal Ops is instrumental in bringing structure, transparency, and strategic discipline to the budgeting process, ensuring that the legal department's resources are optimally allocated to support the organization's objectives while maintaining the flexibility to respond to unforeseen challenges.

Policy and guidelines repository

Legal Ops has an important task in establishing and maintaining a centralized repository for all legal and compliance-related policies and guidelines. Ideally, this single source of truth should encompass not only documents produced by the legal and compliance teams, but also other policy materials issued by other central functions such as finance, HR, procurement, and operations. However, in larger organizations, attempting to consolidate everything from the outset can prove overwhelming and difficult to manage. A more pragmatic approach is to begin with legal and compliance content, setting a robust example that can inspire and guide subsequent rollouts across the organization.

One version of the truth

The benefits of a central repository are clear. By providing a well-organized, up-to-date, and easily navigable collection of all active policies, guidelines, and related documents, organizations empower employees to find the information they need swiftly and accurately. Guided search features and intuitive self-service capabilities direct users to the most relevant documents for their queries, reducing search frustration and the risk of outdated or conflicting guidance being followed. To ensure ongoing relevance and accuracy, each document should have a clearly assigned owner responsible for regular updates and necessary amendments. Legal Ops oversees the maintenance of this repository, tracking document changes, collecting feedback from both owners and users, and ensuring that the framework remains robust and responsive to organizational needs.

Self-servicing opportunities

In addition to formal policies, the repository can also house practical legal guidance notes designed to address routine queries. For frequently asked or standard questions, AI-enabled chatbots provide a significant advantage, guiding users directly to pertinent answers in seconds.[5] By training these tools exclusively on company-approved materials, organizations can deliver prompt, accurate responses while ensuring information integrity. These AI agents also offer valuable analytics by reporting on usage patterns and the types of questions posed. Such insights enable Legal Ops to tailor guidance and resources to evolving user requirements, enhancing both efficiency and user satisfaction.

While self-service tools are increasingly effective, traditional approaches like extensive "legal playbooks" are often less useful in practice. I refer to them provokingly as "knowledge graveyards". Sizable playbooks can quickly become outdated, unwieldy, and difficult to navigate. Instead, leveraging generative AI models has revolutionized the way employees can access legal guidance for standard queries. When trained and adjusted for legal tasks, these models are able to deliver precise, up-to-date answers to standard queries instantaneously.[6] The issue of reliability, referred to as AI-model hallucinations, exist but there are novel ways to address this and frankly AI-glitches are less frequent and less grave than human error or misguided interpretation.[7] As an example, AI-bots are very capable at answering standard queries like, "Can you remind me of my signing authority?" or "Can I accept this dinner invitation from a client?", where the model will talk the individual through policies and checklists leading to the correct answer.

Beyond digital solutions, a proactive approach to knowledge-sharing can drive greater engagement and understanding. Rather than relying solely on static documents or traditional classroom training, Legal Ops can facilitate interactive, dialogue-based workshops tailored to specific legal topics or challenges. These sessions, ideally hosted in partnership with client teams, foster real conversation and practical learning, which can be reinforced by concise written summaries or follow-up advice. Exploring innovative formats such as videos or podcasts can further enhance communication, making complex information more accessible and memorable. Crucially, Legal Ops should avoid the assumption that simply making extensive documentation available will guarantee its effective use – clear, engaging, and targeted communication is far more likely to ensure vital knowledge reaches those who need it most.

Employee-centric policies

Moreover, it is important to recognize that policies are often written with a regulator audience in mind, laden with legal jargon and complex language. While this may satisfy formal compliance requirements, it frequently renders such documents inaccessible to frontline employees. To maximize impact, policies should be distilled into concise, straightforward statements that communicate key messages with clarity. Practical examples and illustrative scenarios are far more effective than lengthy, technical policy papers in driving understanding and compliance among the wider workforce.

Legal Ops is instrumental in delivering not just a repository of documents, but a dynamic, user-friendly knowledge ecosystem. By combining advanced digital tools, clear accountability, and innovative communication strategies, Legal Ops ensures that legal and compliance guidance is accessible, relevant, and fully aligned with business needs.

External counsel management

Legal Operations takes care of establishing a robust framework for instructing external counsel and monitoring related expenditure. It is worth noting that a significant proportion of the legal department's budget, often approaching 80 percent (excluding IP registration and maintenance costs), is allocated to outside counsel. Therefore, it is critical for Legal Ops to ensure that this investment delivers maximum value, by securing high-quality legal services, eliminating unnecessary costs, and making certain that external support is both efficient and accurate.

Strategic partnerships

The principles and standards that govern the work of in-house legal teams must equally apply when engaging external counsel. The objective is to work with top-tier experts who provide clear, precise, and actionable advice, rather than simply offering a generic view or abstract legal opinion. Achieving this is best realized by developing strategic partnerships with panel law firms. Importantly, such arrangements should not be so restrictive as to prevent the team from instructing (highly) specialized experts or innovators outside the designated panel when the situation demands it. Despite this flexibility, the majority of the legal budget is typically allocated to carefully selected and well-managed panel firms, ensuring a consistent, high-quality service.

Investments on both sides

Building these partnerships with leading law firms requires investments from both sides. The in-house legal team must take the time to familiarize external counsel with the nuances of the business, its strategic objectives, and the specific challenges it faces. In turn, external counsel are expected to immerse themselves in the relevant areas of law, proactively engage in creative problem-solving, and keep the in-house team informed of important legal developments or emerging trends. Counsel are not "guns for hire" but develop a deeper relationship and connection with the business, even a sense of care and pride due to a long-term commitment. This reciprocal relationship fosters a deeper understanding and ultimately leads to more effective legal support.

Counsel management tool

A sophisticated counsel management tool, often combined with matter management as explained above,[8] is indispensable in overseeing the engagement of external counsel. As new legal matters are recorded or updated, the system can automatically identify when outside expertise is required and estimate the associated costs. This enables the prompt initiation of instructions to panel firms directly within the tool, streamlining cost forecasting, invoicing, and payment processes. The tool provides visibility into whether the team is receiving good value from its panel advisers or if there are instances of overcharging for relatively straightforward tasks that do not warrant extensive research. The tool can highlight anomalies, such as an unexpectedly high number of associates assigned to a single matter. Leveraging artificial intelligence, the tool can automatically review billing narratives and invoices in real time, flagging any irregularities to both the instructing lawyer and Legal Ops for further investigation. Furthermore, the platform allows in-house lawyers to rate the performance of external counsel, providing valuable feedback that can be used by general counsel to hold meaningful discussions with key contacts at panel firms and inform decisions on future appointments.

Legal Operations is a fundamental driver of efficiency and productivity within legal departments. By implementing effective frameworks for external counsel management, and harnessing technology to ensure transparency and accountability, Legal Ops ensures that legal budgets are used wisely and that the department consistently receives best-in-class support. Positioned at the heart of the general counsel's office, Legal Ops is ideally placed to deliver these benefits, underpinning the legal function's strategic contribution to the wider organization.

References

1 Financial Planning & Analysis (FP&A or equivalent terms/functions) as well as Sales & Operations Planning (S&OP) are both core capabilities for planning, forecasting, and reporting. Lawyers can learn a lot from these specialists and Legal Ops is the right function to build this bridge.

2 See chapter 15: Prompting is the new drafting.

3 Although professional rules may require external counsel to keep separate records and documentation, allowing direct access to company records and relevant documents greatly enhances effective collaboration.

4 Further explanation can be found here: www.ibm.com/think/topics/zero-based-budgeting.

5 See Part 4: Legal Leaders Fit for the Future – the Artificial Intelligence Challenge.

6 See Solutions for the legal profession, in chapter 14.

7 See The state of play in Artificial Intelligence, highlighting latest innovations around small language models (SMLs), which provide bespoke services with increased accuracy, in chapter 14.

8 See Matter, document, and knowledge management, in chapter eight.

Part Three:
The practice and techniques of legal leadership

This third part of the book is about bringing the first two together – building a winning culture for the team as well as developing a strategy and plans that deliver superior results. This starts with questioning what leadership truly means, particularly within the context of legal teams. Leadership involves more than simply overseeing resources and tasks. It involves inspiring, empowering, and uniting individuals around a common purpose and shared vision, especially when faced with rapid change and uncertainty.

This part of the book will address several key questions:

- What defines effective leadership and how does it differ within the legal profession?
- Which leadership techniques have proven successful in practice and how can these be adapted to meet the unique challenges faced by legal teams?

This discussion will offer practical strategies for leaders to address setbacks and failures constructively, thereby promoting resilience and adaptability within the rapidly changing environment of today.

By weaving together the threads of a winning culture and superior planning, legal leaders will be equipped with the necessary tools and insights needed to guide their teams confidently towards long-term success.

Chapter 9:
What is leadership?

Leadership extends far beyond managing resources or processes. At its core, leadership is about guiding, inspiring, and empowering others to achieve a shared vision, even in the face of uncertainty, challenge, and constant change.

The quintessence of leadership

Leadership is about stepping forward and taking on responsibility. It is about proactively seeking opportunities to make a positive impact on both the business and the team. Leadership is not a solitary pursuit. Instead, it is about fostering a cohesive, purpose-driven team where collaboration and shared goals take precedence over individual achievement.

In a complex and multifaceted organization, a well-led team can accomplish what individuals working in isolation cannot. Leaders create unity by aligning diverse experts, talents, and perspectives towards a common purpose, ensuring that the team is positioned to make a difference where it truly matters. By nurturing a sense of collective responsibility and encouraging open communication, leaders empower their teams to respond effectively to challenges, adapt to change, and deliver results that exceed the sum of individual contributions.

Leadership vs management

There is a clear and important distinction between management and leadership. Management is largely about maintaining the current state of affairs – it involves administering and overseeing established processes, ensuring the functioning of existing procedures and diligently avoiding significant errors. Managers tend to focus on stability, keeping their heads down and responding to issues as they arise, rather than proactively seeking out new opportunities or challenges.

By contrast, leadership is a much more dynamic and forward-thinking concept. True leaders look beyond day-to-day operations and actively anticipate what the future may hold. They take the initiative to shape and develop their teams, fostering growth and encouraging continuous improvement.

Leaders are driven by the goal of creating ongoing value for the organization, not just preserving what already exists.

Leaders know how to remain composed and resolute when faced with turbulent situations. They keep their focus, trust their instincts and have confidence in their own capabilities. They become the rock that provides the foundation of structure and support for the entire team. During periods of uncertainty, they blend a sense of optimism with a clear-eyed view of reality.

Rather than being content with the status quo, leaders embrace change, remain curious, and seek out learning opportunities. They understand that success in business requires constant evolution and they strive to ensure that both they and their teams grow in tandem with the organization's needs. Through this proactive, adaptable approach, leaders help their teams thrive in the face of uncertainty and ensure lasting positive impact.

Leading is more than doing

For legal leaders, the challenge extends beyond simply building a productive organizational culture and winning strategy. Legal leaders must actively build and nurture successful teams.

It's akin to having all the ingredients for a remarkable dish laid out on the table. Their mere presence and an award-winning recipe don't guarantee a delicious meal. Just as a skilled chef must thoughtfully combine ingredients, devise a method of cooking, manage timing, oversee the kitchen's operations and equipment, and ultimately present the finished dish to the customer, so too must legal leaders bring together the various plans, talents, and personalities within their teams.

At a larger scale, when kitchens grow and more sous chefs and assistants are involved, it becomes essential for the head chef to lead and coordinate the whole brigade. Like master chefs, legal leaders need to strike the right balance between direction and control on the one hand, individuality and freedom for creative artistry on the other. This orchestration mirrors effective teamwork in legal departments, where leaders must not only guide and support their colleagues but also ensure that everyone is working together towards common objectives. The process demands planning, strict adherence to fixed rules (like timing in the kitchen), clear communication, and the ability to adapt as circumstances evolve.

Ultimately, the responsibility of the legal leader is to coordinate and harmonize the collective efforts of the team. Instead of personally undertaking every task, the focus should be on achieving outcomes at scale. This means that the primary role of the legal leaders is, as the name indicates, "to lead". Leading is driving the team to function as a cohesive unit of professionals towards a predefined goal. Each member contributes their parts and expertise, never losing sight of the bigger picture and, through their combined efforts, they deliver outstanding results as a collective that would not be achievable acting as individuals.

This brings to mind a story from my time in leadership training with the paratrooper division more than 30 years ago (but still relevant). This story perfectly illustrates the delicate balance between hands-on involvement and effective leadership. During one of our exercises, I was tasked with leading a platoon to unload ammunition from a seven-ton lorry. As is customary in the paratroopers, there was a standing battalion record for the fastest unloading and my commanding officer made it clear that he expected nothing less but my platoon not only to meet but to surpass this benchmark.

Fueled by the challenge, I gathered the men, delivered a rousing speech, and encouraged them to rise to the occasion. The energy was palpable and in my eagerness to inspire, I led from the front – literally climbing into the lorry myself and working alongside the team, keeping morale high and pace brisk. The men responded brilliantly. Together we unloaded the lorry at an impressive speed, and it seemed as if we might set a new record.

However, halfway through the operation, my commanding officer called me aside and pointed out a glaring oversight. In my single-minded focus on speed and motivation, I had neglected to establish any clear system for storing the ammunition in the bunker. The result was utter chaos – boxes of ammunition scattered randomly across the storage area with no order or method to the madness. What we gained in speed, we lost in organization. My officer remarked: "Never forget – when you are fully immersed in the work, you are not truly leading and you risk losing sight of the bigger picture".

This experience was a powerful lesson in leadership. It underscored that there is a vital distinction between doing the work and overseeing the work. A leader must strike the right balance between rolling up their sleeves and maintaining the necessary perspective to coordinate, plan, and adjust to ensure long-term success. Don't get me wrong – you earn a lot of credit and engagement from the team by leading the way, acting as a role model and setting the pace through your own actions. But it is not enough to simply participate. True leadership requires stepping back, assessing the situation, and ensuring that all elements work in harmony. Both active involvement and strategic oversight are crucial and neglecting either can undermine even the most well-intentioned efforts.

Leadership is a conscious decision

Above all else, leadership is a conscious decision. It requires a deliberate commitment to step forward and accept the responsibilities, uncertainties, and inherent risks that come with guiding others. Choosing to lead means embracing vulnerability, recognizing that there are no guarantees of success and that mistakes are inevitable along the way. It involves willingly putting yourself in situations where your actions, decisions, and particularly shortcomings are visible to others. This openness to exposure is a testament to the courage and authenticity that true leadership demands. Ultimately, there is no alternative – to lead effectively, one must be prepared to venture beyond the comfort zone, accepting that occasional missteps are part and parcel of the journey towards growth and meaningful impact.

Key qualities of leaders

Leadership encompasses several essential qualities and character traits. The most important are outlined below.

Humility, empathy, and care

A defining quality of effective leadership is humility. True leaders resist the temptation to elevate themselves above others. They remain grounded and approachable, always prepared to acknowledge their own limitations and shortcomings. This humility is not a sign of weakness but a source of strength, for it enables leaders to listen attentively to their teams, to value different perspectives, and to learn and grow alongside those they lead. Such openness fosters an atmosphere of mutual respect, where everyone feels comfortable contributing ideas and feedback, confident that their voices matter.

At the heart of authentic leadership lies empathy – the ability to genuinely care for and understand the people who comprise the team.[1] Great leaders recognize that leadership is fundamentally about people, not processes or numbers. They take a personal interest in the wellbeing, aspirations, and challenges of each team member, demonstrating compassion and emotional intelligence in their everyday interactions. This human touch is a powerful force in cultivating trust and loyalty. When individuals feel seen and supported, they commit wholeheartedly to the collective mission.

Dedication, support, and commitment

Supporting and committing to the team is another foundation of outstanding leadership. Rather than viewing their position as a status symbol, exemplary leaders see themselves as partners in their team's journey. They invest time and energy in the development of their people, actively seeking opportunities to recognize and reward dedication, hard work, and excellence. This creates an unspoken agreement – as team members contribute to achieving organizational objectives, their leader is equally committed to supporting their professional growth and success. Such a partnership builds a strong foundation of trust and motivates everyone to strive for shared goals.

Visionary leadership

As indicated above, proactive forward-thinking distinguishes leaders from managers. Leaders look beyond the present moment to anticipate change, identifying emerging trends and potential obstacles before they materialize as crises. By encouraging their teams to embrace innovation and continuous improvement, leaders help prevent stagnation and complacency. They inspire their teams to see challenges as opportunities for growth and to adapt strategies proactively in pursuit of progress.

Culture architect and builder

Culture building is a vital aspect of the leader's remit. Leaders are the architects of the organizational environment, setting the tone through their own values, beliefs, and behaviors. By consistently modelling the standards they wish to see, even when under pressure, leaders ensure that integrity, collaboration, and innovation become embedded in the team's culture. This consistency inspires confidence and creates a safe space for individuals to contribute ideas, experiment, and take calculated risks without fear of retribution.

Inspirator and motivator

Inspiration and motivation are central to a leader's impact. By clearly articulating a compelling vision of success and celebrating both milestones and individual contributions, leaders lift morale and encourage others to reach their highest potential. Expressing sincere gratitude and recognizing achievements, no matter how small, reinforces the value of each team member and drives collective engagement.

Delivering results with excellence

In addition to being strategists and planners, leaders must excel at execution. Operational excellence means setting clear, achievable objectives for both the team as a whole and for individual members, aligning incentives and organizing resources effectively to maximize collective performance. Leaders monitor progress, adapt plans in response to shifting circumstances, and ensure that everyone remains focused and engaged even as priorities evolve.

Adaptability, agility, and change

Adaptability and a commitment to ongoing learning are indispensable in the ever-changing landscape of modern work. Leaders recognize that perfection is an illusion and are unafraid to experiment, acknowledge mistakes, and adjust their course based on lessons learned. By cultivating a culture where setbacks are viewed as opportunities for growth rather than sources of blame, leaders empower their teams to take intelligent risks and remain agile in the face of uncertainty.

Role model

Perhaps most importantly, influential leaders serve as role models. They lead by example, demonstrating ethical conduct and unwavering integrity, particularly in challenging circumstances. Their actions speak louder than words. For example, by sharing office spaces with colleagues or by always being visible and approachable, effective leaders break down barriers and reaffirm their commitment to collaboration and shared success. Such behavior not only increases productivity but also strengthens the sense of unity within the group.

A service, not a privilege

Ultimately, true leadership is grounded in service, not privilege. It is a responsibility undertaken with humility, self-awareness, and the willingness to adapt one's approach to suit both the situation and the individuals involved. Exceptional leaders are acutely aware that their primary role is to accomplish the mission and serve their teams. They remain determined and yet flexible and responsive as they guide their people towards meaningful and lasting achievement.

References

1 See Empathy and care, in chapter one, for further details as to why empathy is critical for building winning team cultures.

Chapter 10: Leading the team with mission tactics

While qualities such as charisma, intelligence, and interpersonal skills can contribute to effective leadership, they are neither exclusive nor sufficient. Most leaders are made, not born. Many are placed in positions of leadership because someone recognized their potential to handle greater responsibilities, larger teams, or more complex challenges. However, moving into a leadership role is not a guarantee of success. Skills and approaches that served in previous roles may not translate seamlessly to new contexts.

Leadership is a continuous journey of self-discovery, adaptation, and growth. It relies on experimentation, reflection, and a willingness to learn from both triumphs and mistakes (more from the latter). The best leaders recognize that their development is ongoing – what worked yesterday may not suffice tomorrow. Embracing this mindset allows leaders to remain effective, resilient, and relevant as they guide their teams through ever-evolving landscapes.

One highly effective concept of pragmatic leadership is *Auftragstaktik*, also referred to as mission command or mission-oriented tactics.[1] This concept established a novel way of working and leadership. Rather than ordering subordinates what to do in every detail, *Auftragstaktik* delegates the decision-making authority to those facing immediate situations. This delegation, and its willing assumption in practice, ensures optimal, agile, and speedy decisions and actions. *Auftragstaktik* operates within a clearly defined framework that requires the entire team to understand the plan, its intention, and objectives as well as the overall picture. Though rooted in the military, *Auftragstaktik* applies widely to all forms of leadership and is key for modern decision-making, particularly in an uncertain and volatile environment.

Origins of mission tactics (*Auftragstaktik*)

Auftragstaktik emerged as a direct response by the Prussian army to the challenges posed by the increasingly dynamic and unpredictable battlefields of the mid-19th century. For centuries, wars took place on open fields where opposing forces fought until one side won, often within hours. One of the last examples of this traditional style of warfare was the Battle of Waterloo of 1815.

On 18 June 1815, nearly 200,000 soldiers converged in a single, monumental clash, just outside Brussels. Both Wellington and Napoleon Bonaparte led their armies from the front – one can still visit to this day Napoleon's famous command hill from which he directed his troops. Leadership resembled the strategic maneuvering of chess pieces across the board. However, methods of communication on the battlefield were rudimentary, relying primarily on visual signals such as flags and sounds from bugles or drumbeats. Although Napoleon remained physically very close to his forces (apparently even in striking distance of enemy sharpshooters) and could observe the unfolding battle, these basic forms of communication were insufficient for conveying complex orders or adapting quickly to changing circumstances. This limitation became painfully evident when Napoleon ordered his Marshal Ney to lead the cavalry in a reconnaissance operation against the English and Allied positions. Unfortunately, Ney misunderstood the directive, interpreting it as an order for a full-scale cavalry assault. The result was disastrous – the French cavalry charged headlong into unfavorable terrain, encountering deep ditches near the farm of *Papelotte* on Wellington's left flank, where many riders and horses were lost, severely weakening Napoleon's cavalry force.

Compounding the issue, the British army introduced the innovative carré-formation, which was a defensive square that proved almost impenetrable to cavalry attacks. This tactical development left the French cavalry exposed and vulnerable, resulting in further losses and diminishing their effectiveness for the remainder of the battle. The absence of sufficient cavalry support was a critical blow to Napoleon, especially during the pivotal final phase of the battle in the late afternoon. As his Imperial Guard captured *La Haye Sainte*, a highly strategic defense position at the center of the battlefield, and dangerously advanced through the English lines, cavalry support could have had made the difference. Shortly afterwards, however, fresh threats for Napoleon's army emerged when Prussian forces entered the battlefield on his right flank, dramatically shifting the momentum of the engagement.

Waterloo revealed the necessity for new military leadership and decision-making methods. Advances in technology created deadlier weapons capable of destroying entire armies with one single barrage. As a result, troop formations became more widely dispersed, challenging traditional leadership and communication structures.

The Prussian army recognized that centralized command and control were no longer feasible amidst the chaos and rapid developments typical of modern warfare. Instead, it became clear that empowering lower-level commanders to make decisions in response to immediate situations was essential for keeping the initiative and seizing opportunities as they emerged. But in order to keep the army organized and in formation, delegation of authority and decision-making had to follow a prescribed framework.

This realization paved the way for the development of mission tactics, a concept developed by Helmuth von Moltke, who served as the chief of the Prussian General Staff from 1857 to 1888.[2] Its core message remains highly relevant, offering both the benefits of decentralized decision-making and a framework for leaders to maintain overall control.

Key features of mission tactics (*Auftragstaktik*)

Prussia was the first state to understand that, in modern warfare, actions could not be pre-planned in meticulous detail.[3] Every situation in war is unique and requires a unique response. Decisions had to be made on the basis of incomplete, inaccurate, or even conflicting information. Mission tactics were developed as a response to these challenges. The strategy and its objectives – the "what" – were defined within a clear framework. As to the "how", however, frontline leaders had been given operational freedom to determine the best course of action based on the particularities of the specific situation.[4]

While highly convincing in its basic conception, the main challenge is to make mission tactics work as a leadership concept, particularly under the pressure of warfare. The dogma of mission tactics highlights seven focus areas that are essential for operating this leadership concept in practice:

1. *Development of independently thinking leaders. Auftragstaktik* requires a new type of leader – the "thinking leader". First, thinking leaders have the ability and desire to assume responsibility and make decisions. This is the core of leadership. Second, thinking leaders have the analytical ability to assess situations quickly. Third, thinking leaders require creative abilities to develop decisive action speedily. Fourth, thinking leaders execute their decision with excellence. These four elements must be present in candidates that will become thinking leaders and are the main criteria in the recruitment process.

2. *Understanding that leadership is making decisions.* This is not a privilege but a duty of every leader. Situations call for decisions, though they might not demand immediate action. Sometimes the wisest choice is to wait until the factors guiding decisions are better understood. However, this delay should stem from a deliberate choice, not from indecision. Any situation requires careful analysis and a deliberate decision (*Entschluß*). Leaders take pride in decision-making and willingly own the decision-making process; not always the decision itself as this could be something that requires further elevation, approval, and potentially amendments to the plan. But the starting point is the situational decision of the operating leader, rather than leaving the situation unresolved and requesting guidance from the hierarchy. For Prussia, this duty of decision-making requires from the leader moral courage, self-reliance, and self-confidence. All will come with practice if the process of decision-making is taught early in leadership development.
3. *Definition and explanation of the plan.* Leaders need to understand clearly the wider picture and the plan in full. Orders must enable leaders to understand clearly and fully the mission at hand and its core objectives. Most importantly, superior leaders must clearly communicate their *intent* (and purpose of the plan). Prussian's dogma stresses that, when carrying out tasks, leaders should always focus on the intent as the single most important parameter in the decision-making framework. Any action taken by the leader had to conform with the articulated intent.
4. *Acceptance that there is no perfect solution and a certain a degree of imperfect outcomes.* The ideal is to develop a reasonable plan swiftly and to execute it with energy and dispatch. Adjusting a decision later is manageable, but acting quickly offers more benefits than delays from excessive deliberation or overthinking. In general, speed is more important than precision.
5. *Common language and terminology.* Decision-making follows precisely a predetermined scheme or checklist. The decision-making framework is the same for all situations and constantly repeated and trained. As with standard operating procedures for pilots, leaders recognize every step of the process and take comfort from it. As a result, frontline leaders will feel confident and capable of making quick decisions while working within the established framework.

6. *Presence.* The leader is where the action is. Mission tactics and leading from the front are not mutually exclusive. Mission tactics enables decentralized and quick decision-making but superior leaders are always visible to help. It is not expected that they do the job of the operational leaders, but should the situation require a material change of the plan, they are there. Supervision is done in a manner to encourage initiative and maintain self-confidence of leaders. In turn, leaders make every effort to act transparent, regularly inform their superiors of developments, and to escalate situations that require higher input.
7. *Relationship and trust.* Superiors are responsible for choosing and training thinking leaders. Prussia practiced this in a coaching-style relationship. Through regular practice, superior leaders became better at communicating the plans and their intent. Recipients provide regular feedback after the order-giving process (*Befehlsausgabe*), which is the mission briefing. Every decision-making drill followed a precis analysis. Causes of miscommunication or misinterpretation were discussed and ideally eliminated. This close relationship resulted in mutual trust and commonality of thinking. Mistakes – either during the briefing or during the operational decision-making process – were considered essential for the learning process. Best marks were given not for the best decisions but for the best thinking and problem-solving process.

The next level – creating a team of teams

Mission tactics is a great concept for decentralized, empowered decision making within a predefined framework and escalation process. It does not solve one problem though – how can we assure that the dispatched and decentralized teams collaborate effectively with each other? Mission tactics still follows a linear, top-down approach by focusing on the relationship between the mission-giving superior leader and the operational leader in the field. But in today's world there is not just one operating team but multiple teams. Operating leaders might have a great collaborative relationship with their superiors but not necessarily with each other. Hence, in order to be truly effective, operating leaders must work in a "team of teams", sharing knowledge and enabling each other to win.

Concept of a team of teams

This is the concept of "Team of Teams" that General Stanley McChrystal developed as military leader in Iraq facing the threat of Al-Qaeda.[5] McChrystal analyzed the early success of Al-Qaeda in detail and adopted a flexible response to address this novel threat. From the outset, it was hardly explainable how a group of poorly trained and equipped individuals could challenge the mighty US military with its spy satellites, drones, intelligence, communication infrastructure, and dominating weaponry. And yet, Al-Qaeda was keeping the upper hand and the US military struggled to combat this novel threat.

The reason for Al-Qaeda's success was, according to McChrystal, due to the way it operated in a decentralized, network fashion. A central leadership provided strategic direction and a core ideology while local cells and affiliates had a high degree of autonomy to plan and execute operations, often without central leadership being aware of the detailed plans and objectives. This structure made it incredibly resilient and difficult to dismantle as the loss of one cell, or even members of central leadership, did not cripple the entire network. Moreover, Al-Qaeda expertly leveraged the chaos and lack of effective governance of failing states like Iraq, Afghanistan, and Syria. As Mao said, "The guerilla must move among the people as a fish swims in water".[6] Al-Qaeda replaced the collapsed (or where still existent, highly corrupt) state systems, like administration and judiciary, with their own trials which were largely accepted by the people because they provided, despite of all of their fundamental restrictions and shortcomings, a basic framework for physical security and civil order.[7] Furthermore, Al-Qaeda developed a global network for recruiting, training, and financing. Using guesthouses, training facilities, and various front businesses, Al-Qaeda was able to attract and process recruits around the world. This decentralized system was hard for the military, traditional law enforcement, and intelligence agencies to combat.

McChrystal analyzed and concluded that the US response must mirror Al-Qaeda's approach in order to be successful. As to operations and decision-making, he named it operating a "team of teams". Similar to what Al-Qaeda made so successful, he required the decentralized operating teams to connect and collaborate through the network. This does not cover only the military but administration and intelligence services as well. McChrystal advocated total transparency so that information could flow freely across the entire organization. One piece of information might be of relatively minor importance for the discovering team, but it could become a game changer if put into the right context. Every member, from the lowest rank to the highest, needs to have a comprehensive understanding of the overall mission, context, and actions of other teams. To accomplish this, McChrystal highlighted two key components – mindset and structure.

Mindset and trust

A "team of teams" requires a shared consciousness and the belief that collaboration is absolutely crucial for the success of the enterprise. Most important are (radical) transparency and information sharing. By giving access to crucial information to everyone on a real time basis, every team member can understand the broader context of the mission and is made aware of most recent developments. Breaking down information silos is a mindset that requires a high level of trust, particularly between frontline leaders.

Bonds of trust among team members are the fundamental building block of an effective team. In the military, this bond is built through joint experiences in situation of stress, which could be training or combat experience. Paratroopers often have a very high degree of trust and sense of affiliation, resulting in an "esprit de corps" due to the joint experience of the parachute jump. Overcoming fear and physical challenge builds this level of genuine trust. This is not only a rational belief in another person's capabilities or competences but also in character and values as the team overcomes extraordinary challenges together. Not pursuing self-interest but devoting fully to the success of the team makes the difference and builds a "band of brothers".

This level of trust and cohesion is not easily replicated in the corporate world, particularly in large organizations where team members are widespread, working from different locations. But trust is essential for effective teamwork and it is the responsibility of legal leaders to build this culture of trust and shared consciousness, as discussed in more detail above.[8]

Structure

A "team of teams" requires further the right structural framework so that this spirit of joint collaboration is lived in practice. For McChrystal, this was an inter-agency routine where representatives of all authorities, departments, and agencies came together to exchange daily operational updates. The purpose of the meeting was to share knowledge and to collaborate, hence every representative could offer or request help for specific projects. Another structural element were joint task forces where members of the military, intelligence unit, and administration work together to find solutions for specific tasks. This structure creates an "us" mentality beyond the traditional realm.

This is of high relevance for the structure of legal teams. It is key to bring the right people together periodically so that the established bond is lived in practice. At the same time, you want to be mindful and cautious not to schedule too many meetings, as time for internal communication and administration is "non-working spend", taking away time from your lawyers to give legal advice to their clients. A certain degree of alignment in relevant meetings is, however, necessary to bring a "team of teams" to life.

References

1 Also called "Mission Command" by the US and British Army, see Risso, "Misson Command and Leadership in Operations since 1991", Centre for Army Leadership (2010), www.army.mod.uk.

2 "On Strategy" (1871). Interestingly v Moltke is quoting Napoleon as he summarised the new way of thinking: "In this sense one should understand Napoleon's saying: "I have never had a plan of operations. Therefore, no plan of operations extends with certainty beyond the first contact with the main hostile force."

3 Von Clausewitz, "Vom Kriege" (1832): "Drei Viertel derjenigen Dinge, worauf das Handeln im Kriege gebaut wird, liegen im Nebel einer mehr oder weniger großen Ungewissheit." "Three quarters of those things upon which action in war is based lie in the fog of a greater or lesser uncertainty."

4 See Vego, "Auftragstaktik Leads to Decisive Action," published May 2025, www.usni.org/magazines/proceedings/2025/may/auftragstaktik-leads-decisive-action.

5 General Stanley McChrystal, *Team of Teams: New Rules of Engagement for a Complex World*, Penguin, 2013.

6 Mao Zedong, *On Guerilla Warfare* (1937).

7 This also explains why the Western-backed Afghani leaders collapsed within weeks after the US exit in August 2021. Even during the darkest days of the Taliban, their Sharia-based trials provided a rudimental framework of security and order. This was something that the people did not get from corrupt warlords, despite their support from the West.

8 See Trust, in chapter two.

Chapter 11: Operational leadership – keeping the team on track

Effective communication and genuine connection with the team are fundamental responsibilities for legal leaders. Leadership, as articulated in the *Auftragstaktik* philosophy, is not about choosing between visibility and decentralized decision-making. Rather, it is about integrating both approaches to foster a dynamic and responsive environment. A leader must be present where activities unfold, engaging directly with the challenges and opportunities faced by the team.

True leadership cannot be exercised from the isolation of luxurious corner offices or exclusive executive suites. Leaders must proactively seek to build relationships with team members at every level, transcending traditional hierarchical boundaries. This approach aligns with the principles of the "team of teams" methodology,[1] which emphasizes close, frequent interactions throughout the entire organization. Such connectivity not only strengthens bonds but also enhances the collective effectiveness of leadership, ensuring that decision-making is informed, inclusive, and adaptive.

My own experience in the military over three decades ago offers a compelling illustration of this principle. An analysis of the 1982 Falklands War conducted by the British Army identified a critical success factor – British officers used the two-week sea voyage to the islands as a unique opportunity to establish strong rapport with their soldiers.[2] They listened attentively to individual concerns and took time to prepare their teams mentally and emotionally for the challenges ahead. This investment in connection and preparation proved invaluable once the troops were deployed. The units operated as cohesive teams, demonstrating remarkable adaptability and resilience in response to the unpredictable and often chaotic conditions of the battlefield.

In stark contrast, the report highlighted the shortcomings of the Argentinian forces. Their officers withdrew from the frontline, distancing themselves from the soldiers, who were left without guidance or support – sometimes even displaying a lack of discipline, such as smoking in defensive positions at night. This disconnect eroded morale and hindered the ability of the fighting units to respond effectively to the rapidly changing realities, referred to as the "fog of war".

These lessons from military leadership are directly applicable to the legal profession. Leaders must strive to be accessible and engaged, fostering strong relationships not only in formal settings but also in everyday interactions. By remaining attuned to the needs, perspectives, and aspirations of each team member, legal leaders can cultivate an environment where adaptability, collaboration, and trust flourish. Ultimately, it is this culture of connection, both top-down and across all layers of the team, that empowers individuals and elevates the performance of the entire organization.

Establishing a leadership team

The foremost priority for any senior leader with elevated responsibilities (like chief or general counsel) is to form a strong and cohesive leadership team (or executive committee). This foundational step must begin at the very top of the function, as the leadership team sets the overall tone, culture, and expectations for everyone else. If those at the helm are unable to work together effectively, it is unrealistic to expect the wider organization to operate harmoniously. The behavior and unity of the leadership team serve as a powerful example for all employees, shaping attitudes towards teamwork, communication, and problem-solving throughout the business. Ultimately, the success of the entire organization is built upon the strength and effectiveness of its executive committee. Without this, any attempts to foster cohesion or high performance at other levels are likely to fall short.

Purpose of the leadership team

Everything begins with a clear sense of purpose. Why does your leadership team exist? Is its role simply to provide a platform for the leader to bask in the limelight and receive unwavering praise from loyal supporters? Or is it more akin to a "family" gathering of different factions, where territories are negotiated and conflicts escalated to the godfather for resolution? Perhaps it resembles an ancient Athenian *Ostrakismos*, where democratic ballots are cast and decisions are solely adopted anonymously. Or is the leadership team best compared with a *politburo*, governed by its own distinctive, sometimes opaque, decision-making conventions.

The reality is that legal leadership teams can embody all of these characteristics to differing degrees, depending on the personalities involved and the prevailing organizational culture. Personally, I have always preferred the concept of the leadership team acting as the beating heart of the law department – a collegiate body of equals, where every voice is genuinely heard and every vote carries weight. Decisions are taken by the executive committee as organ (almost like a board) and not solely by the formal leader. In order to get full alignment, the formal leader can ask the team to vote or go around the group and ask individuals their opinion. I aways felt that the phrase "business is not a democracy" is often used to justify weak leadership and relies too much on unearned formal authority, which cannot sustain or replace real leadership.

The collegial approach, however, depends on ensuring that the right individuals are selected to represent each business unit, region, category, or function within the legal leadership team. If representatives lack the requisite experience, leadership qualities, or skills, a more directive style of leadership as a temporary solution may be warranted to maintain effectiveness and direction.

Importantly, the legal leadership team should be much more than a routine staff meeting. It offers a unique opportunity to collaborate with senior professionals who are, in their own right, accomplished legal leaders and experts in their fields. When these team members are empowered to participate actively in steering the department, the overall leadership is strengthened and becomes far more effective. In many ways, this is comparable to managing a national sports team – your team comprises seasoned players who require less micromanagement and are able to contribute strategic insight and initiative. By fostering a culture of consensus, where decisions are shaped collaboratively, you not only leverage the collective expertise of the group but also enhance the impact and acceptance of those decisions across the wider department.

Ultimately, a legal leadership team thrives when it transcends the confines of simple reporting or directive management. It should be a forum for robust dialogue, constructive challenge, and shared ownership of outcomes. The more you can harness the diverse experience and perspectives within your team, guiding by consensus wherever possible, the greater the effectiveness of your leadership and the more enduring the positive influence on the organization as a whole.

Structure of the leadership team and span of control

Effective leadership teams should reflect the business and legal team structures, balancing alignment with organizational design and optimizing governance for legal functions.

Global leadership teams should include all legal leaders in charge of advising central business units, divisions, and functions. In addition, all lead counsel for the regions or central geographies should be present. I recommend including also the legal leaders that support central functions like operations, governance, HR, and finance. And of course, if not already included in the first group of personnel, the leaders of legal branches like IP, litigation, and compliance.

All in all, you need to ensure that you have the right leaders assembled to obtain diverse perspectives from all operating units present. They actively contribute to the decision-making process, providing specific (unit and regional) perspectives so that when the decision is taken, it will have the desired acceptance and impact.

Ideally, the core membership of your leadership team should consist of between eight and 12 regular participants. This range represents an optimal "span of control" for the group to function efficiently and fulfil its intended purpose.[3] If you have fewer than eight members, you risk missing out on vital perspectives, as key representatives from important business units may be absent. This can compromise the completeness of your discussions and limit the team's ability to distribute responsibilities effectively, as well as to cultivate meaningful and constructive debate within the group.

On the other hand, exceeding 12 regular members can introduce its own set of challenges. As the group expands, it becomes increasingly difficult to ensure that every voice is genuinely heard during meetings. Often, the conversation is dominated by a handful of more vocal individuals – sometimes for the right reasons, but just as often, not. This dynamic can dilute the quality of dialogue and decision-making. In addition, logistical issues arise. Scheduling becomes notably more complicated, particularly if you value holding regular one-on-one sessions alongside your main team meetings. The larger the group, the harder it is to maintain consistent connections with each member, which can undermine the cohesiveness and trust essential to a high-functioning leadership team.

For meetings with a specific or exceptional purpose, it is entirely appropriate to invite additional contributors, such as colleagues from human resources or communications, whose expertise is directly relevant to the topics at hand. However, it is generally advisable to limit permanent membership of the legal leadership team to those whose regular input is indispensable. This helps preserve the focus, confidentiality, and trust-based intimacy that are so crucial for candid dialogue and effective collective leadership.

Striking the right balance in team composition is about more than just numbers. It is about ensuring diversity of thought while maintaining an environment where open, honest participation is possible. A well-sized leadership team leverages the broadest possible range of insights without losing the clarity of purpose and strong personal connections that smaller groups foster. Regularly reviewing team membership in light of changing business needs can help you maintain this delicate equilibrium, ensuring the leadership team remains agile, representative, and impactful.

Interestingly, Jensen Huang, CEO of Nvidia, is pursuing a different approach that reminded me of ex-FIAT's Sergio Marchionne. Huang encourages a more fluid, direct, and collaborative approach to leadership. In response to a rapid changing environment he prefers to have direct access to key leaders so that he can get input when needed instead of following the traditional chain of command. Apparently, Huang works directly with 50 leaders, who are his direct reports.[4] Similarly, ex-FIAT Chrysler CEO Sergio Marchionne favored a direct, highly centralized management style, which reflects the high number of direct reports (around 40). This high number was a result of his turnaround efforts and the stage of development in which his company was.

Like so many things, the optimal span of control and team structure depends on the specific situation and the purpose you give to your leadership team. In times of more directive and assertive leadership, temporarily bigger teams have the advantage of increased control, better flow of information, and quicker decision-making and execution. Having all critical leaders in one meeting eliminates ambiguity and room for politics as you are in control and have direct access to everybody. It also depends on your ability as a leader how many direct reports you are able to handle without neglecting your other duties (too much). More matured teams comprised of very loyal members who fully support your vision and strategy need less care and it is not required that everybody sits regularly in the leadership team. The magic formula requires experimenting and adjusting. As a leader you should leave time after your leadership team meetings and challenge yourself whether the meetings have delivered what you expect them to do. If not, use the levers at your disposal to adjust.

Team meetings

Meetings! Have you ever stopped to consider just how much of your day is taken up by meetings? I vividly recall my first day working in-house after almost a decade in private practice – I was astonished by the sheer volume of meetings on the schedule. It left me wondering: are all these hours billable or is there simply not enough substantive legal work for us to tackle? This shift was puzzling, and it took a while before I truly understood how meetings operated and what steps I could take to make them genuinely effective.

Meetings are necessary but the fewer the better

As essential as meetings are, it's important to recognize that genuine progress rarely happens within them. While meetings serve as a platform for discussion, debate, and alignment, which are all vital for effective teamwork, the true measure of success lies in whether team members follow through on what has been agreed, not just superficially but in earnest.[5] This crucial work is carried out after the meeting, not during it. Therefore, the more time consumed by meetings, the less opportunity there is for the team – and for you as a leader – to take meaningful action. In this respect, meetings are a form of "non-working spend" – they are necessary for leadership, administration, and alignment, but real value is only realized when decisions are implemented and put into effect. Consequently, scheduling fewer but more purposeful and productive meetings is preferable.

Purpose, process, and outcome

All meetings require a clearly defined purpose, process, and expected outcome. The purpose is the intended goal or objective of the meeting. It defines its agenda and the required (or necessary) participants. A clearly defined purpose helps participants understand why they made precious time during the day available, what is expected of them in the meeting, and why this is a good investment of time. Without a well-defined purpose, a meeting quickly loses focus and drifts into a general discussion, almost a chat, which leaves participants confused (or bored) rather than aligned to take action.

Examples of meeting purposes include to inform (share updates or communicate important news), explain (clarify complex topics or provide detailed context), brainstorm (generate new ideas or solutions collaboratively), challenge (question existing assumptions or encourage critical thinking), align (ensure that all participants are on the same page regarding objectives or strategies), or decide (make a choice together as a team). The closer the meeting's purpose aligns with the unique benefits of live conversation – such as immediate feedback, real-time clarification, or spontaneous idea generation – the more impactful its outcome will be. For instance, if the purpose of the meeting is simply to inform, it may be more efficient to use alternative, less time-intensive forms of communication such as email, a memo, or a quick video message. However, your leadership team might benefit from hearing your interpretation of the news you wish to share and having the opportunity to ask questions. Important news is often best shared live, as it allows for immediate feedback and discussion, ensuring everyone is fully informed and engaged. Another clear benefit of having a meeting to share information is if the news is not only communicated top-down but all members of the leadership team have a slot in the agenda to update the leadership team of important developments in their respective areas or key priorities to come for this week.

Meeting purposes such as brainstorming, challenging, or debating require more time and an appropriate environment. Mining for conflict and challenging ideas is necessary but delicate. You cannot achieve the full benefits of these types of meetings if you try to squeeze them into your weekly tactical team sessions.

If you really want to go deep, you need to set the scene. Take the team somewhere they can open up, leave behind the constraints of their day jobs and their egos and truly focus on finding the right outcome together. For example, consider holding a dedicated offsite brainstorming retreat or scheduling a separate meeting specifically for open debate, away from day-to-day operational discussions. Creating this kind of setting encourages psychological safety – when people feel safe to express their ideas without fear of judgment, teams are much more likely to arrive at innovative solutions.

Live meetings are also absolutely critical when you need to get the team behind a controversial decision you want them to take. Ideally the leadership team works as a college and decisions are taken unanimously. But at times, the team is divided and despite best and numerous efforts, a consensus cannot be reached. If you trust your instincts and take an executive decision, you need to ensure that all members are truly behind it. Disagree but commit. This requires facetime and direct conversation in the meeting.[6]

The second element – the process – is the "how" you are going to achieve the purpose of the meeting. It is the structured agenda and the series of steps you will take during the meeting to achieve its objective. A good process ensures that the meeting flows smoothly, stays on track, and allocates time efficiently. Nothing is more frustrating than never being able to go through the full agenda of the meeting. This reveals a lack of purposeful planning and meeting leadership.

For leadership team meetings, I recommend rotating the chairperson position at regular intervals. My coach first suggested this to me after I described how I led our meetings, always with enthusiasm and drive. On the one hand, bringing high energy to a meeting can be infectious – when I set an energetic tone, others often feel encouraged to participate more actively. However, there is a potential downside – if I dominate with my own energy and ideas, I am likely to unintentionally stifle others' contributions, sometimes making it feel as though I am "taking all the oxygen out of the room". In these situations, colleagues might become passive observers of what I jokingly call the "Thomas Show", rather than stepping up and taking real ownership of the meeting themselves.

Rotating responsibilities for chairing the meeting is therefore a valuable way to increase engagement and sharpen focus across the team. When diverse colleagues take the lead, they each bring their own priorities, perspectives, and problem-solving approaches. For example, a newcomer to the role may introduce fresh ideas or be more willing to experiment with new formats, whereas someone else might prefer a focus on substance – a particular legal problem, a new law, or a business challenge. This diversity not only enriches the process and broadens the collective outlook but also leads to more creative solutions and a stronger sense of shared ownership within the team.

Furthermore, rotating leadership is especially effective for encouraging participation from those who might otherwise remain on the sidelines. While some team members are excellent critical observers (and prefer themselves in this role), they are more comfortable pointing out problems (of and to others) than offering constructive solutions. By inviting them to chair a meeting, you give them a chance to experience first-hand the complexities of leading a group and finding viable answers. Putting them under the spotlight means moving them from the role of critical bystander to that of solution-oriented leaders. In this way, rotating the chair not only fosters inclusivity but also takes negativity out of the room and helps develop advanced leadership skills across the team.

I tried both in the past – rotating leaderships for every meeting or changing in regular intervals, say every six months. For weekly tactical meetings, I have a preference for changing every six months as it takes some time to take control of the meeting dynamics. I also want to give the newcomer an opportunity to experiment and try novel things, which is difficult if you change too often in short intervals. I generally give the appointed chairperson a lot of leeway in terms of how to run our team meetings. I only ask for two things – I want to see the agenda 24 hours in advance and have ten minutes at the start of every meeting to call out the most important items like business updates or progress reports on key projects or initiatives.

Further on process, withstand the temptation to give in when colleagues suggest "Let's take this offline". This can be a valid and fair challenge if a statement is tangential to the agenda and the discussion drifts off point. But it could also be used as code for trying to avoid discussing openly a controversial item on which the team is not aligned. As the legal leader, it falls to you to be alert to such dynamics and to address them transparently within the group setting. The leadership team is the right forum to have this discussion. It is not for one-on-ones or coffee breaks. If you allow this regularly, it will foster a culture of office politics and devalue the power of the team. By ensuring that difficult subjects are addressed openly in meetings, you reinforce the value of healthy dispute, shared decision-making, and strengthen the power of the team as college.

The third element – the outcome of the meeting – should be tangible results or deliverables, such as a decision, a set of action items, a clear and common understanding of a problem, or an agreed plan. While a bias for action is beneficial, it is important not to move forward prematurely, especially if the team is not fully committed to the proposed solution. If not all team members are convinced or ready to "disagree but commit", follow up action is required.[7]

Ensuring a clear outcome means that the meeting concludes with concrete results, leaving no room for ambiguity about what has been decided and what will be implemented. This clarity is essential not only for accountability but also for maintaining team momentum. As the legal leader, it is your responsibility to ensure this clarity. Although you may delegate the chairperson role to a team member, as leader you must step in if you sense the discussion has not yielded a clear outcome or direction. I find it helpful to begin with, "Let me summarize..." at the end of discussions. This signals a transition to clear outcomes and ensures everyone is aligned. Although it always reminds me of Lord Alan Sugar in the BBC TV series "The Apprentice" ("Let me summarize..." is a phrase he uses before candidates get fired), it is an effective way to bring the discussion to resolution and show the path forward.

Liturgy of leadership team meetings

Much like a liturgy provides a structured order and a set of rituals for a religious service, the schedule of your leadership team meetings should also adhere to a consistent sequence designed to support connection and fulfil the team's overarching purpose. For legal leadership teams, the regular cadence of these meetings is fundamental – not only for maintaining alignment but also for fostering a sense of unity and shared direction within the group.[8]

Weekly operational meetings

The primary focus of weekly team meetings should be operational and transactional in nature. These gatherings are intended to address immediate priorities. What are the key activities and deliverables for the current week? What is "hot" this week? Which issues are emerging that require swift team attention? Where should you, as the team leader, direct emphasis and resources? Who within the team needs additional support and who wants to raise pressing concerns or flag obstacles before they escalate?

The agenda for these weekly sessions should be carefully crafted to mirror this purpose, ensuring that discussions remain targeted and relevant to the week's objectives.

To maximize productivity and respect everyone's time, it is advisable to keep these meetings to no more than 60 minutes, preferably scheduling them early in the week to set the tone and direction. In the context of global leadership teams, managing disparate time zones can pose a significant logistical challenge – some colleagues may have to join at the crack of dawn, while others stay on late into the evening. It is therefore an act of fairness and good leadership to rotate meeting times periodically, so that the inconvenience is shared and does not consistently fall on the same regional team members.

Monthly deep-dives

In contrast to the weekly meetings, which are predominantly operational, the primary purpose of monthly team meetings is to provide a forum for strategic reflection and in-depth discussion. These sessions are invaluable for delving into significant issues that have surfaced during the more tactical, weekly gatherings – allowing the team to dissect challenges, explore root causes, and engage in robust debate. Such meetings create a safe space for critical evaluation and constructive conflict, both of which are essential for genuine progress and innovation within the team.

Monthly meetings also serve as a checkpoint to review thoroughly the advancement of ongoing projects and key initiatives. This is the time to take stock of what has been achieved, identify any obstacles, and recalibrate strategies where necessary. In addition, these gatherings present a fitting opportunity to update the team on important developments in the business and legal landscape, ensuring that everyone remains informed about changes that could impact their area of responsibility.

Given the strategic and detailed nature of these discussions, I recommend allocating between two and three hours for monthly meetings. This duration strikes the right balance – it allows for comprehensive debate and gives each team member the chance to voice their perspective, while also preventing the session from dragging on and losing momentum. Meetings that are too brief risk glossing over vital topics or stifling contributions from quieter voices, whereas excessively long – especially virtual – sessions can lead to fatigue, disengagement, and diminished productivity. To get the most out of these extended meetings, it is helpful to structure the agenda thoughtfully, build in short breaks, and encourage active participation from all attendees.

Annual planning meetings

Annual meetings represent a pivotal moment for the leadership team to engage in thorough and far-reaching strategic discussions. In my experience, there are typically two major annual gatherings in the corporate calendar, each playing a vital role in shaping the long-term direction of the team and, by extension, the wider organization. Given their significance, I strongly advocate for hosting at least one of these sessions as an offsite event. Stepping away from the regular work environment fosters deeper connections among team members, provides space to address and resolve any simmering disagreements, and encourages honest dialogue that may not occur in the usual day-to-day setting.

Holding these meetings in person and away from the office not only injects a sense of occasion but also creates lasting memories for participants.[9] By tackling issues that have been impeding progress – those challenges recognized by the entire team as barriers to success – you can generate a renewed sense of momentum and collective purpose. The shared experience of finding solutions together often strengthens the bond within the team and reignites enthusiasm for the year ahead.

The first of these annual meetings is dedicated to comprehensive planning for the forthcoming year. I recommend scheduling this strategic session in the fourth quarter, once the organization's broader operating plans have been formulated and can provide clear guidance for the legal team's priorities. During this meeting, each team member should arrive well-prepared to present their key initiatives and explain how their work will support the overall business objectives. This collaborative setting also provides an opportunity for other central functions – such as compliance and intellectual property – to share their priorities, ensuring alignment and synergy across the team.

The culmination of this annual planning meeting is a robust and clearly articulated operating plan for the legal team. After extensive, constructive debate and alignment, each team member leaves with a solid understanding of their priorities and responsibilities for the coming year. This clarity not only empowers individuals but also enhances accountability, ensuring that everyone is committed to driving the agreed objectives forward. By investing time and energy into these annual meetings, you lay the groundwork for a more unified, effective, and forward-thinking leadership team.

Annual talent review

The second annual meeting that is firmly embedded in my yearly schedule is the annual talent review. This session holds particular significance, as it allows to take a step back and look beyond immediate performance metrics to evaluate the broader trajectory of the team member's development. To gain the most meaningful insights, it is best to schedule the talent review at a time well separated from annual performance assessments. This ensures conversations are not overly influenced by recent events or short-term results, but instead focus on long-term growth, potential, and the real impact of the development opportunities that have been provided. This also keeps the discussion separate from performance bonuses, reducing the risk of distress or defensiveness from line managers concerned about employee motivation if they have to deliver the message.

During the talent review process, three key questions should be considered:

1. To what extent have team members leveraged opportunities for growth and development during the review period?
2. Are their personal development plans advancing in alignment with both their individual ambitions and organizational expectations?
3. How effectively do they incorporate feedback and do they continue to demonstrate a commitment to ongoing learning or have they reached a plateau in their career progression?

The methodology of the exercise should be anchored in a framework for monitoring and facilitating long-term professional development such as the Roles, Skills, Succession and Progression chart (Table 2) in chapter five.

It is my firm belief that people are the greatest asset. Much like a football team aspiring to win the World Cup, success is directly tied to the caliber and development of talent. With this in mind, the focus of the annual talent review is not simply to categorize individuals or assign labels, such as those found in the traditional nine-box grid. In practice, most people end up in the safe, undistinguished middle box, which offers little value or actionable insight. Similarly, the simplistic labels of "ready now" or "ready in two to five years" fail to capture the complexity and individuality of each person's journey.

What truly matters to me is understanding each individual's ambition and how that aligns with the team's core values and strategic direction. I place particular emphasis on recognizing team members who take the initiative, contribute to collective success, and consistently demonstrate commitment to both their own and the team's development. Continuously pursuing new learning opportunities and preparing for the next step in their career are both strong indicators of positive momentum and future readiness.

However, the annual talent review is not solely about celebrating achievements. It is equally important to identify areas where team members have further learning needs or potential blind spots. Openly discussing these aspects allows to focus and allocate resources more effectively, ensuring that everyone receives the guidance needed to progress by overcoming challenges and realizing their full potential.

The ultimate goal of the annual talent review is to enable managers to prepare updated, dynamic talent development plans. These plans should not be the product of isolated opinions but should instead reflect the collective feedback, insights, and experiences of the entire leadership team. By pooling perspectives, one can more accurately identify opportunities for growth, create targeted development pathways, and ensure that every individual is supported in their journey. In doing so, not only is talent nurtured and further developed but also a robust foundation is laid for the future success of the organization as a whole.

In summary, adopting a structured and predictable sequence for leadership team meetings, akin to a liturgy, promotes clarity, engagement, and a shared sense of purpose. It is essential to regularly review both the timing and structure of these meetings to ensure they continue to serve the needs of all participants, fostering both operational efficiency and team cohesion.

One-on-ones

While some leaders, such as apparently Jensen Huang, CEO of Nvidia,[10] have taken the bold step of eliminating one-on-one meetings with direct reports to prevent the creation of information silos, I continue to see value in maintaining these bilateral conversations. Huang's approach aims to foster transparency and collective problem-solving by discouraging private exchanges that might withhold information from the broader team. However, the effectiveness of one-on-one meetings largely depends on the maturity and culture of the team and its individuals.

In my experience, one-on-one meetings serve several indispensable purposes which cannot be easily replicated in a group setting. Firstly, these sessions provide a safe space to delve deeply into issues that might be highly specific to an individual's role, responsibilities, or business area – matters that may not be pertinent to the wider team. This allows for a more tailored and efficient problem-solving process, ensuring that unique challenges are addressed with the necessary attention.

Secondly, one-on-ones foster an environment of candor and vulnerability. Team members are generally more open to receiving feedback and less likely to become defensive when they are not in front of an audience. Sensitive subjects, personal development needs, or admissions of difficulty are more comfortably discussed in private, enabling real progress and mutual understanding. It is in these confidential conversations that individuals often feel empowered to acknowledge weaknesses or seek help, thereby accelerating their growth and enhancing team resilience.

Thirdly, the coaching aspect of one-on-one meetings is invaluable. These sessions offer the opportunity to support colleagues in overcoming specific leadership challenges or navigating complex situations. Coaching is inherently individualized and cannot be effectively conducted in a larger forum, where time constraints and broad agendas often prevent deeper exploration of personal or professional obstacles. Weekly team meetings tend to focus on transactional updates, while monthly gatherings are better suited to collective priorities, leaving little room for individual coaching and support.

Reflecting on a recent conversation with a CEO, I was struck by his observation that around 80 percent of his daily discussions are difficult ones. This prompted me to consider my own experience as a leader. While I fully recognize that providing honest and sometimes challenging feedback is a necessary part of driving the team forward, I have found that, for me, the majority of conversations are not that difficult. In fact, I believe feedback is often a positive and motivating force one that inspires growth, builds confidence, and strengthens team cohesion.

This contrast with the CEO's perspective led me to reflect on my own approach. Although difficult conversations are sometimes unavoidable, I have never found them to dominate my day-to-day leadership to the extent he described. My focus has always been on balancing critical feedback with encouragement and recognition, believing that people thrive when their efforts are acknowledged and their achievements celebrated.

For example, I recall a recent conversation in which I commended a team member for taking the initiative to streamline a process that had previously caused frustration across the team. By highlighting the positive impact of their actions and linking it to our wider objectives, I saw their confidence grow and engagement deepen. These are the kinds of interactions that make leadership rewarding and, I believe, enable teams to flourish.

Ultimately, whilst it is essential for leaders to address challenges and have honest discussions, I find that fostering a culture where feedback is as much about encouragement as it is about correction leads to greater satisfaction and better results for everyone involved.

As another interesting perspective, I worked with one inspirational business leader whose philosophy was to treat one-on-one meetings as *my* time, dedicating the entire session to my needs and concerns rather than imposing his own agenda and queries. This approach encouraged me to come prepared, raise the topics most pressing to me, and leave with actionable solutions and renewed clarity. It was not only empowering but fostered genuine trust and engagement and I have often replicated this model in my own leadership practice.

That said, flexibility is key. It is not that one-size-fits-all and allowing reports to set the agenda may not deliver the desired outcome. With some reports, I have found it beneficial to set the agenda myself – circulating discussion points in advance to ensure a focused, productive conversation that leads to clear outcomes. While the dialogue remains two-way, this approach prevents meetings from drifting into unfocused chat, ensuring that both parties' objectives are met. Ultimately, the most effective one-on-one meetings are those adapted to the personalities and needs of those involved, blending structure with openness and direction with responsiveness.

In summary, in my view, bilateral one-on-one meetings remain a cornerstone of effective leadership. They not only facilitate targeted problem-solving and honest dialogue but also strengthen relationships and foster a culture of continuous growth and support. By thoughtfully balancing when to listen, when to coach, and when to direct, leaders can ensure that these meetings fulfil their true potential as instruments of individual and organizational development.

Optimism is a choice

Effective legal leadership becomes much more attainable when you genuinely enjoy your work and openly express this enthusiasm to your team. Demonstrating visible joy in your role not only boosts your own energy but is infectious, inspiring your colleagues to engage more fully and approach challenges with a similar spirit. Cultivating optimism is a cornerstone of strong leadership. It fuels resilience, motivates teams through adversity, and helps create a vibrant, productive work environment. Importantly, optimism does not mean ignoring difficulties or glossing over legitimate concerns. Instead, it is about communicating a steadfast belief in the team's ability to navigate obstacles and achieve positive outcomes, as has been proven time and again through shared experience.

A genuine passion for the work, coupled with an optimistic outlook, forms a virtuous cycle within high performing legal teams. When leaders approach challenges with confidence and positivity, it encourages team members to rise to the occasion, view problems as opportunities to demonstrate capability, and derive fulfilment from overcoming adversity. This mindset is crucial – the greatest growth and most valuable contributions often emerge from tackling tough situations head-on. Were the waters always calm, one might reasonably question the need for a world-class (and hence expensive) legal team at all.

Apparently also leadership abides by the laws of physics – the amount of energy you invest in your team is reflected back to you. Energy in, energy out.[11] If you project negativity and dwell on frustrations, you can expect morale to dip. Conversely, if you share optimism and drive, your team is far more likely to respond in kind, channeling that energy into concerted effort. Both positivity and negativity are contagious. As a leader, you set the emotional tone.

Of course, authenticity is paramount. Not every leader is a natural optimist, but the choice remains – focus on the positive aspects and potential of your work, or dwell on its frustrations and limitations. It's a conscious decision whether to emphasize confidence in your team's skills or to let fear of challenges take center stage. If you demonstrate belief in your collective abilities and lead with enthusiasm, your team will be inspired to exceed expectations.

Optimism is also a critical driver of resilience and effective problem-solving. Leaders who maintain a positive perspective see setbacks not as insurmountable failures but as temporary hurdles or valuable learning experiences. This approach encourages perseverance, creative thinking, and a sense of calm under pressure, all of which are vital in the legal profession where uncertainty and complexity are the norm. Experience shows that with determination and teamwork, solutions are always within reach.

Reflecting on my own career, I recall a time when the company was acquired by a competitor. This was a period fraught with uncertainty and anxiety for the legal team. Despite being at the heart of the transaction and busier than ever, morale suffered as colleagues worried about job security ("Are we all getting fired?"). Rather than succumbing to pessimism, I encouraged the team to view the situation as an opportunity to excel and prove our value. We focused on what we could control, which was delivering the deal, a smooth closing, and a flawless transition. Ultimately, our efforts paid off. Many team members secured rewarding roles in the new organization, while those who chose to move on found desirable positions, aided by the valuable experience gained during the transaction. In such moments, an optimistic leader provides hope and stability, but this must be coupled with realistic planning. Empty reassurances are no substitute for actionable strategies.

Evidently, optimism must be grounded in reality. There is a clear distinction between maintaining a positive outlook and slipping into denial or wishful thinking. Overpromising or sugarcoating challenges erodes trust and can lead to disappointment. For naturally optimistic leaders (like me), self-awareness is crucial. One effective strategy is to actively seek alternative perspectives – for example, by consulting a known pessimist or ultra-cautious member in the team, or by constructing a thorough pros-and-cons analysis that takes potential pitfalls seriously. Allowing time for reflection can also help ensure a balanced view. Often a situation seems much clearer after a good night's sleep. This practice of periodic reflection and challenge is essential for credible and trustworthy leadership.

An insightful illustration of the balance between optimism and realism is found in the Stockdale paradox, named after Admiral James Stockdale, who survived eight years as prisoner during the Vietnam war.[12] Stockdale observed that the POWs who clung to blind optimism, expecting to be released by certain dates, (for example) were often those who did not survive. Repeated dashed hopes led to despair. Similarly, those who surrendered to cynicism and lost all hope also fared poorly. The key to survival, according to Stockdale, was to combine unwavering faith in eventual success with the discipline to confront harsh realities head-on.

This paradox lies at the heart of resilient leadership – holding onto hope and confidence in ultimate victory, while also facing the most brutal facts of the present situation. Optimism may be fueled by faith, confidence, or hope. But self-awareness ensures that leaders don't lose sight of the real challenges they face. In complex or novel situations, failures are inevitable at first. The path to success involves rigorous analysis, learning from mistakes, and persistent effort. Each small victory builds knowledge and confidence, fueling further optimism, while honest acknowledgement of the hard work and sacrifices required keeps expectations grounded.

Ultimately, leadership is a marathon, not a sprint. Successful leaders demand perseverance, patience, and strength. We celebrate our abilities, progress, and successes on the way while remaining clear-eyed about the long journey ahead.

Developing effective incentive structures

Just as in economics, incentives are pivotal in shaping a culture that drives the desired behaviors and outcomes. Throughout my career, I have witnessed both extremes – on the one hand, rigid meritocracies and on the other, environments where everyone is generously rewarded, regardless of performance. The optimum, however, lies somewhere between these two poles.

The dangers of poorly constructed incentives are well-documented and can lead to significant unintended consequences. A classic illustration is the frequently cited example of the Soviet nail factory, where output was measured solely by weight.[13] Predictably, the factory began producing large, heavy nails that met the quota but were impractical and went unsold, while the country continued to need smaller nails. The incentive system failed to align with actual requirements, resulting in wasted resources and unmet needs.

Similarly, the story of the Vietnamese rat plague provides a cautionary tale.[14] In an attempt to curb an infestation in Indochina, the French colonial authorities offered a bounty for each rat killed and presented to officials. Unfortunately, the scheme backfired – people began breeding rats to maximize their earnings, which undermined the original purpose of the incentive and exacerbated the problem rather than solving it.

Closer to home, empirical studies reveal how misaligned incentives can foster precisely the opposite of the intended behavior. One particularly striking study caught my attention. Researchers examined the impact of attendance bonuses on absenteeism among apprentice workers at a German retailer.[15] They assigned apprentices to two groups – one was offered a financial bonus and the other extra holiday for perfect attendance. Surprisingly, neither group saw a reduction in absenteeism. In fact, the monetary bonus increased absenteeism by an average of 50 percent. Follow-up surveys revealed that the introduction of a reward for attendance shifted perceptions of what constituted acceptable conduct. Rather than feeling intrinsically obligated to attend, workers felt entitled to take time off, rationalizing that attendance was now transactional rather than expected. This demonstrates how incentives can inadvertently reshape social norms and, in some cases, undermine core values.

This phenomenon is equally relevant when considering performance incentives for teams. If bonuses are awarded for simply meeting basic expectations – such as granting an overly generous target bonus to those who merely do their jobs – the effect is likely to be counterproductive, eroding the drive for exceptional performance. Such systems may inadvertently foster a sense of entitlement rather than a culture of striving for excellence. Furthermore, if bonuses are used as a substitute for competitive base salaries, the incentive becomes a mechanism to patch over structural pay issues rather than reward true achievement. The risk is that team members come to expect these elevated rewards as standard. Any subsequent adjustment, even if performance remains strong, will likely be perceived as a disappointment, leading to demotivation. If top grades and top bonuses are not exclusively awarded to exceptional achievements, the team risks stagnating in a culture of entitlement and mediocrity.

Conversely, an overly rigid meritocratic system can also have negative consequences. Meritocracy is, in principle, a commendable method of recognizing individuals based on achievement rather than background, connections, or entitlement. However, if it becomes an unforgiving, winner-takes-all scenario, it can encourage people to cut corners or engage in questionable practices to secure financial rewards. History is replete with examples of "rogue" traders or employees who, acting in self-interest, have exposed their companies to significant risk. Even the most principled among us can succumb to the temptation of shortcuts during crises or under mounting pressure, making decisions that provide short-term gains but jeopardize long-term stability. One example is deferring essential maintenance to achieve immediate cost savings, which often leads to greater problems later.

Leaders must recognize these pitfalls and strive for balance. An effective incentive system should align individual aspirations and motivations with the broader interests of the company and its stakeholders. This requires thoughtful moderation, ensuring that rewards encourage not only high performance but also long-term responsibility and ethical conduct.

For this reason, I have always approached the measurement of legal team performance with caution, especially when it is based solely on short-term business outcomes. Lawyers are integral to the wider organization, and while their contributions must support overarching performance, their responsibilities extend beyond immediate business metrics. Ultimately, their duty is to uphold the interests of the company and all its stakeholders, safeguarding long-term stability and ethical standards.

Although financial incentives are undeniably important, they are not the sole motivator for legal teams. True fulfilment comes when compensation is commensurate with the value an individual brings to the organization, both in the present and for the future. However, excessive rewards are unnecessary and can be counterproductive. In fact, non-financial incentives often prove to be even more powerful. Recognition, promotions, expanded responsibilities, increased decision-making authority, shared values, job security, a vibrant workplace culture, humanity, humor, and a sense of belonging are all critical motivators. It is incumbent on leaders to develop genuine relationships with their teams, to understand what inspires and drives them and to tailor incentives accordingly.

The art of designing effective incentives lies in understanding that people are motivated by a wide array of factors, not just money. By nurturing relationships, promoting personal growth, and recognizing achievement in a holistic way, leaders can foster a culture where individuals are inspired to excel. Not out of entitlement or fear, but through genuine ambition and shared purpose.

Management by Walking Around

Allocating time during the workday to engage directly with team members is a highly effective leadership practice. There is name for it – leadership literature refers to this as Management By Walking Around (MBWA). The origins of this approach can be traced to various leadership cultures, such as Toyota's *genchi genbutsu* ("go and see for yourself"), which encourages managers to spend time on the shop floor, identify issues firsthand, and propagate best practices through continuous improvement initiatives (referred to as "*kaizen*"). Similarly, Hewlett-Packard, under the guidance of its founders, Bill Hewlett and David Packard, institutionalized informal office visits by managers, later recognized in leadership studies as a model practice.[16]

One clear advantage of MBWA is its positive impact on motivation. Individuals generally appreciate attention and when leaders actively approach and listen to employees, demonstrating genuine interest and understanding of their unique situations and challenges, it conveys empathy and care. This approach helps break down hierarchical barriers, fostering transparent dialogue between leaders and staff. Personal interactions build trust and increase leaders' approachability.

However, MBWA can backfire and fail to achieve its goals. If not executed with authenticity and respect, it may be misinterpreted as unannounced supervision and micromanagement. Engaging team members in discussions about their challenges or ideas raises expectations. Without follow-up actions, acknowledgment, or implementation of suggestions, disappointment and frustration may arise, negatively impacting productivity and morale.[17]

Despite these potential pitfalls, MBWA remains an invaluable tool for legal leaders seeking to strengthen team connections. Regular, authentic conversations drive higher engagement and foster stronger bonds. The benefit of spontaneous discussions is that feedback is direct and unfiltered, free from corporate jargon or stylized presentations. When talking to the team, be yourself and authentic. Resist the temptation to simply waft into open offices like royalty but instead make time for a genuine conversation.

Personally, I dedicate considerable effort to MBWA – typically at least twice weekly, preferably towards week's end when workloads are somewhat lighter. I have long advocated for an open-door policy, making initial contact with team members straightforward. It is usually apparent whether team members are available for conversation and, in most cases, they welcome the opportunity for meaningful interaction.

Conversations often begin with personal inquiries, such as "How are your children?" or "How was your recent marathon?". Not to intrude, but to express sincere interest. For example, I pay particular attention to colleagues returning from maternity leave, acknowledging the adjustments in their lives involved. These discussions can also touch on hobbies or notable experiences, always reflecting a genuine interest in the individual. Nevertheless, MBWA should extend beyond casual exchanges. I am keen to understand how the team is managing their responsibilities, whether they grasp and support our strategies, and how they perceive central initiatives such as new legal operations projects. Questions such as, "How is the new matter management system working for you?" or "Are you able to access necessary templates and best practices?" frequently prompt valuable discussions, particularly with business-facing legal lawyers.

While MBWA at headquarters is easy, I have not yet achieved the same level of success with virtual MBWA as I have in in-person settings. Physical presence allows for more intuitive timing and rapport; attempts to "cold call" employees lack the same ease and comfort. I do reach out to remote team members on specific topics but these interactions are more formal and differ from spontaneous hallway conversations. During my visits to our overseas offices, I devote significant time, often exceeding 60 percent, to team engagement through one-on-one meetings, dinners, and market visits with rotating colleagues.

Recently I heard the story of a business leader who chooses not to book hotels while travelling internationally, instead opting to sleep on planes and arrange meetings at airports. My personal approach could not be further away from this practice. In contrast, my aim is to visit offices specifically to meet with team members in person, aiming to understand and connect with them. This type of interaction typically does not occur in airport settings. These interactions consistently prove to be highlights of my travels, reinforcing the primary goal of building strong team relationships.

Leadership is not a popularity contest

While forging a strong rapport with your team is fundamental to effective leadership, it is crucial not to confuse leadership with a quest for popularity. Sustainable leadership is not about canvassing for approval or seeking to be liked at all costs. The desire to be well-regarded is an understandable human trait, but as leaders, especially within the legal profession, our guiding principle must not be popularity. If we become preoccupied with polling for support or tailoring our actions to win favor, we risk losing sight of our core purpose and responsibilities.

True leadership involves crafting a clear vision and championing that vision with conviction. Although it is essential to involve the team in developing this vision and collaboratively building the strategy, the responsibility for execution ultimately rests with the leader. There will inevitably be times when making the right decision demands courage, as it may not align with popular opinion. Leaders must be prepared to make difficult, sometimes unpopular, choices for the greater good of the team or the wider organization. Trust your instincts as leader. If you shy away from these moments of truth, someone else will step in to fill the void, potentially to the detriment of your team's cohesion and progress.

This leads to a fundamental leadership dilemma. What takes ultimate precedence, the mission or the people? While I have the utmost respect and genuine care for every member of my team, my primary duty as a legal leader is to deliver the outcome articulated in the mission statement. Succumbing to resistance at the first sign of challenge would mean abdicating this responsibility. If every decision is put to a popularity test or subject to team approval, effective leadership soon gives way to indecision and respect is eroded. Worse still, such an approach can foster a toxic culture of gossip and internal politics, where leadership devolves into little more than a popularity contest and the leader becomes captive to fluctuating public opinion – something even seasoned politicians find difficult to manage.

To avoid this pitfall, I prioritize transparency and dialogue. I invest significant time in thoroughly explaining my decisions, inviting feedback, and welcoming constructive challenge from the team. However, once a decision is made, I expect unified action. I expect our team members to get behind me and, if not in initial support, *disagree but commit*. This principle ensures that even those who may have reservations align behind the collective goal, strengthening team solidarity and effectiveness.

In addition, it is vital not to deflect responsibility or hide behind senior management when communicating decisions that may be unpopular. Once you have committed to a course of action, regardless of its origins, it becomes your responsibility to stand by it and own the outcome. Blaming others erodes your authority and diminishes your influence as a leader. Instead, by taking ownership you reinforce your credibility and, leading by example, foster a culture of accountability within your team.

Conflict management

As leaders, we play a pivotal role in conflict management. Effective teamwork requires healthy conflict – constructive, at the right time, and in the right place. In heated debates, the mark is quickly overstepped and what was meant to be constructive turns personal. Leaders need to pick up on this tension and bring the team back to the usual rhythm of harmony.

As leaders, we hold a pivotal responsibility in managing and resolving conflicts within our teams. A certain level of conflict is not only inevitable but also necessary for effective teamwork. It is often through robust discussion and the healthy exchange of differing perspectives that the best ideas emerge. However, there is a delicate balance to strike. Constructive conflict must occur in an appropriate setting and at the right moment, ensuring that disagreements remain focused on the issues. It is all too easy for the conversation to cross the line from productive to personal, which can threaten team cohesion and morale. In these moments, leaders must be attuned to rising tensions and act swiftly to steer the group back towards a collaborative and respectful environment.

Resolving conflicts within a team requires a combination of emotional intelligence, clear communication, and impartiality. First and foremost, leaders must foster an atmosphere of trust where team members feel safe to express their views openly, knowing that their opinions will be heard and respected. When disagreements arise, it is important to address them directly rather than allowing issues to fester beneath the surface. This may involve facilitating open dialogue, encouraging each party to articulate their perspective and actively listening without judgement.

Effective conflict resolution also demands that leaders remain neutral, focusing on the underlying issues rather than the personalities involved. By identifying common ground and shared objectives, leaders can guide the team towards solutions that benefit everyone. Sometimes, it may be necessary to remind team members of the collective mission and the value of diverse viewpoints in achieving innovative outcomes. Setting clear expectations for respectful behavior and intervening promptly when discussions become unproductive are also key responsibilities.

Moreover, leaders should model the behaviors they wish to see, which are demonstrating patience, empathy, and a willingness to compromise where appropriate. Providing feedback constructively and encouraging a culture of continuous learning helps ensure that future conflicts are handled even more effectively. Ultimately, successful conflict management is about restoring and maintaining team harmony, so that energy is channeled towards shared goals rather than internal strife.

References

1 See The Next Level: Creating a Team of Teams, in chapter ten.
2 See BBC, "Our Falkland War: A frontline story", published on 7 June 2022, https://www.bbc.co.uk/
3 See Ideal span of control in chapter seven on Organizational design.
4 The New York Times Deal Book 2023, in which Huang explains why he has 50 direct reports. Available on YouTube. Similarly, Meta's Mark Zuckerberg works directly with a group of 35 leaders. Apparently, he does not hold formal leadership meetings. Alignment is found through bilateral conversation or meetings with those who are essential for the particular project or initiative.
5 See the "Disagree but commit" paradigm, in chapter two.
6 "Disagree but commit" is sometimes easier said than done and requires a dedicated conversation.
7 *Ibid.*
8 See Lencioni, *Death By Meeting* (2004) for additional insights.
9 See the "Spirit of Malente" as unifying momentum in chapter two.
10 Sarah Jackson: "Six Tips from Nvidia CEO Jensen Huang on how to run a company and manage your team", 29 November 2024, businessinsider.com
11 As stipulated in the first law of thermodynamics: energy cannot be created or destroyed; it can only be transformed from one form to another.
12 From Jim Collins, *Good to Great* (2001), www.jimcollins.com.
13 Thomas Sowell, cited in: Koch, *The Science of Success* (2007), page 95.
14 Rolf Dobelli, *The Art of Thinking* Clearly (2014).
15 *The Economist*, 10 October 2024, "Bartleby: When workplace bonuses backfire." The article cites a research project conducted by Altifian, Sliwka, and Vogelsang from the University of Cologne and the Frankfurt School of Finance and Management.
16 See Peters and Watermann, *Search of Excellence* (1982).
17 See the 2013 study conducted by Anita Tucker (Boston University) and Sara Singer (Stanford University) assessing MBWA in 19 hospitals, cited in *The Economist*, Bartleby "Leaving the Seat of Power," 20 February 2025.

Chapter 12: Leadership in successful talent acquisition

Effective recruitment is integral to successful legal leadership. The ability to source and select individuals who demonstrate not only superior legal skills but also align with the core values and behaviors essential to building a high-performing team is critical to success. In today's market, exceptional talent remains scarce. While numerous candidates may possess some desired skills or attributes, it is notably challenging to identify individuals excelling across all key competencies. Heightened competition for top professionals has created what is often described as a "war for talent". High-caliber candidates are discerning in their choices, weighing factors such as organizational culture, sense of belonging, opportunities for professional growth, and reputation alongside financial remuneration. The latter is no longer the decisive factor.

Recruitment forms a key pillar of the people strategy crafted by legal leaders.[1] It is important to resist the urge to fill vacancies hastily with suitable candidates capable merely of performing the role. Instead, each opening should be viewed as a strategic opportunity to enhance the department's talent pool, prioritizing candidates with the right mindset and potential to drive the team forward.

From a leadership perspective, effective legal recruitment comprises two primary components. First, it necessitates a robust and adaptable process for identifying and attracting leading legal professionals – one that is consistently applied across the entire departmental hiring, while retaining flexibility for specific requirements. Second, personal involvement in recruitment is invaluable. I regard participation in the selection process as a direct responsibility, typically meeting all new hires either through comprehensive interviews or 30-minute discussions, depending on the role's importance and seniority. I want to be convinced that the candidate can fulfil the value proposition we had assigned to this role, embodies our core values, and has the potential to bring the team forward. This approach also provides candidates with the opportunity to engage directly with leadership, ask questions, and gain insight into departmental expectations. Moreover, this visible investment by the GC serves as recognition for candidates, offering a competitive advantage in the war for talent. My experience confirms that such engagement is highly beneficial and represents time well invested, given the pivotal role of recruitment in team success.

Who are we looking for?

It is critical to seek out and recruit individuals who are not only intelligent and highly skilled, but who are also empowered to succeed through genuine autonomy. Rather than forcing new hires into rigidly defined, micromanaged roles – which risks producing an army of uniform corporate "tin soldiers" – the goal should be to cultivate a diverse group of individuals whose varied perspectives fuel creative thinking and innovation. It is essential to avoid the trap of selecting candidates simply because they are familiar or share personal similarities, as I once did early in my career. Instead, our focus should be on attracting true talent – people who are not just outstanding legal professionals, but also dynamic team players who show initiative, challenge constructively, and energize those around them to push the team forward.

The ideal team player

In very general terms, reflecting the importance of effective teamwork for legal departments, the aim is to identify ideal team players. In that respect, my thinking is influenced by Patrick Lencioni's work on the ideal team player.[2] According to Lencioni, three main character traits or virtues need to stand out. Ideal team players are humble, hungry, and smart.

1. *Humble* means that they are not egoistical but empathic and genuine team players with integrity and honesty.
2. *Hungry* refers to energy and passion for the work they are doing. They are self-motivated and committed to get things done.
3. *Smart* means that ideal candidates have great people skills and connect well with others.

If candidates are hungry and smart but not humble, they could be described as "skillful politicians". They are unwilling to support team decisions and only progress their own agenda and self-interests.

If candidates are humble and smart but not hungry, Lencioni refers to them as "lovable slackers". There is a lack of commitment to work hard for the team and deliver results. There is limited energy, no proactive approach, and no initiative.

If candidates are humble and hungry but not smart, they could be "accidental mess-makers", meaning that they lack people and communication skills, which has the potential to derail or at least distract the team effort.

Objectifying the assessment

From my own experience, I have learned that recruitment requires a structured and objective approach.[3] Initially, I made the mistake of relying on personal preference and intuition when selecting candidates, focusing more on who felt familiar rather than what the team truly needed. This method was ultimately biased and ineffective, and a thorough failure analysis of my recruitment outcomes revealed the pitfalls of such subjective decision-making.

Moreover, while recruiting candidates based on general qualities as described above like humility, drive, and (emotional) intelligence is a positive first step, it is insufficient for ensuring successful recruiting. Legal leaders must go beyond these general traits and identify the precise competencies, experiences, and personal qualities required for a particular role. This is especially critical when filling senior or strategic positions, where the stakes and expectations are considerably higher. It is essential to define these requirements precisely within the job description and not defer to the general template provided by HR.

For example, if the role involves leading a transformative "change" initiative then proven leadership capabilities, strategic vision, and experience in change management become highly important. In contrast, when recruiting for a leadership position within a team that has been plagued by dysfunction, internal conflict, or a lack of trust, the priority shifts. Here, the ideal candidate over-indexes in people skills with the ability to rebuild relationships, foster collaboration, and restore a healthy, positive team culture as a priority. Another illustrative scenario is hiring a sole practitioner to establish a presence in a newly entered market. In this context, the candidate must possess exemplary organizational and prioritization skills, as she or he will be required to manage an overwhelming workload and navigate the complexities of setting up operations from scratch. The ability to remain focused, resilient, and adaptable is paramount. Without these attributes, the individual risks being overwhelmed by the demands of the role and failing to make a meaningful impact.

To ensure objectivity and consistency in the hiring process, I have developed an assessment framework anchored in four key categories. These categories serve as the cornerstone for evaluating candidates, though their relative importance and weighting may be adjusted depending on the specific requirements of the role.

By systematically scoring candidates in each category and providing a clear rationale for each assessment, legal leaders can make informed, objective decisions that balance technical proficiency with the personal qualities essential for team and organizational success.

- *Legal skills* encompass not only a robust education and proven experience in the legal field, but also a genuine enthusiasm for the law itself. I view these skills as non-negotiable – they are the cornerstone upon which all other capabilities rest. A candidate must demonstrate both technical competence and relentless curiosity, continuously seeking innovative and practical legal solutions to complex challenges. Candidates should be ambitious to become the go-to person for a particular area of law, brand, or type of business. It is this blend of solid grounding and creative thinking that enables a legal professional to deliver consistently outstanding results and make a meaningful contribution to the team.
- *Energy and drive* reflect both the personal motivation to achieve individual goals and the capacity to inspire momentum within the wider team. I look for candidates who not only exhibit discipline and perseverance in their own work, but who also bring a contagious positivity that lifts those around them. This means taking ownership, showing resilience in the face of setbacks, and maintaining a proactive, results-oriented approach. It is about fostering a "play-to-win"[4] mentality, where delivering superior outcomes is balanced with the ability to energize and encourage others to strive towards shared objectives.
- *Smart with potential* pertains to a candidate's interpersonal skills and intrinsic values. Here, I assess their capacity to build rapport, communicate effectively, and respond thoughtfully to feedback. The willingness to listen, adapt, and learn from others is vital for personal progression and for contributing positively to team dynamics. In addition, I seek evidence of ambition and the potential for growth – individuals who are not just content to perform their current role, but who aspire to develop, take on greater responsibility, and help shape the future of the team.
- *Business acumen and influence* are about a candidate's ability to understand the business environment in all its complexity. An exceptional

candidate will grasp the company's strategic objectives, operational realities, and the wider market landscape. He or she is capable of translating legal expertise into actionable, practical advice that aligns with business imperatives. Equally important is the skill to communicate legal advice persuasively, earning trust and influencing decision-makers at every level of the organization.

By evaluating candidates across these four dimensions, I ensure a holistic assessment that balances technical excellence with the attributes necessary to thrive in a dynamic, high-performing legal team, as shown in Figure 3.

Legal skills

- Passion for law
- Solid academic education
- Curious and constant learner
- Creative but realistic
- Problem solver mindset
- Able to build own legal brand

Energy and drive

- Hungry self-starter
- Takes initiative and delivers
- Able to prioritize – gets things done
- Disciplined and accountable for results
- Energy-giver to the team (optimism is a choice)
- Challenges status quo and drives continuous improvement

Smart with potential

- Empathetic with good people skills
- Humble but ambitious
- Honest and transparent
- Caring for colleagues and the team
- Listens and open to feedback
- Bigger roles/leadership potential

Business acumen and influence

- Passion for business, playing to win
- Solid business understanding with curiosity
- Able to build trust with business leaders
- Clear, practical, and convincing advice
- Courageous and unbiased

Figure 3: The talent assessment matrix.

I now rigorously assess every candidate across four core dimensions, dedicating ample time to explore each area during the interview process. To maintain objectivity and provide a useful reference, especially given the large number of applicants I encounter, I assign each candidate a score out of ten for each category. In addition, I document a concise rationale to explain my reasoning and highlight any standout qualities or concerns. This dual approach, combining quantitative scoring with qualitative insights, enables meaningful comparison between candidates and creates a clear record of the factors influencing my judgement. Ultimately, this method helps safeguard against unconscious bias and ensures that recruitment decisions are based equally on technical merit as well as on the behaviors and values that contribute most positively to the team and the wider organization.

Interviews and the recruitment process

Recruiting top legal talent is challenging, as candidates often present only their strengths. Ultimately the aim is to identify those who are outstanding legal talents, and not only excellent at job interviews. A structured approach helps reveal genuine potential beyond impressive interviewing skills.

Go deep, listen, and observe

When it comes to interviews, I consciously avoid the conventional path of relying solely on standardized, HR-prepared questions. Instead, I dedicate significant time and effort to devising bespoke conversational themes that genuinely probe into what is necessary for success in the role. My interviews are never rushed – I take the time needed to go deep, which could extend to two hours or more for senior or critical roles. To break down the barriers of rehearsed answers, I often suggest a walk or a lunch, using these informal settings to get beneath the surface and truly understand the individual behind the CV.

I am particularly drawn to responses from candidates that showcase genuine originality and inventive legal thinking. It is immediately apparent when someone is actively listening and engaging in the discussion, bringing fresh perspectives to the table. In contrast, my interest wanes rapidly when candidates simply present rehearsed success stories or revert to a standardized "achievement pitch", rather than directly addressing the question asked. In the extreme, it feels like watching a politician on camera who makes a statement that bears little relevance to the question asked. Well-considered answers that get straight to the heart of the question are far more compelling. Originality in thinking trumps perfection in presentation.

I make it a point to invite candidates to talk about legal matters they are genuinely proud of and then probe further to discern the specific nature of their involvement. It is not uncommon for candidates to reference significant achievements, sometimes including high-profile cases or notable clients, only for it to emerge that their personal input was limited – perhaps as one of many team members simply fulfilling an expected role. While teamwork is of course very important, I am more interested in hearing about situations where candidates can clearly articulate their own unique contributions, the challenges they personally overcame, and the tangible impact they made personally.

On occasion, I might ask the candidate in interviews to collaborate with me in developing a strategy or plan for the team. This often leads to an engaging and inspiring discussion. I am also careful to ensure that ample time is set aside for candidates to ask their own questions. This not only creates a genuine dialogue, it also allows candidates to assess the opportunity and cultural environment in detail, and offers valuable insights into what matters most to candidates. The nature of their enquiries and the way they ask them can be highly revealing, often providing insights into their priorities, values, and level of preparation.

I once worked with a very experienced legal leader who would begin interviews by asking candidates to tell him a joke. His intention was to break through the practiced façade and observe how individuals responded to the unexpected. While the joke itself was irrelevant – and most struggled to deliver one – their reactions offered insight into their adaptability and authenticity. Personally, I find such approach a little intrusive and prefer to foster meaningful discussion through more considered questioning.

Bottom line, I must believe the candidate can excel in the role as defined with its particular profile and requirements. Candidates also have to convince me of their potential and ambition to deliver results and to grow within the team as a genuine team player. I am looking for something special that the candidate contributes to the team. Conversely, if the candidate fails to convince me beyond doubt during the interview process, it is hard to believe that the candidate has the ability to influence business leaders in practice.

Candidate's self-awareness

Assessing self-awareness is another crucial aspect of my interview process. Everyone has strengths that come naturally and areas where others excel more easily. The key is to recognize and openly acknowledge both. As Sun Tzu famously said, "If you know yourself and your enemy, you will win every battle". Mature candidates are typically more willing to discuss their weaknesses and, more importantly, to explain the strategies they employ to compensate for them. For example, one memorable candidate revealed to tending to act quickly – sometimes at the expense of thoroughness. To counterbalance this, he had established a routine of double-checking his work and collaborating with detail-oriented colleagues. Such candor and proactive self-correction are hallmarks of both self-awareness and professional adaptation.

Panel diversity

At the outset of each recruitment round, we assemble a diverse interview panel, drawing members from different parts of the legal team to ensure a broad spectrum of perspectives. I am committed to fostering true diversity so that all parts and aspects of the team are included and represented. While the job description serves as the principal script, the lead recruiter briefs the panel thoroughly and encourages interviewers to pursue promising lines of enquiry as they see fit. The aim is to assess each candidate holistically, leaving no aspect unexplored. The panel reconvenes shortly after the interviews to share observations, with the lead recruiter guiding the discussion and recording detailed notes.

Final call

Ultimately, I believe that the final hiring decision should rest with the lead interviewer, who is typically the line manager responsible for the candidate's day-to-day management and long-term development. However, this responsibility must be exercised prudently. The lead interviewer cannot simply override well-founded concerns raised by the panel. Instead, there must be consensus that the chosen candidate is not only suitable for the immediate needs of the team but also possesses the potential to grow and lead the team forward in the future.

In certain cases, particularly where communication skills appear less developed than desired, a written assessment can provide valuable additional insight. This need not be a lengthy, footnote-loaded legal memorandum. A succinct email to a business leader outlining the issues and recommending a course of action can be far more instructive, revealing both clarity of thought and communication style.

Finally, it is important to bear in mind that the ideal candidate is not necessarily the smoothest interviewee. Some individuals excel at presenting themselves but may lack the discipline, organization, or determination to follow through on their promises. Therefore, it is essential to probe thoroughly across all assessment dimensions – technical skills, cultural alignment, motivation, and communication – to ensure a well-rounded and accurate evaluation of each candidate's true suitability.

References

1 See Talent acquisition strategy in chapter five.

2 Lencioni, *The Ideal Team Player, How to Recognize and Cultivate the Three Essential Virtues* (2016).

3 According to Bartleby, *The Economist* of 18 December 2025, "How to conduct a job interview", structured job interviews have the most predictive value of any recruitment method, quoting a 2022 study of Paul Sackett of the University of Minnesota and his co-authors. "An unstructured interview, in which hiring managers make things up on the fly and reach decisions based on gut instincts, has less than half the predictive validity of a structured one."

4 In reference to *Playing to Win*, a 2013 HBR title written by former Procter & Gamble CEO, A.G. Lafley.

Chapter 13:
Case study – navigating the VUCA world

In the contemporary legal environment, leaders find themselves navigating an increasingly turbulent landscape characterized by volatility, uncertainty, complexity, and ambiguity, collectively encapsulated in the VUCA framework. Although the term VUCA originated within military circles to describe unpredictable and swiftly changing conditions, it has since become strikingly pertinent to the legal sector. Today's legal leaders are not only expected to respond effectively to rapid change but also to anticipate unforeseen challenges, ensuring that both their clients and teams remain resilient, adaptable, and aligned with strategic goals in the midst of continual disruption.

The reality is that VUCA is a universal phenomenon. No organization or leader is exempt from its effects. Rather than viewing VUCA purely as an obstacle, it can and should be embraced as an opportunity for growth and differentiation. The more adept we become at reading and interpreting shifting circumstances, the more sophisticated our intelligence-gathering and forecasting capabilities, and the more agile and decisive our leadership, the greater the advantage we create. Not only for our legal teams but for the business as a whole.

Legal leaders must therefore cultivate a mindset and organizational culture that welcomes change, encourages proactive horizon scanning, and supports rapid yet thoughtful decision-making. By continuously scanning the legal and regulatory environment for emerging trends and potential disruptions, leaders can position their teams to act swiftly and effectively when new challenges arise. This proactive approach strengthens both the quality of legal advice provided and the overall value delivered to the business.

Ultimately, the key to thriving in a VUCA world lies in the ability to transform uncertainty into strategic advantage. By fostering agility, resilience, and a commitment to continuous learning within their teams, legal leaders can not only weather the storms of disruption but also seize opportunities for innovation and growth, ensuring that the legal function remains a critical enabler of organizational success.

Understanding VUCA and its impact

VUCA encapsulates the core challenges facing legal leaders today:

- *Volatility:* Describes a situation of pace and unpredictability of rapid change, such as sudden regulatory shifts, technological breakthroughs, or rapid market fluctuations. This can change established norms overnight without warning. For example, a dramatic and unforeseen change in regulatory requirements or an unexpected legal reform can put the entire business operations in a country at risk and demand immediate action.
- *Uncertainty:* Describes a situation of lack of clarity about future events or outcomes, often due to incomplete information. There is consensus that change will happen, but timing and extent remain unclear. For instance, after winning the election, the new governing party will introduce a new trade policy with increased tariffs, but the timing and exact level of new duties remain unclear.
- *Complexity:* Describes a situation of multiple, interconnected, interdependent, and potentially changing variables where their respective impact on the total outcome remains unclear. Cross-border transactions, multi-party and multi-jurisdictional litigation are all examples of complexity in legal practice.
- *Ambiguity:* Describes a situation where information is unclear, incomplete, or even contradictory. It requires interpretation without clear precedents or rules. Dealing with AI is a good example for a situation of ambiguity as it does not fit into the present regulatory framework. The upsides of using AI are multi-fold but there are also great risks for the existing legal system.

Leadership responses to VUCA

Traditional top-down planning and rigid hierarchies often fall short in a VUCA environment. Instead, legal leaders must foster a culture that is agile, adaptive, and resilient. *Auftragstaktik*[1] or mission tactics is a powerful tool to address VUCA challenges in preparation for the unpreparable. Unite the team behind the vision, decentralize and authorize rapid decision-making within a predefined teamwork, foster radical information transparency, and value a speedy response over a perfect outcome.

Volatility – acting with agility and speed

When faced with rapid change, leaders should prioritize agility. This means making swift, informed decisions without losing sight of core values and the long-term vision. Leaders are prepared to adapt or correct previous decisions if necessary. Material one-way decisions that are difficult to reverse are postponed as long as possible until the situation becomes clearer. Scenario planning, regular risk assessments, and flexible resource allocation allow leaders to reroute plans quickly while keeping the team focused on the ultimate goal. Investing in horizon scanning, which is actively seeking intelligence on emerging trends, can provide early warning and better preparedness.

Uncertainty – embracing informed experimentation
Uncertainty demands a proactive approach to information gathering and intelligence sharing. Legal leaders should cultivate diverse networks, both within and outside their organizations, enabling them to access a broad range of perspectives. Encouraging a culture of "hope for the best, plan for the worst" helps teams develop contingency plans and remain ready to adapt. Transparent communication and regular scenario analysis also help clarify potential risks and responses.

Complexity – simplifying and integrating
Complex environments require leaders to simplify wherever possible. This might involve breaking down large projects into manageable components, integrating cross-functional teams into a unified "team of teams", and leveraging technology to streamline workflows. Prioritizing clarity, setting clear roles and responsibilities, and focusing on critical issues help reduce confusion and enable more effective collaboration.

Ambiguity – taking incremental steps
In ambiguous situations, leaders should avoid making irreversible decisions until more information becomes available. Instead, they can adopt an iterative approach – moving forward in small, reversible steps and regularly reviewing outcomes. This allows teams to learn quickly, adjust course as needed, and keep options open. Encouraging experimentation and learning from small failures fosters innovation and builds confidence in navigating the unknown.

Embracing VUCA as an opportunity for growth

While the VUCA world presents undeniable challenges, it also offers legal leaders the chance to generate a competitive advantage for the company. It is important to remember that these challenging circumstances are not exclusive to any single individual or company. Rather, they are a shared reality for everybody. There is no universal playbook for best navigation through the VUCA world. In light of rapidly changing situations and facts, assessments and decisions require constant revision and adaptation. In this regard, stakeholder and expectation management is essential for success as legal advice in a VUCA environment differs fundamentally to what some clients might be used to. By embracing agility, fostering resilience, and preparing for the unexpected, legal leaders can turn uncertainty into opportunity and ensure their organizations are fit for the future.

The agile manifesto and its ways of working

The key to excelling amidst the complexities of VUCA is to adopt an agility framework, a concept whose relevance has endured since its inception. Agility emerged as a cornerstone of contemporary leadership and organizational practice through the "Manifesto for Agile Software Development," drafted in February 2001 by 17 visionary software experts at a retreat in Snowbird, Utah.[2] This manifesto arose from widespread dissatisfaction with the prevailing "heavyweight" methods of software development, such as the rigid waterfall model, which relied on exhaustive documentation and sequential planning. These traditional approaches were regularly derided for their slow pace, excessive bureaucracy, and inability to adapt to evolving needs or late-stage changes. Lengthy upfront planning and meticulous specification meant that projects often failed to respond to new challenges or opportunities, resulting in costly overruns or outright failures. Moreover, these methods tended to discourage meaningful collaboration, with limited interaction among developers, business stakeholders, and customers throughout the project lifecycle.

Seeking a more effective and collaborative approach, the authors of "The Agile Manifesto" articulated four fundamental values that continue to underpin modern agile methodologies:

1. *People over processes.* Successful projects center around highly motivated teams, supported and trusted to deliver results. Rather than treating work as an assembly-line process, organizations should foster an environment that encourages creativity, problem-solving, and sustainable work rhythms. Open, face-to-face communication is vital, as it enables employees to suggest improvements and managers to remove barriers to collaboration.

2. *Responding to change over following a fixed plan.* Detailed, long-range project plans often become obsolete before they are executed. Teams should create a strategic vision but only plan for tasks that remain relevant in the short-term. A willingness to adapt and learn, even late in a project, ensures alignment with client needs and enhances outcomes. Embracing change keeps teams responsive and closer to the customer.
3. *Working prototypes over excessive documentation.* Rapid experimentation and the creation of tangible prototypes allow innovators to test ideas in real market conditions. This approach fosters quicker learning, greater job satisfaction, and more valuable output. Teams should pilot solutions with select customers, gather feedback, and iterate swiftly. Disputes should be settled through practical experiments and suggestions rather than lengthy debates or appeals to hierarchy.
4. *Customer collaboration over rigid contracts.* Speed to market and cost efficiency are paramount. Since customers rarely know precisely what they want at the outset, specifications must evolve throughout the process. Frequent prototyping, ongoing market validation, and continuous collaboration ensure that development stays focused on delivering genuine customer value.

Practical considerations

The principles of agility are particularly evident in effective crisis management. Frequently, organizations assemble cross-functional task forces at short notice to tackle urgent and complex challenges, drawing on expertise from a range of disciplines to rapidly generate practical solutions. This collaborative but focused approach enables teams to address critical issues efficiently and adapt to fast-changing circumstances. However, it is important to recognize that operating in a constant state of crisis is unsustainable. Business success is more akin to running a marathon than a sprint and maintaining such an intense pace indefinitely can lead to burnout and diminish long-term effectiveness.

Instead, legal leaders should harness the strengths of agile methodology in a targeted manner, deploying "sprints" when rapid response is required, but ensuring that the overall team rhythm remains sustainable. By deliberately applying agile practices – such as forming multidisciplinary teams for defined periods, encouraging open communication, and continuously learning from iterative feedback – organizations can balance the need for speed with the importance of resilience. This approach not only enables swift resolution of urgent matters but also supports the long-term health and productivity of the team, ensuring that business objectives are met without sacrificing wellbeing or creativity.

Consider, for instance, the sudden introduction of new packaging regulations in a major export market. This is an unforeseen development that has caught the entire industry off guard. As an emerging market, the legislative process is not as transparent and inclusive as hoped for. On substance, these new regulations appear puzzling, offering little justification from a business, environmental, or consumer benefit perspective. Nonetheless, compliance with the newly mandated packaging materials has become non-negotiable for any organization wishing to maintain its market presence.

Addressing such an unexpected and complex challenge cannot be accomplished through traditional, hierarchical channels alone. Instead, it necessitates the rapid formation of a cross-functional, agile team drawn from across the organization and beyond. At the heart of this team should be the business leader responsible for the specific export market, as they are uniquely positioned to consolidate and interpret all relevant information pertaining to local operations and customer needs.

Alongside business leaders, lawyers and technical regulatory specialists advise on the interpretation of the new rules, pathways to implementation, transition periods, and acceptable alternatives, in constant dialogue with key government stakeholders, at the working as well as the political level. The procurement team must also be engaged from the outset, tasked with sourcing compliant materials at speed and negotiating with suppliers to ensure continuity of supply chains. Equally vital are contributions from government affairs and legal experts, who are responsible for engaging with regulatory authorities and educating both internal and external stakeholders about the operational challenges posed by the new rules. Working collaboratively, these specialists can develop and present well-founded alternative proposals to regulators – solutions that not only meet the legal requirements but also offer improved outcomes from environmental or societal perspectives. The credibility of such proposals is greatly enhanced by robust scientific evidence, ideally provided by the organization's R&D function.

Where possible, this approach should transcend the interests of a single organization. Coordinating an industry-wide response, rather than merely voicing concerns from one company, carries significantly more influence with policymakers. By uniting competitors and peers in a shared advocacy effort, the industry can present a compelling, collective case for regulatory flexibility or refinement, thereby increasing the likelihood of a favorable resolution.

This scenario illustrates the essence of an agile response within a VUCA (volatile, uncertain, complex, and ambiguous) world. It demonstrates how organizations can mobilize multidisciplinary teams, break down silos, and collaborate at speed to navigate unforeseen challenges effectively. Such agility ensures not only compliance and operational continuity but also positions the business as a proactive and credible partner to regulators and stakeholders alike, turning disruption into an opportunity for constructive engagement and innovation.

VUCA strategies for legal leaders – embracing agility and adaptability

In conclusion, effective strategies for navigating a VUCA environment do not necessarily demand the invention of an entirely new set of leadership tools. Instead, the most successful organizations are those that foster a culture where initiative, empowerment, and trust are actively encouraged and embedded at every level. Such a culture enables teams to respond swiftly and creatively to unforeseen challenges, leveraging the collective strengths and insights of their members. A certain degree of imperfection is accepted and decisions have built-in resilience so that they can be revised and adapted where and when necessary.

Interestingly, the principles underpinning this approach are not new. The concept of *Auftragstaktik*, developed by Helmuth von Moltke nearly two centuries ago, remains highly relevant and instructive for today's legal leaders. *Auftragstaktik*, or "mission command", emphasizes the importance of clearly communicating intent and desired outcomes as framework, while granting leaders the autonomy to determine how best to achieve these objectives based on their expertise and situational awareness.[3] This philosophy empowers teams to adapt dynamically as circumstances evolve, rather than relying solely on rigid instructions or hierarchical decision making.

For legal leaders operating in the modern VUCA world, embracing such an approach means creating an environment where initiative is valued, and employees are trusted to make decisions on the frontlines. It involves providing clarity of purpose, encouraging open communication, and supporting continuous learning from both successes and setbacks. By drawing on these time-tested principles, legal teams can remain agile, resilient, and well-equipped to tackle the complex and rapidly changing challenges of today's business landscape:

- *Empower agile teams:* Enable teams to make decisions rapidly and autonomously, especially those on the frontlines who are closest to emerging issues. Grant them the authority and trust to experiment, iterate, and respond swiftly to new challenges. Encourage teams to prototype solutions, pilot them with select stakeholders, and adopt a cycle of continuous feedback and improvement.
- *Champion adaptability:* Lead by example in demonstrating flexibility and openness to change. Recognize that setbacks and evolving circumstances are inevitable in a volatile and uncertain environment. Celebrate lessons learned from mistakes and pivot quickly when necessary. Make adaptability a core organizational value, ensuring that teams are comfortable revisiting decisions and modifying strategies as new information emerges. Acknowledge that agility is a key asset in navigating constant flux.
- *Set dynamic expectations:* Prepare business leaders and stakeholders for a fast-paced, changeable operating environment. Reinforce the principle that advice and decisions must be revisited as facts change. Avoid complacency by regularly challenging the status quo and encouraging contingency planning. Develop not just a single alternative (Plan B), but multiple backup options (Plans C, D, E, and F) to ensure readiness for various scenarios. This multi-layered approach ensures organizational resilience and responsiveness.
- *Strengthen communication channels:* Maintain open, transparent, and regular lines of communication throughout the organization. Ensure that crucial messages are clear, consistent, and easily understood. Establish mechanisms for frontline teams to report new developments, escalate issues, and share insights promptly. By actively listening to those closest to change, organizations can gain a competitive advantage by responding to threats and opportunities ahead of the curve.
- *Build organizational resilience:* Invest in contingency planning and cross-functional training to ensure teams can adapt to unexpected events. Foster flexible working arrangements that allow rapid redeployment of resources as circumstances dictate. Cultivate reserves, be it additional personnel, financial resources, or technical capacity, that can be mobilized at short notice. This proactive approach minimizes disruption and supports sustained success, even in the face of adversity.

- *Harness technology effectively:* Leverage legal technology tools and automation to streamline routine and administrative tasks. By digitizing and automating repetitive processes, legal teams free up valuable time for strategic analysis, creative problem-solving, and innovation. Stay abreast of emerging technologies and integrate them thoughtfully to improve efficiency and enhance decision making.
- *Network with purpose:* Actively engage with professional associations, regulatory bodies, and industry peers to remain informed about evolving trends, regulatory changes, and best practices. Establish collaborative relationships and participate in industry-wide initiatives. This proactive networking not only expands organizational knowledge but also positions legal leaders to shape and influence the broader regulatory and business landscape.

References

1 See Leading the team with Mission Tactics, in chapter ten.

2 Rigby, Sutherland, Takeuchi, "Embracing Agile", *Harvard Business Review*, May 2016; Brosseau, Ebrahim, Handscomb, Thaker in: McKinsey & Company, "The journey to an agile organisation", published May 2019.

3 See chapter ten.

Part Four:
Legal leaders fit for the future – the Artificial Intelligence challenge

In part four, we set our sights on the horizon, examining what it means to deliver outstanding legal leadership in the years ahead. As the landscape continues to evolve at pace, effective legal leaders will not only steer their teams with clear intent but will also actively equip them with the skills, adaptability, and resilience required to meet future challenges. This involves fostering an environment where innovation, continuous learning, and agility are at the forefront, ensuring legal professionals remain prepared to navigate uncertainty and seize new opportunities as they arise. By anticipating emerging trends and embracing technological advances, legal leaders can confidently guide their teams towards sustained success in an increasingly complex world.

Since the emergence of major law firms in the 1980s and 1990s, the legal industry has remained largely untouched by genuine disruption. The prevailing business model has endured for over a century, with current revenues for the largest firms soaring into the billions. Despite this financial growth, the traditional partnership structure continues to dominate law firms, with the career path to partnership remaining the norm, albeit with modifications. Remuneration of lawyers is still primarily based on hours worked and the only significant innovation has been the widespread practice of offering substantial discounts on standard rates to attract or retain clients.

However, the legal profession now stands at the threshold of a profound transformation. The rise of artificial intelligence (AI) promises not only faster and more cost-effective legal services but also the potential for greater accuracy, creativity (as it spots patterns otherwise undetected), and more reliable outcome prediction. Although we are still in the early stages of this shift, a range of specialist AI solutions tailored for legal work have begun to appear. *Harvey*, named after the protagonist of the television series "Suits", is arguably the leading player in this space, boasting around 500 clients, revenues exceeding $100m and a market valuation of $5bn.[1] Harvey's partnership with A&O Shearman (renowned for its technology accelerator, FUSE) has further accelerated its growth. Other noteworthy competitors include

Luminance (based in the UK), *Legora* (Sweden), and *Noxtua* (Germany), the latter having announced a partnership with the law firm CMS. Harvey has secured a collaboration with LexisNexis, one of the largest repositories of legal data, potentially granting it exclusive access to its content. Nevertheless, all legal AI agents operate on similar underlying platforms and confront comparable challenges.

Despite the promise of these tools, adoption within the legal sector remains minimal. According to research by Gartner, only one percent of the world's largest 5,000 companies currently employ AI in their legal operations.[2] Security concerns are the principal barrier to wider adoption, even surpassing worries about reliability and the risk of AI "hallucinations" producing incorrect or misleading outputs. Yet, the potential for efficiency gains is enormous. Salesforce, for example, estimates that its proprietary AI agent, originally named *Agentforce*, will save the company 9,500 hours annually in staff time devoted to compliance and risk management tasks.[3]

The question remains, are Large Language Models (LLMs) truly capable of delivering the disruptive change to the legal industry many anticipate? Historically, legal practice has been thought to require nuanced human judgement – balancing legal arguments is not a purely mathematical exercise but rather demands careful consideration of the broader context and circumstances. Achieving justice often involves weighing what is fair and right in unique or unprecedented situations.

Recent developments suggest that LLMs are rapidly closing the gap. In 2023, GPT-4 not only passed the US bar exam but ranked among the top ten percent of human test-takers, according to OpenAI.[4] However, legal leaders must recognize both the capabilities and the limitations of these technologies. While LLMs can produce plausible-sounding answers and excel in structured environments like exams, true legal work often demands deeper insight and ethical judgement – qualities that may remain the domain of humans, or possibly advanced humanoid AI in the future.

To navigate this evolving landscape, legal leaders must gain a robust understanding of the technology – the mechanisms that drive AI, its constraints, and associated risks. They must also design organizational structures and workflows that clearly define the interfaces between human expertize and AI-driven processes. Ultimately, the profession's ability to adapt will determine whether it thrives in an AI-transformative world, turning technological disruption into a catalyst for innovation and progress.

References

1 *Financial Times*, "How a former junior lawyer created a $5B AI legal start-up", 15 September 2025.
2 *Financial Times*, "AI agents still need a human in the mix for legal tasks," 4 September 2025.
3 *Ibid.*
4 https://openai.com/index/gpt-4-research/

Chapter 14:
The state of play in AI

When discussing artificial intelligence (AI) or the concept of superintelligence, we are referring to advanced systems that have the capability to learn from vast quantities of data, discern patterns, and make decisions in the absence of explicit, step-by-step instructions from human programmers. This process is broadly known as machine learning, a subfield of AI that has enabled a wide array of innovative applications across numerous sectors.

Large Language Models (LLMs) such as OpenAI's GPT, Google's Gemini, Microsoft's Copilot, and Anthropic's Claude have gained significant attention in recent years for their remarkable ability to generate human-like language and assist with a variety of tasks, from drafting documents to translating text. However, these models represent just one facet of the expansive AI landscape.

AI encompasses several other key domains, each with its own set of capabilities and use cases:

- *Computer vision*. This branch of AI allows computers to process, interpret, and analyze visual information from the world, much like the human eye. Applications range from facial recognition systems used at airports and on smartphones, to object detection in autonomous vehicles and quality control on manufacturing lines.
- *Reinforcement learning*. Here, AI agents are trained to make a series of decisions by receiving rewards for desirable actions. This approach is widely used in robotics – where machines learn tasks through trial and error – as well as in developing AI that can compete against humans in complex games such as chess or Go. Reinforcement learning also plays an important role in training LLMs.
- *Speech recognition*. This technology enables machines to process and understand spoken language. Voice assistants like Siri and Alexa rely on speech recognition to interpret user commands, transcribe audio, and facilitate hands-free interaction with devices.
- *Traditional machine learning*. In this area, AI is used to analyze structured datasets to make predictions or classify information. Common

examples include credit risk assessment in financial services, where algorithms evaluate the likelihood of loan default, and spam filtering in email systems, where messages are categorized as legitimate or junk based on learned patterns.

In essence, while LLMs have brought AI into the public consciousness due to their versatility with language and information processing, they are just one part of a much broader technological revolution. The full spectrum of AI includes systems capable of seeing, listening, learning from experience, and reasoning across structured and unstructured data, all of which are steadily transforming how individuals and organizations operate in an increasingly digital world.

Generative vs agentic AI

It is important to delve deeper into the nuanced distinction between generative AI and agentic AI, as they represent two fundamentally different approaches to artificial intelligence. Generative AI refers to systems designed to create content (be it text, code, images, or other media) as a response to prompts provided by users. Current examples such as GPT, Gemini, Copilot, Claude, and DeepSeek excel at handling single-step tasks – they can draft documents, produce summaries, translate text into various languages, or assist with brainstorming, but always as a direct reaction to human input. Their capabilities are impressive, yet their scope is typically restricted to the completion of well-defined tasks, much like a skilled writer producing prose based on an idea supplied by someone else.

Agentic AI, on the other hand, marks a significant evolution in artificial intelligence by functioning as an autonomous problem-solver. Instead of simply responding to prompts, agentic AI is capable of managing complex, multi-step workflows. Agentic AI mirrors the adaptive and goal-oriented nature of human intelligence. When presented with a desired outcome or objective, agentic AI does not wait for further guidance but instead proactively devises a plan, executes the necessary steps, monitors progress, and revises its strategy as circumstances require. To accomplish this, agentic AI orchestrates a variety of generative AI tools, directing them as needed to fulfil different components of the overall task. In essence, if generative AI is akin to a brilliant author who can craft elegant text from supplied ideas, agentic AI is the project manager – it recruits the author, oversees the manuscript, develops launch and marketing strategies, coordinates production, and determines pricing and sales tactics. All done in one single, continuous workflow process.

Although agentic AI in 2025 is still in its infancy, it is already making its mark in enterprise-level automation. For instance, Microsoft's *Copilot* can autonomously analyze threads within Outlook emails, verify the status of ongoing projects in SharePoint, generate draft action plans in Word, and schedule follow-up meetings in Outlook. Copilot is cable of streamlining entire workflows with minimal human intervention. Similarly, Salesforce's *Agentforce* operates as a customer service agent by processing support tickets, retrieving customer purchase histories from the Customer Relationship Management (CRM) system, consulting inventory software for relevant products, issuing refunds through financial software interface, and closing tickets – all in an integrated, automated manner. Closer to the legal sector, the AI agent *Harvey* is advertised as an agentive AI that reviews contracts, checks liability clauses against the company's approved risk playbook, flags deviations, and generates a redline with suggested alternative language for negotiation. Again, all in a continuous workflow without the need of human intervention.[1]

The emergence of agentic AI signals a paradigm shift in how businesses and professionals can leverage artificial intelligence. Rather than merely automating isolated tasks, agentic AI systems are poised to manage entire processes, adapt to new information, and coordinate complex activities. For that reason, agentic AI has the potential to completely reshape how organizations approach problem-solving, decision making, and operational efficiency in the digital age.

Large language models

Within the legal profession, large language models (LLMs) have emerged as particularly significant technological tools. Acting as the core engine powering generative AI, LLMs are sophisticated statistical prediction machines. These models are trained on vast datasets to anticipate the most probable next word in a sequence of text, enabling them to generate language that closely mirrors human writing and reasoning with remarkable proficiency. This capability, though rooted in the seemingly straightforward act of predicting subsequent words, becomes incredibly powerful when scaled up and applied to legal documents and workflows.

From language prediction to universal interface

LLMs function as statistical prediction machines. Their core and original task is to predict the most probable next token in a given sequence, be it a word, word segment, or character. This is achieved by breaking down input text into machine-readable units called tokens, which are then transformed into numerical representations known as embeddings. These embeddings capture the semantic meaning and relationships between words – words with similar meanings are mapped closer together in this multidimensional space.

The remarkable predictive abilities of LLMs are powered by their transformer architecture. A foundational deep learning structure is now standard in advanced AI systems. Unlike earlier models, transformers can process all elements of a sentence or even an entire document simultaneously, rather than sequentially. This enables LLMs to grasp long-range dependencies and contextual relationships across words, phrases, sentences, and idiomatic expressions with astonishing precision. As a result, these models can generate coherent, contextually aware responses and perform complex reasoning tasks, solidifying their role as the backbone of modern AI-driven solutions.

Language processing, however, is one facet of the broader methodology underpinning LLMs. It is anticipated that LLMs are progressing beyond their origins as generators of text and language, evolving into universal interfaces and sophisticated reasoning engines. Their expanding capabilities are expected to allow them to interpret user goals, devise logical plans, and execute complex actions across a diverse range of digital environments.

LLMs also serve as the foundational layer in agentic AI systems. However, for these models to make autonomous, strategic decisions, they require a higher-level organizational framework. This is provided by the emerging generation of LLMs – often dubbed "LLM 2.0" – which act as orchestrators or project managers, coordinating multiple generative models to achieve multi-step objectives. The underlying structure enabling this coordination is known as "reasoning and acting".

For instance, when given a prompt such as "list the ten biggest cities in France by population", a traditional LLM 1.0 would typically search for existing published top ten cities rankings and select the most corroborated answers. By contrast, an LLM 2.0 would decompose the request into discrete, logical steps – first, it would research the current populations of major French cities, then it would rank these cities mathematically from largest to smallest. This approach mirrors human problem-solving by planning, executing, and verifying each stage of the process.

This multi-step reasoning is also evident in more complex tasks, such as travel planning. Consider the instruction: "Find the best flight to London on 23 December and book a luxurious hotel for two nights". An advanced LLM would break this down into a series of actions – querying flight booking interfaces (so-called APIs to booking agents like Google Flights or airline websites), analyzing prices, searching hotel APIs, analyzing reviews to meet "luxurious" criteria, comparing total costs, and finally booking through the relevant APIs. At each step, the model must determine which external tool or database to consult – a process known as tool selection or coordination. These tools might include search engines, other LLMs, calculators, code interpreters, or specialized databases. After each action, the LLM receives feedback (an observation), assesses whether this outcome moves it closer to the goal (e.g., identifying the best flight based on price, number of stops, or preferred airline), and adjusts its plan accordingly. If an error or unexpected result occurs, the LLM revises the remaining steps. If the criteria are met, it proceeds to finalize the booking.

As a further example, the same reasoning methodology can be applied to more specialized domains such as legal contract review. Suppose an AI agent is tasked with ensuring a procurement contract aligns with a company's standard template and inventory of previously signed agreements. If the contract is based on the company's own template, this verification is relatively straightforward. However, reviewing a third-party template is more complex. The AI must first analyze which provisions and rules are included in the foreign draft, paying particular attention to whether the parties' obligations are clearly defined. For product or service specifications, the agent might connect to the company's warehouse or production IT platform. When examining payment terms, the tool references the company's standard practices as defined in its financial IT system, accepting or revising deviations according to pre-set tolerances. For risk allocation, AI compares warranty and indemnity clauses against approved standards and the repository of existing contracts. If a vendor seeks to cap liability at the contract level, the tool might rewrite the clause to set the cap at an insurance level or reject any limitation entirely, depending on company policy.

Breakthrough with neural network technology

AI did not originate with the advent of LLMs. AI stretches back several decades. Early AI systems were designed to tackle specific, well-defined tasks using structured data. Classic examples include automated customer call routing via decision trees and product recommendation engines based on predetermined rules. These traditional systems relied on human engineers to encode logic – the familiar "If... then" correlation. While these rule-based solutions proved highly effective for repetitive, standardized tasks, they were inherently limited in scope and often struggled to adapt when faced with unfamiliar or evolving contexts.

LLMs, by contrast, represent a paradigm shift in the field of artificial intelligence. Rather than being explicitly programmed to follow particular rules, LLMs are trained on vast and diverse collections of unstructured data, including text from books, websites, blogs, conversations, computer code etc. Through exposure to this immense data landscape, LLMs learn by identifying patterns in language, discerning subtle relationships between concepts, and recognizing signals in communication – some of which may even lie beyond human awareness and only emerge through mathematical analysis. This fundamental difference endows LLMs with a level of flexibility and adaptability that was unattainable with earlier rule-based AI systems. Whereas traditional AI was designed to automate tasks already well understood, LLMs are engineered to navigate complexity, uncover hidden patterns, and reveal interdependencies that may have previously eluded human discovery.

The true innovation underpinning LLMs is their reliance on neural network technology. Neural networks are software technology inspired by the architecture and functioning of the human brain. They belong to a subfield of machine learning known as deep learning. Within a neural network, millions of artificial neurons are organized into layered structures, forming an adaptive system that continuously learns from mistakes and refines its outputs. These networks consist of input and output nodes, linked by numerous layers of interconnected neurons. When data is introduced, it can traverse many possible pathways through the network, yet only one path ultimately leads to the correct answer. At each node, the network makes a prediction about the next step and immediately checks whether its guess was accurate. For each new data point, this process repeats and, over time, correct pathways receive higher weighting than incorrect ones, facilitating self-directed learning and improvement.

To better conceptualize neural networks, imagine them as a GPS navigation system operating without a map. In a typical navigation scenario, there is a starting point and a destination. The algorithm determines the optimal route, weighing multiple choices such as motorways versus country roads, current traffic conditions, access to petrol stations or charging points and so forth. While many routes exist, only one is optimal, judged by criteria like travel time, fuel efficiency, or traffic density. Similarly, neural networks replace the traditional map with millions of artificial neurons, each possessing unique attributes, akin to road junctions with distinct characteristics. The network must decide which pathway through the "neural map" best achieves the desired outcome.

The impact of neural networks on AI systems is nothing short of transformative. In traditional machine learning, human experts were required to train the system to achieve a specific goal. For instance, if the objective was to identify images of cats, traditionally a software engineer would need to manually collect, label, and curate thousands of pictures, defining distinctive features of cats such as the number of legs, eye and ear shapes, tail length, and fur color.[2] This process might also involve correcting for dataset imbalances – for example, if the system is only trained on pictures of white cats, it would struggle to identify black ones as cats. In contrast, deep learning harnesses the power of neural networks to process all available images automatically. The system detects recurring patterns, such as shapes and features and – through a process of trial and error – determines which characteristics are truly distinctive for cats. It then applies this learned knowledge to new data, making intelligent, autonomous decisions. The hallmark of deep learning is its ability to self-improve at extraordinary speed, requiring minimal human intervention while delivering remarkably accurate results.

The process of training LLMs

To effectively perform their tasks, AI agents must undergo a comprehensive training process. Although these agents possess the capability to independently recognize patterns and derive accurate conclusions, they still require a foundational reference which is a substantial pool of data from which to learn. The initial stage, known as pre-training, involves feeding enormous datasets into the system to establish what is called the foundation model. The objective of this phase is for AI to master the intricacies of grammar, syntax, semantics, and general knowledge about the world. The data sources are predominantly unstructured and span the internet, supplemented by books and articles. Due to the sheer scale of information processed, this phase is highly resource-intensive. For example, training sophisticated models like GPT-4 can require 60 to 90 days of uninterrupted computing power.

Once the foundation is laid, the model advances to a second stage – supervised fine-tuning. Here, the focus shifts to teaching the model how to follow instructions and interact in a conversational manner. Unlike pre-training, this phase utilizes a much smaller, carefully curated dataset assembled by human trainers. The aim is to enhance the model's precision, efficiency, and relevance to real-world applications. The effectiveness of this step is closely tied to the quality of the labelled data provided. Any biases or inaccuracies within these datasets can have a direct and lasting impact on the model's performance and reliability.

During supervised fine-tuning, human trainers create examples of exemplary interactions, guiding the model to transition from merely predicting the next word in a sequence to generating responses that fulfil the intended instructional purpose. This sets the stage for the third and final phase – reinforcement learning from human feedback (RLHF). The primary goal here is to align AI's behavior with established safety protocols, ethical standards, and practical utility. Human reviewers systematically rank the model's responses according to their usefulness and adherence to these standards. This feedback is compiled into a new preference dataset, which serves as the basis for developing a reward model. AI then learns to anticipate the type of reward score a human evaluator might assign to each possible response, encouraging it to generate outputs that maximize predicted human approval and utility. This iterative process is repeated multiple times, reinforcing the agent's tendency to produce beneficial, safe, and ethically sound results by default.

It is important to note that the overwhelming majority of content used in training LLMs consists of unreviewed material sourced from publicly available publications. In contrast, the data utilized for fine-tuning and RLHF represents only a tiny fraction of the overall dataset. This imbalance helps explain why certain issues, such as bias or inaccuracies, may occasionally arise in these systems.

Table 4: The process of training LLMs on content. Source: Gemini (Oct 2025)

Training phase	Purpose	Data size (scale)	% of total data
1. Pre-training	Establishes foundational knowledge and language fluency across a broad range of topics	Trillions of tokens (commonly exceeding 1,000,000, 000,000 tokens)	Approximately 98–99.99%
2. Supervised fine-tuning (SFT)	Develops the ability to follow specific instructions and enhances task competence	Tens of thousands of examples (typically 10,000–100,000 prompt-response pairs)	Less than 1%
3. Reinforcement learning from human feedback (RLHF)	Refines behavior, safety, and ethical alignment through human-guided feedback	Hundreds of thousands of comparisons (commonly 50,000–300,000 ranked pairs of responses)	Less than 0.1% (often closer to 0.01%)

ESG challenges

Artificial intelligence is accompanied by underlying challenges that must not be overlooked. Firstly, the sheer scale of computational resources required to train and operate AI systems results in a considerable environmental impact. The energy consumption associated with powering advanced data centers and performing large-scale model training contributes to a substantial carbon footprint, raising concerns about sustainability and ecological responsibility.

Beyond environmental issues, the ethical dimension of AI's development and deployment extends to the creation of responsible data supply chains.

Training and maintaining AI models is not an entirely automated process. It relies heavily on human involvement. Much of this work falls to data enrichment or annotation workers who are frequently based in countries such as the Philippines, Kenya, and India.[3] Often under demanding working conditions, these individuals are tasked with the laborious process of classifying, labelling, and verifying data to ensure the models function effectively.

Several investigative reports have drawn attention to the challenging and sometimes exploitative working conditions faced by these data workers.[4] Issues such as low pay, long working hours, and inadequate workplace conditions are allegedly common within this workforce. Such conditions highlight the importance of integrating considerations for data workers into Environmental, Social, and Governance (ESG) assessments. This should include applying existing frameworks and standards for fair working conditions, conducting thorough assessments, and establishing verification mechanisms to monitor and improve conditions where necessary. By leveraging established fair labor practices and ensuring robust oversight, organizations can promote more ethical and sustainable AI supply chains, ultimately supporting the development of responsible and sustainable artificial intelligence.

LLM failures and biases

The immense datasets used to pre-train LLMs mirror the vast, unfiltered, and frequently unverified information found across the internet. LLMs, by their very nature, lack the ability to innately differentiate between true and false, or moral and immoral, content. To address this shortcoming, human intervention during the training phase – specifically, through reinforcement learning from human feedback (RLHF) – is crucial. This process involves humans evaluating and ranking responses generated by the model, assigning higher ratings to those deemed helpful, safe, and non-toxic. Over time, the model learns to internalize these standards, thereby developing an understanding of safety and ethical boundaries. As a result, contemporary LLMs are less likely to produce harmful or dangerous content, even when explicitly prompted to do so.

Recent advancements in safeguards and oversight mechanisms have made it increasingly unlikely for previous failings to resurface. A notable early example was Microsoft's "Tay" chatbot, launched in 2016. Tay, short for "Thinking About You", was designed to engage with users on (then) Twitter and improve its conversational skills through real-time human interaction.

However, within just 16 hours of its launch, Tay was overwhelmed by a coordinated campaign of malicious users feeding it racist, sexist, and hateful content. Lacking any built-in legal or moral filters, Tay quickly began to echo and even promote this harmful material, including highly offensive statements and quotations attributed to Adolf Hitler.[5] This prompted Microsoft to take the chatbot offline almost immediately. The Tay incident served as an early and stark warning of the need for robust safety protocols and vigilant supervision when developing AI agents.

Conversely, in 2024, Google's Gemini model sought to counter criticism regarding biased image generation, such as producing images of CEOs or judges primarily featuring white male figures. To promote diversity, Google implemented a feature ensuring that all images depicting people reflected a wide range of ethnicities and genders, even in contexts where historical accuracy would suggest otherwise. This "alignment bias" led to images of Vikings, Popes, the Founding Fathers, or German WW2 Landser featuring individuals from a variety of backgrounds, genders, and ethnicities which, while well-intentioned and at times hilariously entertaining, compromised historical realism.[6] In response to significant public debate and political intervention, including an executive order from President Trump aimed at "Preventing Woke AI in Federal Government",[7] Google subsequently adjusted the system to balance the objectives of diversity with the need for factual and historical accuracy.

For AI systems to function with a semblance of a "moral compass", they must be capable of classifying content, whether by source (such as prioritizing reputable, balanced journalism) or by grouping information that reflects largely undisputed facts. This approach enhances both the ethical standing and the accuracy of AI-generated outputs. However, prioritizing content from specific, high-quality sources introduces a new set of challenges, particularly in the realm of copyright law. For instance, in December 2023, *The New York Times* filed a lawsuit against OpenAI and its main investor, Microsoft, alleging that millions of copyright-protected articles were used to train LLMs without permission, thus exceeding the bounds of fair use.[8] This legal case underscores the potential risks for LLM creators who assign undue weight to content from sources – doing so could increase the likelihood of models reproducing substantial portions of copyrighted material, thereby exposing developers to significant legal liability.

It is essential to recognize that biases are inherent in all LLMs – not as isolated or deliberate flaws, but as systematic tendencies shaped by multiple factors. Biases can be defined as consistent, repeatable patterns in which the model produces outputs that reflect societal prejudices or statistical imbalances, often resulting in inaccuracies. The primary source of bias lies in the input data itself. Since machine learning models can only be as representative as the data used to train them, any existing imbalances or stereotypes within the training corpus are likely to be ingrained and potentially amplified by the model. A second source of bias may arise from choices made during the design, structuring, or training methodology of the AI system. Because LLMs are rewarded for detecting and repeating patterns, there is a tendency for such models to reinforce and intensify historical or present stereotypes. Third, as seen in the Gemini example, overcorrection or excessive efforts to address historic biases can introduce new forms of distortion, such as overriding factual accuracy in pursuit of diversity or representation.

Biases in LLMs have become a contentious issue in political discourse.[9] Research indicates that most LLMs exhibit a left-leaning tendency, often favoring responses that align with Democratic or progressive viewpoints in the US. Any attempt to restrict the model's training to non-contentious information risks accusations of censorship and infringement upon free speech. In truth, all AI systems contain overt or subtle biases, many of which may be difficult – if not impossible – to fully eliminate. Achieving genuine neutrality is a complex challenge, given that there is no universal consensus on what neutrality entails. Nevertheless, it is possible to train LLMs to present a plurality of perspectives, thus making their outputs more balanced, though potentially less persuasive.

Importantly, the issue of bias in AI extends beyond accuracy and political debate. The European Union's AI Act,[10] for example, specifically prohibits systems that threaten fundamental rights, many of which involve algorithmic discrimination. One notable example is "social scoring" – the use of AI by public authorities to classify individuals based on behaviors, characteristics, or predicted traits, which can result in unfair or detrimental treatment in unrelated settings. Even if overt indicators such as race or gender are excluded from training data, models may still infer these characteristics from proxies such as language use, names, or educational backgrounds. This is particularly problematic in high-risk domains, such as employment, access to essential services, law enforcement, and judicial administration, where the EU AI Act mandates that developers and users must implement robust, measurable, and auditable safeguards to prevent discrimination and document their efficacy.

Hallucinations

Hallucinations are a result of current LLM architectures, which excel at pattern recognition and text generation but lack true factual understanding. As described above, LLMs function as prediction engines and their training data often contains errors. Hallucinations occur when models generate fluent, confident responses that are plausible but factually incorrect – sometimes inventing information. This happens because LLMs are designed to guess when uncertain, rather than admit "I don't know", which might cause user frustration. In addition, the vast majority of LLMs' training data is unverified and often includes fiction or conflicting facts. Human feedback can worsen hallucinations if convincing but inaccurate answers are rewarded over cautious ones that acknowledge uncertainty.[11]

In order to overcome hallucinations, new reasoning models have been developed that are available in modern agents like GPT-5.[12] These models do not immediately provide responses to prompts. Instead, they reconsider their initial response through repeated queries to check for contradictions or confirmations, refining the final output through several cycles. While this approach does not ensure flawless results, it helps lessen instances of hallucination. For legal AI agents, combining the technology with reputable legal databases (such as LexisNexis, WestLaw, Bloomberg Law, or Thomson Reuters' Practical Law) appears to be the most effective strategy for minimizing hallucinations to an acceptable range. Studies indicate that this retrieval-augmented generation significantly reduces hallucinations, bringing them in line with levels observed among human legal professionals not using AI on handling similar tasks.[13]

Security

LLMs have several well documented security vulnerabilities.

Public servers

General and free-to-use LLMs run on public servers outside secure enterprise IT environments. This exposes companies to distinct and elevated security threats triggered by data leakage and disclosure of business secrets and confidential information. User prompts containing confidential information could be recycled and become part of the training data of LLMs, potentially appearing in a response to an unrelated user's query at a later stage. Many free or consumer tier-AI services state in their terms of service that user input and output may be retained and used for future versions of the model.

In March 2023, a bug in ChatGPT's model caused the disclosure of other users' chat history, including in some instances the disclosure of personal information. A study led by Stanford University showed that GPT-2 could memorize and reproduce sensitive personal data such as social security numbers, full names, and email addresses.[14] Following these incidents and the growing awareness of this risk, many companies have implemented strict policies or even banned the use of public or publicly-accessible AI agents for work-related tasks.

Prompt injections

LLMs have another inherent and systemic security problem.[15] The core of the problem is that LLMs cannot distinguish between data and instructions. When the tool receives a prompt to rewrite text, it will rearrange content. When it receives a command, it will execute it. For the AI agent, both operations are the same. As a result, LLMs are vulnerable to a type of cyberattack called "prompt injection". This occurs where malicious instructions are hidden in content prompted to the tool. For instance, a user could instruct the AI agent to summarize a thousand-page external document, cross-reference its content with private files on a user's hard-drive, and then send an email with the outcome to the team. However, the external document may also include – unknown and unseeable to the user – the instruction to copy personal files of the user stored on the hard drive and send it to hacker@malicious.com. The agent will execute both orders with the same accuracy. There is no inherent safety feature in the tool to distinguish between content and instructions.

The Economist calls this security vulnerability a "lethal trifecta". For it to occur, three conditions must be present. First, the LLM needs exposure to outside content (a prompted document or emails). Second, it has to have access to private data (like access to a company's ERP, passwords, email inboxes etc.). Third, the LLM is able to communicate independently with the outside world. If all three conditions are met, AI agents are vulnerable to hidden prompted cyberattacks.

Exposure to prompt injections is an inherent LLM risk, on top of general cyber security risks. Although there has not been a massive cyberattack facilitated through a prompt injection (current incidents were typically caused by individuals being tricked to release their password and access codes) this risk is real. Microsoft reported a novel attack technique named *EchoLeak* that has been characterized as a "zero-click" vulnerability that allows bad actors to exfiltrate sensitive data from Microsoft 365 Copilot's context without user interaction. Microsoft issued a security patch in June 2025 that mitigated the identified risk.

One solution could be to restructure the architecture of AI agents. Just the removal of one leg of the "lethal trifecta" reduces the cyber-risk significantly. Where an agent is fed with outside content and needs to have access to enterprise data, it should not be able to communicate externally.

Solutions for the legal profession

The legal sector is witnessing a surge in AI, many of which assert that they have tackled the most pressing challenges associated with AI adoption in the legal professional field – namely, ensuring safety, accuracy, and reliability. These AI legal agents are typically built upon general large language models (LLMs) such as GPT or Gemini. However, what sets them apart is the incorporation of specialized frameworks tailored to overcome the inherent limitations of standard LLMs, particularly within the highly secure, risk-sensitive, and context-dependent realm of legal practice.

The unique demands of the legal profession introduce a number of stringent requirements that significantly constrain how AI can be used.[16] Foremost among these is the obligation to uphold client confidentiality – an ethical cornerstone for lawyers. It would be ethically impermissible for legal professionals to input confidential or privileged client information into public or widely accessible AI systems, as this could expose sensitive data to third parties or allow it to be reused for ongoing AI training. As a result, any legal AI solution must guarantee absolute non-retention of client data. Furthermore, to preserve legal privilege, these systems must be deployed within secure and fully auditable enterprise environments, whether that be via robust cloud infrastructure or on-premises servers designed to meet regulatory standards.

Another critical consideration is the duty of competence owed by lawyers who remain personally accountable for any errors or lapses in judgement.[17] The repercussions of professional negligence in law are severe and far-reaching. For example, submitting fictitious case citations ("hallucinations") can undermine the credibility of an entire legal brief and constitute far more than a mere oversight. Legal professionals must therefore have a comprehensive understanding of the risks and benefits associated with AI technologies in their work. Excessive reliance on AI, without appropriate oversight, may attract regulatory scrutiny and sanctions.

Legal reasoning itself is founded upon the requirement that every argument be substantiated by precise and citable sources, such as laws, regulations, or case law. Arguments lacking verifiable authority are dismissed as conjecture and hold no sway in legal proceedings. Accordingly, LLMs that cannot produce accurate and verifiable citations are of limited utility in the legal sector and depending on them could be deemed negligent. There is also ongoing debate about whether current LLMs are sufficiently trained to recognize the subtleties and intricacies of differing legal jurisdictions, or whether they are prone to "dominance bias", which can lead to erroneous outcomes.

In response to these multifaceted challenges, legal AI agents are engineered to satisfy three foundational requirements – robust data security, minimization of hallucinations, and the ability to produce verifiable sources for every claim made. By meeting these standards, such agents aim to provide trustworthy and compliant support to legal professionals, while safeguarding client interests and upholding the integrity of the legal process.

Security features

To ensure robust security, legal artificial intelligence solutions are predominantly developed as enterprise-grade platforms that avoid any uncontrolled or unsecured connections to external networks. Typically, these legal AI systems are deployed within dedicated private cloud environments or integrated directly into a client's own Virtual Private Cloud (VPC) infrastructure. This approach establishes a highly secure and isolated "sandbox" environment in which all client data is handled and processed. The isolation provided by this sandbox guarantees that sensitive client information remains completely segregated, ensuring it is never mixed with data from other organizations or exposed to the public internet.

A second critical security aspect is a strict "zero-retention policy" implemented by legal AI models. Under this policy, any confidential client inputs – such as prompts, documents, or other data – are deleted immediately from the AI tool after results are produced. This ensures that sensitive information is not retained, stored, or repurposed for broader AI model training, effectively eliminating the risk of inadvertent data leaks or unauthorized access.

Further reinforcing data security, legal AI platforms employ granular "role-based access control" mechanisms. These systems dictate that access to confidential datasets and advanced AI model functionalities is determined by individual roles, responsibilities, and seniority within the organization. In practice, this means that the permissions granted to an AI agent are closely aligned with the clearance levels assigned to their human counterparts. For example, if employees cannot view board-level documents, AI acting on their behalf is similarly restricted.

To defend against advanced cyber threats, legal AI systems must be engineered with robust safeguards against "prompt injection" attacks. These attacks involve malicious attempts to manipulate AI by injecting harmful instructions or trying to override built-in operational constraints. To counter these risks, sophisticated filters and guardrails are embedded within the input processing layer to identify and block adversarial language or unauthorized requests, especially within the legal domain. These security measures are continuously refined to detect emerging threats and are tailored specifically for legal applications.

Privacy compliance is another cornerstone of these platforms. Legal AI tools feature automated output scanning mechanisms that detect and prevent the unintentional disclosure of sensitive information, such as personally identifiable data, unless there is a clear and justifiable need for such release. This helps organizations adhere to strict regulatory requirements regarding data protection and privacy.

Finally, to demonstrate their commitment to the highest levels of information security, leading legal AI providers – such as *Harvey* – obtain and maintain internationally recognized certifications, including SOC 2 Type II and ISO 27001. These certifications independently verify that the platforms have implemented rigorous internal controls to safeguard security, ensure system availability, maintain processing integrity, and protect both confidentiality and privacy across all operations.[18]

Accuracy and hallucination mitigation

To enhance their accuracy and reliability, legal AI tools are subjected to rigorous fine-tuning using comprehensive and authoritative legal datasets. This process involves training on a vast array of published laws, regulatory texts, and judicial decisions, ensuring that the AI agent is not only familiar with the substantive content of the law but also internalizes the distinctive methods and logical structures that underpin legal reasoning. Mastery of these unique reasoning patterns is essential for any AI intended to operate effectively within the legal sector, as it ensures AI can both interpret complex legal materials and construct sound legal arguments.

Modern legal AI platforms benefit significantly from advanced "reasoning tools".[19] These technologies are specifically architected to tackle challenging logical and analytical tasks, allocating greater computational resources to thorough analysis during inference. This step-by-step approach mirrors the way a human legal professional might develop a plan, systematically considering each aspect of a problem before arriving at a conclusion. By generating an internal chain of reasoning, these models are able to iteratively review and refine their outputs, ultimately producing more nuanced and accurate answers. Such reasoning capabilities are now incorporated in leading models, including GPT-4 (with the o1-preview introduced in 2024) and various other general and domain-specific LLMs.

A distinguishing feature of advanced legal LLMs, such as Harvey, is their use of sophisticated source verification techniques, most notably retrieval-augmented generation (RAG).[20] Instead of merely generating responses based on probabilistic predictions, RAG-equipped tools actively cross-reference their outputs against proprietary or licensed legal databases to verify and corroborate their answers. Examples of connected legal databases include LexisNexis, WestLaw, Bloomberg Law, and Thomson Reuters Practical Law. This approach not only enables access to the full spectrum of laws and judicial precedents, but also to a wealth of practitioner-generated materials, such as contract templates, legal memos, commentary, drafting guides, and more. Every assertion or citation produced by AI is linked directly to a verifiable source, enhancing the traceability and trustworthiness of the tool's output.

RAG technology, which has been available since 2020, fundamentally strengthens "conventional" LLMs by providing an external, highly credible source of truth. This is especially valuable in the legal sector, where the existence of extensive, high-quality content repositories makes legal tasks particularly well-suited to RAG-based solutions.

Unlike traditional LLMs, which are constrained by the infrequency and cost of model retraining, RAG-powered systems can update their vector databases regularly, thereby ensuring that their knowledge base remains current. Furthermore, RAG technology makes it possible to integrate the company's own proprietary materials – such as internal templates, signed and recorded contracts, corporate policies, historic case files, legal memoranda, and operational checklists and playbooks – directly into AI's workflow. This degree of customization allows legal AI agents to deliver highly relevant and context-specific outputs, tailored to each client's unique needs.

The efficacy of these advanced legal AI systems has been empirically tested. On 4 March 2025, Professor Daniel Schwarcz from the University of Minnesota Law School, together with his co-authors, published a study

analyzing the performance of AI-assisted legal work.[21] In the study, 127 participants were tasked with completing six realistic legal assignments.[22] For two tasks, participants worked without AI assistance; for another two, they utilized a reasoning model (such as GPT-4 o1); and for the final two, they used a specialized legal LLM (Vincent AI from VLex, enhanced with RAG capabilities). The findings were illuminating. First, access to either AI agent significantly improved the speed with which tasks were completed. Second, in four of the six assignments, the quality of AI-enabled work was markedly superior, particularly in terms of clarity, organization, and professionalism.

However, the impact of AI on the accuracy of legal research – measured by the precision and usefulness of the results – was mixed. The RAG-powered Vincent AI almost entirely eliminated hallucinations, producing fewer spurious citations than even the control group with no AI assistance. In this respect, Vincent outperformed the reasoning-focused GPT-4 o1. Nevertheless, when it came to the depth and nuance of legal analysis – a critical metric in evaluating the quality of legal work – the specialized Vincent AI lagged behind both GPT-4 o1 and the control group.[23] This highlights an important limitation – while RAG technology is highly effective at mitigating hallucinations and ensuring that cited legal sources are genuine, it does not always guarantee that the AI agent will select the most pertinent legal source required to construct the strongest and possibly winning legal argument.[24]

The study's results suggest that the future of legal AI lies in combining enhanced reasoning capabilities with robust source verification mechanisms like RAG. By integrating these complementary strengths, it may be possible to produce legal AI agents that not only avoid hallucinations and provide verifiable citations, but also deliver the depth, nuance, and analytical rigor required for top-tier legal work.

The preferred answer – dedicated legal AI agents on small language models

In addition to the advancements seen with LLMs, there has been a notable emergence of smaller and more agile alternatives known as Small Language Models (SLMs). These SLMs are specifically engineered to address bespoke corporate requirements, offering a tailored approach that contrasts with the broad, general-purpose capabilities of LLMs. Notable examples of SLMs currently available include Microsoft's Phi-3 and Google's Gemini Nano, both of which demonstrate the practical application of this technology in real-world corporate environments.[25]

The primary ambition behind SLMs is to deliver performance on par with LLMs for highly specialized tasks, but with a significantly reduced operational footprint. Because of their compact design, SLMs are substantially more cost-effective – they can operate efficiently on standard IT infrastructure, utilizing conventional computing processors (CPUs) rather than the powerful, cloud-based graphic processing units (GPUs) typically required for LLMs. This means that organizations can deploy SLMs without the need for extensive investment in cloud computing resources.

A further advantage of SLMs lies in their ability to process data locally. Their "modest" size allows for on-premises deployment, which is particularly beneficial when handling highly sensitive or confidential information, as it eliminates the need to transmit data to external cloud servers. By design, SLMs are trained on more narrowly defined and specific data sets, which not only enhances their relevance to the task at hand but also improves safety and reliability by reducing the likelihood of generating hallucinated or spurious content.

SLMs are inherently more adaptable and easier to retrain than their larger counterparts. Organizations can rapidly update or fine-tune these models to reflect changing requirements or regulatory developments, ensuring that the technology remains aligned with the latest legal standards and business needs. While some LLMs can be adapted for specialized purposes, SLMs excel in this regard due to their modularity and targeted focus.

Another distinctive feature of SLMs is their ability to operate as modular components within a broader agentic workflow. Rather than relying on a single, monolithic LLM to perform all tasks, organizations can assemble a suite of specialized SLMs – for instance, one tool could be dedicated to review, analysis, and summary of large quantities of documents as typically necessary in litigation or M&A transactions. A separate AI agent could run the contract management processes, including review and annotations, renewal and termination, as well as signing and filing tasks. A third model could be in charge of compliance processes including risk assessments, audits, and policy management. This modular approach not only reduces costs but also enhances operational flexibility and resilience.

The rise of SLMs signals a maturing phase in the AI industry. It reflects a shift away from reliance on expensive, energy-intensive, and sometimes error-prone mega-models towards practical, deployable solutions that are highly specialized and fit for purpose. In the context of legal research and analysis, purpose-built SLMs have shown considerable promise in overcoming some of the key limitations identified in current LLMs, such as the risk of hallucinations or the inability to provide nuanced, context-specific answers. As the technology continues to evolve, it is increasingly likely that SLMs will become the preferred choice for legal AI agents, offering a blend of efficiency, reliability, and precision that aligns closely with the unique demands of the legal sector.

References

1 www.marketreportanalytics.com/news/article/harvey-to-roll-out-agentic-workflows-6735

2 Example taken from AWS, https://aws.amazon.com/what-is/neural-network/.

3 China's biggest data factory, MBH, employs over 300,000 data workers. *The Economist*, "China's success at AI has relied on good data but cheap labour has also played an important role," 2 January 2020.

4 www.brookings.edu/articles/reimagining-the-future-of-data-and-ai-labor-in-the-global-south/

5 *The Guardian*, "Tay, Microsoft's AI chatbot, gets a crash course in racism from Twitter," 24 March 2016

6 *The Guardian*, "Google chief admits 'biased' AI tool's photo diversity offended users", 28 February 2024.

7 https://deloitte.wsj.com/cio/how-americas-ai-action-plan-may-help-shape-ai-governance-globally-721966fd.

8 https://harvardlawreview.org/blog/2024/04/nyt-v-openai-the-timess-about-face/

9 *The Economist*, "Donald Trump is waging war on woke AI... but unbiased chatbots may be impossible," 28 August 2025.

10 Regulation 2024/1689 of 13 June 2024, OJ L 2024/1689.

11 Lakera.ai: "LLM Hallucination in 2025: How to Understand and Tackle AI's Most Pertinent Quirk," published 3 October 2025.

12 https://platform.openai.com/docs/guides/reasoning

13 See Accuracy and hallucination mitigation with empirical evidence in this chapter.

14 Rodrigo Fernandez, "Why Your AI Model Might Be Leaking Sensitive Information (and How to Stop It)," neutraltrust.ai published on 7 April 2025.

15 *The Economist*, "Why AI systems may never be secure, and what to do about it; A 'lethal trifecta' of conditions opens them to abuse", 22 September 2005. See also *The Economist*, "How to stop AI's 'lethal trifecta'", 25 September 2025.

16 Instructive read: Mark L. Shope, "Lawyer and Judicial Competency in the Era of Artificial Intelligence: Ethical Requirements for Documenting Datasets and Machine Learning Models", *The Georgetown Journal of Legal Ethics*, 2021 Vol 34, page 191 et seq.

17 ABA, Model Rules for Professional Conduct, Section 1.1: "A lawyer shall provide competent representation to a client. Competent representation requires the legal knowledge, skill, thoroughness and preparation reasonably necessary for the representation."

18 Security Addendum, www.harvey.ai/legal/security-addendum.
19 See From language prediction to universal interface in this chapter.
20 See www.harvey.ai/blog/enterprise-grade-rag-systems.
21 Schwarcz, Manning, Barry, Cleveland, Prescott, Rich: "AI-Powered Lawyering: AI Reasoning Model, Retrieval Augmented Generation and the Future of Legal Practice", 2025 https://dx.doi.org/10.2139/ssrn.5162111.
22 The assignments were: draft an email to a client about defamation claims in litigation; draft a legal memo for a partner analysing whether the insurance covers legal fees; summarize and analyse a class action complaint; draft an NDA; draft a notion to consolidate two pending cases; and lastly draft a persuasive letter that a covenant not to compete was reasonable and enforceable.
23 Schwarcz, page 40.
24 Schwarcz, page 57.
25 See *The Economist*, "Artificial Intelligence – Peak LLM?" 13 September 2025. This article quotes David Cox, Head of AI research at IBM, with "Your HR chatbot doesn't need to know advanced physics." See also in Jassal in: Forbes, "Unlocking the Value of Enterprise AI With Small Language Models," 23 October 2025, www.forbes.com.

Chapter 15: Prompting is the new drafting

Undoubtedly, artificial intelligence will establish itself as an integral part of the legal profession. Legal leaders cannot afford to ignore its presence. While the adoption of AI comes with inherent risks and potential threats, choosing to disregard or reject this technology is not a viable strategy – such an approach will inevitably result in a significant competitive disadvantage. Instead, it is imperative that legal leaders invest the necessary time and resources to thoroughly understand AI – its practical applications, the outcomes it can deliver, and its limitations.

It is important to dispel any misconceptions about AI's capabilities. Contrary to the notion of AI as sentient, humanoid bots possessing human-like intelligence, the reality is far more nuanced. As previously discussed, AI is fundamentally a prediction engine powered by pattern recognition, not a system rooted in rigorous calculation or comprehensive analysis. Although the outputs generated by AI agents can be linguistically convincing and may resemble high-quality legal reasoning, these appearances should not obscure the technology's conceptual boundaries and operational limitations.

Nevertheless, the efficiency gains achievable through the strategic deployment of AI agents are considerable. These benefits should be deliberately woven into the overall strategic framework of the legal function, with ongoing evaluation of the risks and opportunities associated with the technology's use. Rather than viewing AI as a standalone tool, its implementation should be seen as an integrated enhancement to the entire suite of legal services and processes. The adaptation of AI within the legal domain is best regarded as a structured evolution – an upgrade of existing systems and workflows – rather than a radical transformation that supplants human expertise or eliminates the need for professional judgement.

By embracing AI thoughtfully and proactively, legal leaders can ensure their teams remain agile, efficient, and well-positioned to meet the demands of a rapidly changing professional landscape. The key lies in balancing innovation with prudent oversight, leveraging AI's strengths while maintaining a clear understanding of its limitations and the critical role of human insight in legal practice.

Corporate governance

Within the realm of corporate governance and company secretarial operations, artificial intelligence agents are poised to significantly enhance both the efficiency and accuracy of standardized workflow processes. By integrating AI into these functions, companies can establish robust governance frameworks that incorporate multiple checkpoints for legal review, thereby minimizing errors and ensuring compliance with regulatory obligations.

AI agents can streamline the scheduling of board meetings, automatically dispatching invitations and curating agendas informed by previous meetings as well as input from the chairperson and company secretary. Utilizing shared digital journals where topics and priorities are recorded, the system can dynamically adjust the agenda to reflect evolving business needs. During the board book preparation phase, AI can swiftly synthesize and format a wide array of documents, including business updates and financial reports sourced directly from integrated finance platforms. The technology is capable of scrutinizing these materials for inconsistencies or content unsuitable for inclusion in corporate records, flagging such items for further review by legal counsel or company secretary before final approval.

Once the board pack is assembled, the AI agent securely distributes it via encrypted document sharing systems, providing succinct executive summaries of key items. Board members are empowered to interrogate the content according to bespoke prompts, such as comparing current asset utilization figures with historical data over multiple years, thus facilitating more informed decision-making.

During board meetings, AI can independently transcribe proceedings from audio recordings or human notes, producing an initial draft of formal minutes that clearly delineates motions, resolutions, action points, and their respective owners. This draft is then circulated to board members in the appropriate sequence for review and approval. Voting outcomes are recorded separately, ensuring comprehensive audit trails are maintained. Moreover, AI can automatically extract action items, deadlines, and responsible individuals from the minutes, providing ongoing tracking and reminders to ensure timely completion.

AI agents also have the capability to fully automate changes to company directorships, especially when integrated with HR systems. As business roles evolve – through promotions, departures, or new appointments – these changes are reflected in the HR platform, prompting AI to initiate the necessary corporate updates. This includes preparing relevant corporate resolutions, managing any required training for new directors, and filing documents automatically with the appropriate authorities.

In the sphere of legal entity management, AI tools can continuously monitor external regulatory feeds for updates, such as new beneficial ownership disclosure rules or modified tax filing deadlines. Upon detecting relevant changes, the system conducts impact assessments to identify which entities are affected, ensuring that necessary adjustments are implemented promptly. Reorganizations and modifications to ownership structures are managed through dedicated AI-driven workflows, which are instantly mirrored in the entity's organizational chart.

Similarly, standardized intragroup corporate actions such as entity recapitalization, intercompany loans, and dividend distributions among affiliated companies can be efficiently managed by AI agents. These tools ensure accuracy and consistency across these routine-yet-critical activities.

Furthermore, AI can generate regular reports and conduct audits to verify the accuracy of corporate records for the parent company and all subsidiaries. Statutory filings, including statements and annual accounts, are seamlessly handled by AI, which interfaces directly with financial platforms to compile and submit the required documentation. In broader entity management, AI agents are capable of preparing supplementary documents and filings as needed, further reducing the administrative burden on company secretaries and legal teams and enhancing the reliability of corporate governance processes.

Legal monitoring and regulatory watch

AI agents are set to play a transformative role in monitoring and navigating the ever-evolving legal and regulatory environment. Leveraging advanced pattern recognition and natural language processing, these tools can autonomously scan a wide range of authoritative and relevant sources for newly published regulations, legislative updates, and compliance requirements. Unlike traditional monitoring systems that might indiscriminately aggregate every law firm alert disconnected from its impact and value, AI agents can be finely tuned to prioritize and filter information from trusted regulators, industry bodies, and jurisdictions specifically relevant to the organization's business sectors, products, markets, and geographic operations.

Beyond simply identifying new legal developments, AI agents have the capability to proactively predict which additional jurisdictions or regulatory domains might be impacted next, based on emerging trends and historical data. This predictive insight enables organizations to anticipate regulatory changes and prepare in advance, rather than merely reacting after the fact.

Upon detecting relevant legal updates, AI tools can generate concise, actionable summaries that highlight the key changes, transition periods, and critical deadlines. These findings are automatically tagged with pertinent internal business categories – such as HR, tax, product regulation, and compliance, environmental, social, and governance (ESG) matters and more. This structured tagging system, including checkpoints for human verification and oversight, allows for seamless integration into central databases and targeted distribution lists, ensuring that the right stakeholders receive timely and relevant information.

When integrated with the company's enterprise resource planning (ERP) system, AI agents can automatically assess the impact of regulatory changes on existing corporate policies, internal standards, production processes, and product formulations. The tool can rapidly identify areas of non-compliance, flag gaps, and propose detailed remedial action plans, ensuring that the organization remains aligned with its legal obligations.

Moreover, AI agents are equipped to estimate the financial implications of regulatory changes, enabling business leaders to obtain oversight very early in the process. This enables informed decision-making based on detailed impact assessments right from the start. This financial forecasting capability supports effective risk management and enhances the company's ability to remain competitive and compliant in a dynamic regulatory landscape.

In addition, AI-driven legal monitoring tools can extend their predictive analytics to judicial behavior, litigation outcomes, and enforcement trends. By analyzing patterns in court decisions and regulatory enforcement, these agents provide valuable insights that inform legal strategy, compliance planning, and risk assessment. This forward-looking approach transforms legal and regulatory monitoring from a reactive task into a strategic function that underpins robust corporate governance and operational resilience.

Contract management and generation

AI agents are poised to transform the process of contract creation and life-cycle management. Conventional self-service contract platforms typically rely on rule-based, human-designed "If...then" checklists and guided intake questionnaires. Users are led through a series of preset criteria to select the most appropriate contract template for their needs. While this approach streamlines template selection, the result is rarely a truly bespoke contract. Rather, it is the closest fit among available standard templates.

In contrast, AI-driven contract management solutions are capable of delivering genuinely tailored agreements. Instead of requiring users to answer a structured menu of questions, these advanced tools can process unstructured project materials – including project outlines, project approval memos, financial forecasts, email correspondence, and other documents – either uploaded by the user or autonomously gathered. The AI agent then analyses this information, adapting the contract's terms, clauses, and language to reflect the specific requirements of the transaction. For instance, if the system identifies that "fit-for-purpose" performance is critical from the correspondence, it will automatically insert comprehensive representations and warranties to address this priority. Similarly, where the achievement of sales targets in defined regions is a key contractual objective, the AI agent will search its database for robust, proven clauses addressing this issue and integrate them into the agreement.

Moreover, by leveraging sophisticated reasoning models, AI tools can offer transparent explanations for their drafting choices, allowing in-house or external legal counsel to review, validate, or adjust AI's assumptions and recommendations. This collaborative approach not only increases confidence in AI's output but also streamlines the review process, ensuring contracts are both precise and aligned with business intent.

Beyond drafting, AI agents excel at reviewing third-party templates and identifying deviations from a company's own standard agreements and policy requirements. LLMs/SLMs are able to suggest alternative language, drawing upon a repository of model clauses and prior agreements, ensuring consistency and risk mitigation across all contracts. The AI model can generate detailed summaries of its findings and proposed edits, automatically distributing these to the relevant stakeholders for validation and approval before finalization.

For contract lifecycle management, AI tools provide comprehensive monitoring of both contract performance and timelines. By integrating with financial and operational platforms, the system can track whether contractual sales targets or minimum purchase thresholds are being met. The AI will promptly flag any underperformance or missed obligations. It can generate draft notifications or reminder letters for the relevant parties that the business lawyer in charge can submit by simple click. For example, if equipment fails during the warranty period, the system will alert the responsible user and propose a suitable notice of defect letter, ready for immediate dispatch.

Automated alerts are also generated for upcoming key dates, such as renewal windows and termination events. If required, LLMs/SLMs can prepare and send renewal or non-renewal communications, request electronic signatures, and ensure that all related correspondence and executed documents are securely stored and linked within the contract management system.

This seamless and efficient approach to contract generation and management is likely to lead to a significant increase in the proportion of business transactions governed by formal contracts. Historically, many transactions have defaulted to purchase orders with standard terms and conditions due to the perceived complexity and time-consuming nature of negotiating bespoke agreements. By automating and simplifying both the drafting and administrative processes, organizations can mandate contractual documentation for all transactions, greatly enhancing legal certainty and risk management. Not only does this reduce disputes arising from ambiguous purchase orders or reliance on boilerplate terms (*battle of the forms*), but it also ensures that critical product specifications and service standards are properly documented from the outset. This addresses one of the most common pitfalls when seeking recourse against suppliers.

Internal audit and risk assessment

The strategic implementation of AI in internal audit and risk assessment offers transformative opportunities for companies. Rather than conducting periodic, retrospective reviews, internal audit functions can now transition to continuous, real-time oversight of operations and controls. AI-driven systems are capable of monitoring vast streams of transactional data as activities occur, enabling the immediate identification of anomalies indicative of fraud, embezzlement, or other suspicious conduct.

AI agents excel at learning typical behavioral patterns across transactions, user activities, and system controls. They continuously analyze journal entries, vendor invoices, payment processes, discounting, and system access logs, scrutinizing not only the content but also contextual factors such as transaction values, timing, geographic location, and account movement velocity. When a transaction deviates from established norms – be it an unusual payment amount, access attempt from an unexpected location, or abnormal frequency of activity – the system automatically flags it for further investigation.

What sets AI-based audit tools apart is their advanced pattern recognition and adaptability. Not only do they highlight irregularities, but they also provide likely explanations and conduct root cause analyses, offering auditors immediate insights into potential risks or incidents. The self-learning nature of these systems, including ongoing novelty training, significantly reduces false positives and enhances the accuracy of fraud detection. A critical advantage is the feedback mechanism – when a human reviewer confirms a flagged incident as genuine fraud, the AI model instantly assimilates this information, refining its detection capabilities for future cases. This improvement is not limited to a single business unit or region. The benefits are propagated organization-wide, strengthening global defenses against evolving threats.

Beyond internal controls, AI-powered pattern recognition is widely adopted by regulatory authorities. For example, the European Commission utilizes AI to analyze earnings calls and other public corporate communications for indications of anti-competitive behavior.[1] Phrases such as the market being "congruent", "sufficiently disciplined", or "leading and following" pre-agreed price increases may serve as signals or even explicit invitations to collude. The novelty is not the keyword search but the understanding of certain key patterns, announcements, and market reactions that could be symptomatic of prohibited collusive conduct.

By deploying similar AI screening technologies internally – across all corporate documentation, including drafts and speaking notes – companies can establish internal filters, identifying and addressing potential miscommunication early before it is picked up by others.

Equally, AI agents are invaluable for broader corporate risk management. They are adept at detecting vulnerabilities and exposures before they escalate into significant issues. For instance, the system can quickly identify financial risks, such as a customer accumulating large outstanding receivables without proper documentation of extended or collateralized credit lines. Regulatory risks are also promptly detected, with AI agents monitoring changes in legislation and operationalizing impact assessments to ensure compliance across products, services, and even employee travel to high-risk regions.

In the sphere of reputational and brand risk, AI takes "social listening" to a new level. By monitoring external sources in real time – such as news outlets, social media platforms, blogs, and forums – AI agents can provide early warnings of emerging crises, including negative product reviews, ethical supply chain concerns, or public relations issues. These insights enable organizations to respond swiftly and effectively, safeguarding their reputation and minimizing potential damage.

Overall, the purposeful use of AI in internal audit and risk assessment not only enhances the efficiency and accuracy of these functions but also empowers organizations to adopt a proactive, strategic approach to risk management, turning potential threats into opportunities for resilience and growth.

Intellectual property

AI is rapidly becoming indispensable in the creation, administration, and enforcement of intellectual property rights (IP), fundamentally reshaping how organizations manage and protect their valuable assets. The transformative power of AI lies in its ability to deliver speed, scalability, and precision previously not available in the IP domain.

AI in IP creation

During the IP creation phase, AI serves not merely as a tool but as a hyper-efficient research assistant and drafting partner. Its advanced capabilities enable it to optimize the legal robustness and strategic value of IP from the outset. For example, in the context of patent applications, AI has shifted the paradigm away from basic keyword searches towards a deeper, conceptual understanding of inventions. By analyzing technical drawings, project notes, emails, and other preparatory materials, AI agents are able to interpret the underlying essence and business intent of new inventions. This allows for comprehensive screening of authoritative databases, scientific literature, and technical papers to identify prior art or similar innovations.

AI agents, trained on an extensive dataset of successful patent applications, are particularly adept at drafting patent claims and full specifications. They can suggest optimal language, structure claims effectively, and generate supporting descriptive text that meets legal standards while minimizing ambiguity. This not only streamlines the drafting process but also enhances the likelihood of securing robust and defensible IP rights.

In addition, when conducting freedom-to-operate (FTO) assessments, AI tools proactively evaluate the risk of infringing third-party patents. They can identify specific claim elements that may pose infringement risks for a proposed product or process. If a significant risk is detected, the AI system is capable of proposing alternative technical solutions – so-called "workarounds" – that achieve the same objective without infringing existing rights. Both the FTO findings and potential workarounds are presented to the patent attorney, supporting informed decision-making.

Trademark searches also benefit from AI's sophisticated image recognition and text analysis. These systems go beyond mere word mark searches, analyzing logos, 2D and 3D trademarks, and even identifying phonetically similar or closely misspelled marks across global trademark databases, domain registrations, and social media. This comprehensive approach significantly reduces the risk of overlooking potentially conflicting marks.

AI in IP administration

AI agents are able to cover the entire spectrum of IP administration, providing continuous, real-time monitoring of a company's IP portfolio and its external challenges. They track filing deadlines, renewal dates, initiations, and status of opposition proceedings, automatically alerting the team to critical events. Advanced AI agents are employed to continuously monitor IP applications submitted by third parties. These agents systematically evaluate each filing to determine whether it may be invalid, or whether it infringes upon the organization's existing IP portfolio. Should the agents identify any such concerns, they are programmed to automatically prepare and submit formal opposition filings, thereby protecting the company's IP estate without requiring manual intervention. Moreover, AI can forecast which competitor patents are likely to lapse or be invalidated, based on factors such as litigation history and fee payment patterns. This intelligence is invaluable for strategic planning within both the IP and R&D teams.

Furthermore, AI models play a pivotal role in assigning dynamic financial valuations to individual IP assets. By analyzing licensing fees, litigation outcomes, brand reputation, and sales performance, these systems provide up-to-date valuations that reflect an asset's current and potential worth. They can even establish correlations between IP investments – such as registering a suite of related marks or expanding geographic coverage – and their impact, whether through successful enforcement actions or as deterrents to competitors. This data-driven approach transforms IP management from a reactive function into a strategic, forward-looking discipline, enabling legal leaders to prioritize resources and maximize business value.

AI in IP enforcement and brand protection

For enforcement and brand protection, AI leverages advanced computer vision and image recognition to scan vast e-commerce marketplaces – such as Amazon, eBay, and Alibaba – as well as social media platforms and independent websites. AI-powered programs like Amazon's Project Zero exemplify this advancement, with proactive controls reportedly blocking over 99 percent of suspected infringing listings before they reach consumers.[2] Brands can directly remove counterfeit listings, provided they maintain a high accuracy rate, while unique product identifiers (such as Amazon's transparency codes) further strengthen anti-counterfeiting measures at fulfilment centers.

Beyond detection, AI revolutionizes the fight against counterfeiting by enabling sophisticated brand protection intelligence. Like a modern intelligence agency, AI systems aggregate and analyze data from seizures, online posts, and supply chain activity to map out counterfeiting networks. They can identify the individuals or organizations behind illicit activities, uncover logistical routes, and highlight vulnerabilities in the counterfeiters' operations. This intelligence-led approach empowers companies to target enforcement actions precisely where they will have the greatest impact – disrupting counterfeit supply chains and protecting brand integrity.

Strategic value determination

Taken together, these AI-driven capabilities mark a step change in how companies create, manage, and enforce their IP rights. By automating routine tasks, providing strategic insights, and enhancing enforcement efficiency, AI allows legal and IP teams to focus on high-value strategy and innovation. This shift ensures that every IP investment is closely aligned with business objectives and that organizations remain resilient and competitive in an evolving global marketplace.

M&A and litigation support

The benefits of deploying AI agents in mergers and acquisitions (M&A) and litigation are becoming increasingly clear and transformative.

M&A

Advanced LLMs are now capable of swiftly processing and analyzing enormous volumes of unstructured documents, including leases, procurement and sales contracts, operating permits, real estate agreements, IP rights and licenses, as well as employment contracts. This unprecedented processing speed enables AI tools to extract crucial clauses such as termination rights, change-of-control provisions, indemnities, and non-compete covenants. Furthermore, these systems can automatically identify and flag deviations from standard provisions, inconsistencies from standard patterns, and other anomalies. This enables legal professionals to focus their attention better targeted on areas of concern highlighted by AI or uncovered through further investigation.

On the financial due diligence front, AI agents are equally invaluable. They can analyze a wide range of financial documents – statutory accounts, regulatory filings, profit and loss statements, balance sheets and more – extracting key metrics such as revenue growth, debt obligations, and asset valuations. This structured data is then compared instantaneously with historical trends, allowing for the rapid detection of anomalies or irregularities that may warrant further scrutiny. The quality and reliability of these results significantly surpass traditional methods, such as keyword searches or manual checks, ensuring a higher standard of accuracy and efficiency throughout the verification process.

AI also delivers exceptional capabilities in the enterprise valuation process, a domain that, while adjacent to the legal core, is of keen interest to experienced M&A lawyers due to its direct impact on purchase price negotiations. AI-driven tools can rapidly process financial data to estimate a potential valuation range, running sophisticated scenario simulations and predictive models to forecast synergies and cost savings. This empowers legal and financial teams to anticipate post-acquisition financial outcomes with greater confidence, informing negotiation strategies and risk assessments.

Litigation

Similarly, AI agents are revolutionizing litigation support. These tools can ingest millions of documents and instantly organize them by relevance to the specific issues of a case. Specialized LLMs are trained to recognize patterns and language indicative of attorney–client privilege or attorney work product, automatically flagging and quarantining such documents to prevent inadvertent disclosure. AI-driven classification is markedly more consistent and accurate than traditional keyword searches or manual review, effectively eliminating the issue of "reviewer drift" or "reviewer fatigue" where human reviewers may inconsistently judge relevance. Furthermore, LLMs can be tailored to identify particular patterns of relevance unique to each case, enhancing the precision of document review.

Beyond classification, AI agents facilitate the population of structured data into spreadsheets or chronological timelines, helping to build coherent narratives from disparate data points. These capabilities allow legal teams to construct a comprehensive case chronology, streamlining the litigation process and enhancing strategic planning. As AI applications in M&A and litigation continue to evolve, the potential for further innovation and efficiency gains grows ever greater.

However, it is essential to emphasize that, despite the sophistication of these AI tools, final responsibility remains with the human lawyer. Legal professionals must verify and approve all AI-generated outcomes, ensuring ethical standards are upheld and that the use of AI is transparently disclosed – particularly before courts or regulatory authorities. Lawyers cannot abdicate their ethical duties or delegate ultimate responsibility to machines. While the core responsibilities of legal professionals remain unchanged, the allocation of their time has been fundamentally transformed by AI. Previously, up to 80 percent of a lawyer's workload was consumed by manual tasks such as document review, summarization, and record-keeping, leaving only 20 percent for strategic thinking. The advent of AI has reversed this ratio, enabling legal experts to dedicate the vast majority of their efforts to high-level strategy, innovation, and client advisory, while routine tasks are efficiently managed by AI-augmented tools.

In summary, the integration of AI into M&A and litigation processes is not merely an incremental improvement. It is a paradigm shift that redefines the role of lawyers and legal professionals. By automating laborious tasks and providing powerful analytical insights, AI enables lawyers to focus on strategic decision-making, ensuring that legal practice remains both effective and aligned with evolving business objectives in a fast-changing global landscape.

References

1 An illustrative example of a regulator's use of AI to detect prohibited market practices can be found in ECJ judgment, *Michelin v. EC* (T-188/24) of 9 July 2025 in which the plaintiff challenged the legality of the Commission's investigation.

2 https://sell.amazon.com/brand-registry/project-zero.

Chapter 16:
Legal leaders in the AI battle

As legal leaders, we have a fundamental obligation to steer our teams confidently towards a future shaped by artificial intelligence. AI is no longer a distant prospect but has become an established phenomenon that brings with it a multitude of opportunities and challenges. Rather than representing a mere incremental enhancement, AI constitutes a transformative shift – a true disruptor that is redefining the very foundations of the legal profession on an unprecedented scale.

To navigate this era of rapid technological evolution, it is incumbent upon legal leaders to chart a clear course, anchored by vision and foresight. Guiding teams through the complexities of this "AI revolution" requires more than technical know-how. It demands deliberate, strategic leadership and a willingness to embrace change. AI readiness should not be mistaken for a purely technical matter to be delegated to IT specialists. Instead, it is a strategic imperative and a cultural endeavor. Legal leaders must take ownership, establish governance frameworks, and purposefully drive the adoption of AI as an integral part of the team's strategy and daily operations.

This means proactively fostering a workplace culture that is receptive to innovation but at the same time acknowledges with empathy and care the disruptive potential AI can bring to the team. Legal leaders need to ensure their teams are prepared to collaborate effectively with AI tools, rather than resist them. By embracing new technology early, teams position themselves to benefit from innovation instead of being left behind by rapid change.

Security as foundational requirement

The foremost and uncompromising principle when integrating AI into legal practice is robust security. AI deployment must never compromise the security or integrity of company operations. Specifically, it is paramount that no confidential information, sensitive strategic discussions, or privileged communications are ever fed into general-purpose, publicly accessible LLMs. Such practices expose organizations to significant risks of data leakage and breach of client confidentiality, which could have severe legal and reputational consequences.

Corporate policy should clearly reflect this imperative by prohibiting the use of any AI agents that have not been formally approved through enterprise channels. Ideally, companies should implement a blanket ban on non-enterprise sanctioned AI tools to eliminate the possibility of inadvertent data exposure. This is not a matter of preference but a fundamental requirement for protecting sensitive information and ensuring compliance with legal and regulatory obligations.

When engaging third-party vendors for AI solutions, legal and procurement teams must insist on stringent contractual safeguards. Service agreements should include strong assurance clauses, such as zero data retention (ensuring that corporate data is never stored on external systems), a complete prohibition on using corporate data for model training, robust access controls, and comprehensive audit trails. These measures are designed to guarantee that sensitive data remains secure and that all interactions with AI systems are fully accountable and transparent.

It is worth noting that, despite the inherent vulnerabilities of LLMs (particularly to prompt injection attacks – often described as their "Achilles' heel"), the majority of major cybersecurity incidents in recent years have not stemmed from AI missteps. Instead, they have been the result of traditional human errors, such as the inadvertent disclosure of passwords or access codes through theft, deception or manipulation.[1] While early challenges with AI adoption have largely been addressed, the risk landscape continues to evolve, necessitating ongoing vigilance and adaptation.

There are effective strategies to ensure the safe and secure use of AI agents, particularly when these systems are fully integrated within the enterprise IT infrastructure. For legal services, the evolution is towards smaller, purpose-built AI models trained exclusively on verified, authoritative content. These specialized models offer greater control over data handling and output quality, reducing the risk of bias or hallucination and ensuring that legal advice remains accurate, reliable, and secure.

Ultimately, the responsible implementation of AI in legal environments hinges on a combination of rigorous policy, careful vendor management, and ongoing education around both technological and human factors. Security must remain the bedrock upon which all AI initiatives are built.

The need for human intervention

AI is fundamentally crafted to augment and support human judgement, rather than replace it. While predictive analytics can suggest likely outcomes, they cannot replicate the nuanced deliberation and holistic assessment that underpin sound legal judgment. True justice is not a matter of calculating the "most probable result" or following a predetermined sequence. It demands a consideration of the broader context, the evolving nature of facts, and the overarching aim of achieving substantive fairness. The discipline of law requires practitioners to look beyond surface-level data, weighing the totality of circumstances to reach decisions that reflect both the letter and spirit of justice.

Legal systems around the world are increasingly recognizing the necessity of human oversight in the deployment of AI, particularly in high-stakes environments. The EU AI Act, for example, enshrines the principle that all high-risk AI systems must, by default and by design, be subject to meaningful human supervision.[2] This is essential to safeguard health, safety, and fundamental rights. Such systems must be transparent in their capabilities and limitations, enabling human reviewers to understand, monitor, and, if needed, challenge or override AI-generated outcomes. The risk of automation bias means that designated individuals must always retain the authority to pause, disregard, or reverse AI decisions when warranted. Similar standards are echoed in the OECD AI Principles[3] and the UNESCO Recommendation on the Ethics of Artificial Intelligence.[4] This reflects a growing international consensus on the need for robust human involvement in AI-driven processes.

In the legal profession, this requirement for human oversight is not merely regulatory but ethical. Lawyers are bound by duties of competence and supervision, ensuring that their actions uphold the integrity of the legal system.[5] The use of AI does not absolve lawyers of these responsibilities. Instead, it increases the importance of vigilant oversight and informed decision-making. Legal professionals must remain the final arbiters, ensuring that AI is used as a tool to enhance, not diminish, the quality of legal advice and client service.

However, it is also necessary to examine whether AI, in some cases, delivers outcomes superior to existing practices.[6] For instance, legal teams often expend considerable time reviewing mundane, low-value contracts – such as standard vending machine leases – that rarely justify the investment of legal expertise. Traditional proxies, like value thresholds, are used to exempt certain agreements from legal review, but these are often ineffective, as even low-value contracts can contain clauses (e.g., duration, IP rights, indemnities, penalties, jurisdiction, etc.) that pose significant risks. AI agents, by contrast, offer a more sophisticated intake filter, quickly triaging contracts and flagging those that warrant further scrutiny. Recent analysis suggests that while AI may not yet match human judgement in complex legal evaluations, it outperforms manual processes in initial triage, delivering more consistent and qualitative results than cumbersome, rule-based human reviews.[7]

The imperative for human oversight extends beyond legal matters to the broader context of conflict and escalation. Theories of conflict management, notably those developed during the Cold War, emphasized the importance of measured, rational decision-making at every stage of escalation, particularly when the stakes involved potential nuclear confrontation.[8] Leaders relied on structured frameworks to avoid unintended escalation, maintaining control over critical decisions. With the advent of AI in military and strategic arenas, the lines between analysis and action are becoming increasingly blurred.[9] AI systems, benchmarked against elite staff, have demonstrated remarkable capability in assessing situations and recommending optimal responses, regularly outperforming their human counterparts. Yet this raises profound concerns – if one side were to eliminate human safeguards in pursuit of tactical advantage, the risk of uncontrolled escalation could increase dramatically.

The importance of retaining human control over AI-driven decisions in matters of national and global security has been explicitly acknowledged by global leaders. At their summit on 17 November 2024, Presidents Joe Biden and Xi Jinping jointly affirmed the necessity of maintaining human oversight in the deployment of AI, particularly concerning the use of nuclear weapons.[10] Their agreement to enshrine this principle in official communications marks a significant step towards recognizing human oversight and control as essential for the responsible use of AI.

While the stakes may be lower in legal disputes, the underlying principle remains the same – automated legal actions, such as AI agents independently issuing cease and desist letters or initiating court proceedings, are more likely to escalate conflicts than resolve them. Human discretion and the ability to engage in face-to-face dialogue remain crucial to achieving resolution and maintaining trust. Ultimately, the responsible integration of AI in legal practice is not about relinquishing control but about leveraging technology to support human expertise, ensuring that justice remains both effective and humane in an increasingly automated world.

Vision and strategy for the adaptation of artificial intelligence

For legal leaders, establishing a clear vision and strategy for artificial intelligence is not simply an administrative exercise, but a critical driver of long-term success. The starting point must be to articulate precisely why the team is embracing AI and how this aligns with the broader strategy and values of the legal department. Leaders should ask, how can AI meaningfully advance the team's vision to be the trusted business partner, enabling growth and safeguarding the organization's interests?

Rather than approaching AI as an open-ended experiment or a passing trend, its introduction should be guided by a purposeful, phased plan. The deployment of AI tools must be intentional, targeting well-defined objectives that serve the strategic priorities of the team. The most immediate advantages of AI lie in automating routine, repetitive, or administrative tasks – processes that, while necessary, often consume disproportionate amounts of skilled lawyers' time. By freeing up this capacity, legal professionals can focus on higher-value, strategic work such as nuanced legal analysis and effective business partnering.

AI in its current stage of development be understood for what it genuinely is – not a flawless authority or subject matter expert, but rather a diligent and capable support tool that thrives under proper human supervision. Much like a junior associate within a law firm, AI excels at handling foundational tasks, such as drafting the initial version of a memorandum or conducting preliminary research. Like with junior associates, AI's effectiveness is closely linked to the clarity and completeness of the instructions it receives. The more precise and comprehensive the briefing, the better the quality of the AI's work product.

Yet, just as junior associates are prone to occasional errors or misinterpretations, AI systems are not immune from making mistakes. These may result from ambiguous prompts, overlooked nuances, or limitations in the data on which the AI was trained. Consequently, integrating robust human oversight into every stage of AI-supported legal work is essential. Experienced professionals must review, scrutinize, and, where necessary, correct AI-generated outputs and processes to ensure quality and accuracy. From a strategy design perspective, comprehensive checks and balances throughout the workflow are essential for upholding the standards of professional excellence.

Certain areas within legal operations are particularly well suited for early AI adoption. For instance, corporate governance routines, ongoing regulatory monitoring, intellectual property management, and administrative-heavy tasks such as budgeting and matter management are all prime candidates. When evaluating where to begin, leaders should examine current workflows, applying the Pareto Principle or 80/20 rule.[11] If senior lawyers are regularly dedicating significant time to tasks like trademark searches or legal research, this represents a clear opportunity for AI to optimize resource allocation and reduce opportunity costs.

Similarly, where the team relies heavily on ad hoc information-gathering or on external law firm reports for legal and regulatory updates, AI can introduce consistency, speed, and reliability. AI-powered tools can systematize legal horizon screening, ensuring nothing is missed, and reducing dependency on manual efforts or external consultants. However, the core of legal services remains human-led legal advice. AI should serve as an enabler, assisting with research, drafting initial memos or contracts, and providing structured support to inform and enhance legal decision-making.

Crucially, leaders must design robust systems of checks and balances to guard against over-reliance on technology. This includes integrating human checkpoints within all AI-supported processes and, where appropriate, employing a model of "AI supervising AI" to cross-validate outputs. No AI system should operate in isolation or without meaningful human oversight, particularly in high-stakes or complex matters.

Change management is fundamental to successful AI integration. Leaders should set out a clear, staged roadmap for AI adoption – start with smaller pilot projects in well-defined areas, measure and demonstrate tangible benefits and then expand. Rather than vague declarations such as "We will use AI", the strategy should be grounded in specific, measurable objectives and timelines. For example, an actionable target might be: "Enable AI-driven automation for 80 percent of corporate governance processes by the end of the business year". This approach not only clarifies the desired outcomes but also helps track progress and maintain accountability across the team.

Ultimately, the effective implementation of AI within legal functions relies on vision, discipline, and ongoing engagement from leaders. By approaching AI as a strategic, cultural, and operational imperative – rather than a mere technical upgrade – legal leaders can ensure that technology serves as a true catalyst for innovation, efficiency, and excellence in legal service delivery.

Cultivating an AI-ready culture

The principal obstacle to the effective adoption of AI in legal teams is not the technology itself, but rather the human factors – resistance to change, a shortage of relevant skills, and apprehension about the future. In my experience, when discussing the possibilities that AI presents, the question that most often arises is: "Will my job still exist after AI implementation?". These concerns underscore the importance of legal leaders promoting safety and transparency, encouraging everyone to adapt, use AI effectively, and address areas where AI underperforms.

The evolution of roles within the workplace can be likened to the shift from secretaries to executive assistants. Previously, a significant part of a secretary's job revolved around tasks such as note-taking and typing correspondence. Over time, however, the expectations and responsibilities associated with these roles have grown considerably. Today, executive assistants are entrusted not only with administrative duties but also with managing the intricate operations of entire executive offices. They coordinate complex schedules, oversee critical projects, facilitate communication across departments, and often act as strategic partners to leadership. This transformation demonstrates how automation and technology can elevate roles by removing repetitive, low-value work and creating opportunities for professionals to contribute at a higher, more impactful level. Similarly, as AI becomes integrated into legal teams, it offers the chance to move beyond routine tasks, empowering staff to take on broader, more strategic responsibilities, and thus driving both individual development and organizational success.

Leaders play a crucial role in openly communicating both the purpose and the scope of AI within the team's overall vision. It is essential to reinforce that the aim is not to replace human expertise, but to enhance it – enabling team members to shift their focus from routine, repetitive tasks to work that is more strategic and intellectually fulfilling. Given that legal advice fundamentally relies on human judgement, AI should be positioned as a supportive tool – one that complements and strengthens the provision of legal advice rather than replacing the nuanced insight and ethical considerations that only people can provide.

To build trust and acceptance, it is vital that AI solutions are accessible and integrated into the team's daily workflows. AI-powered tools can assist with organizing workloads, summarizing key developments, and supporting the initial drafting of documents. Beyond this, comprehensive AI training must be provided to all staff, empowering them to move from passive users to proactive "AI-augmented lawyers". This means equipping everyone with the ability to craft effective prompts, critically assess AI-generated outputs, and resolve any errors or inconsistencies that may arise.

Illustrating the tangible benefits of AI is key to achieving widespread buy-in. Leaders should showcase practical use cases where AI streamlines and systematizes routine workflows, thereby freeing up valuable time and resources. Appointing "AI champions" within the team can be particularly effective – these individuals can lead pilot projects, demonstrate successes, and act as advocates for further adoption. In addition, establishing dedicated "sandboxes" encourages creativity and builds confidence. Sandboxes are safe spaces where staff can experiment with AI tools without fear of failure or risks to data security.

Importantly, trust in employees must underpin any AI strategy. Rather than restricting access to certain AI functionalities out of concern for potential misuse, such as seeking self-serving employment advice, leaders should err on the side of openness. By granting full access to (corporate approved and secure) AI capabilities, leaders demonstrate confidence in their team's professionalism and integrity. Imposing excessive limits undermines the spirit of empowerment and collaboration that AI is intended to foster and can stifle the very innovation that the technology promises to unlock.

Cultivating an AI-ready culture demands transparent communication, robust training, and unwavering trust in people. Leaders must champion these principles, ensuring that AI is viewed not as a threat but as a powerful ally in delivering ever more valuable and strategic legal services.

AI governance and data readiness

The effectiveness and security of AI systems are intrinsically linked to the integrity of the data they consume and the robustness of the operational protocols governing their use. For legal teams, this means that leaders must prioritize the establishment of a comprehensive data governance framework, ensuring that only accurate, reliable, and secure data is utilized in AI models. Data serves as both the fuel and the foundation for artificial intelligence. If the quality of data is compromised, the outputs generated by AI are likely to be skewed, unreliable, and potentially damaging. Such deficiencies can undermine the entire investment in AI technologies, resulting in reputational harm and operational setbacks.

It is incumbent upon legal leaders to spearhead the development and enforcement of clear, detailed policies, rules, and guidelines that promote the fair and ethical deployment of AI within their teams. The regulatory landscape, exemplified by the EU AI Act,[12] has already set important boundaries, highlighting the reputational risks associated with biased algorithms or erroneous outputs – often referred to as "hallucinations" – in critical systems. To mitigate these risks, a practical approach is to adopt a risk-based governance model, mirroring the categorization framework outlined in the EU AI Act. This involves classifying AI activities according to their level of risk – for example, automated recruitment processes, job application screening, decisions relating to promotion or termination, performance appraisals, social profiling, and emotion recognition are considered high-risk or may even be prohibited. In contrast, AI applications such as content summarization, drafting assistance, language review, and brainstorming typically fall into the low-risk category.

Legal leaders must also set clear parameters around acceptable levels of AI-related risk for each function within their organization. This includes introducing well-defined human checkpoints, commonly referred to as "human-in-the-loop", as well as repeated review mechanisms to identify inconsistencies or foster collaboration.[13] Adopting a "trust but verify" approach is advisable, whereby any legal output generated by AI is subject to rigorous scrutiny, validation, and approval by a suitably qualified team member prior to its integration into legal advice or decision-making processes.

A robust AI governance framework should incorporate a formalized review and approval process for every proposed use of AI. This process should ensure that all applications are thoroughly vetted, with explicit rules regarding the inclusion of external documents in AI prompts, given the inherent vulnerabilities of current large language models. Furthermore, as an additional security feature, it is advisable to restrict AI agents' access to only the minimum amount of data and system resources necessary for the performance of their specific tasks. This principle of least privilege helps safeguard sensitive information and reduces the risk of unintended disclosures or misuse.

Ultimately, as with the adoption of any new technology, success hinges on striking the right balance between rigorous governance and a spirit of encouraged experimentation. Blanket rejection of AI is not necessarily the safest course of action. Legal leaders must consider the existing state of affairs – the current systems and practices underpinning legal operations. In instances where processes are highly manual, overly reliant on individual effort, and lacking adequate resilience, AI can offer a transformative solution. Beyond improving efficiency, the introduction of AI can establish essential guardrails that previously did not exist, enhancing the consistency, reliability, and overall quality of legal service delivery.

By fostering a culture of responsible AI adoption, anchored in strong governance, ethical principles, and ongoing oversight, legal leaders can ensure that technology acts as a powerful enabler rather than a source of risk. This proactive approach not only safeguards the interests of the organization but also paves the way for meaningful innovation and sustained excellence within legal teams.

References

1 Recent examples of cyberattacks and their causes during the last five years include: JLR (2025) – Attackers gained access using stolen credentials (some outdated) and exploited over-permissive access rights; M&S (2025) – Intruders used social engineering (tricking employees) to obtain credentials and deploy ransomware; United Health Group (2024) – Credential theft from a third party service provider and access via a server that lacked multi-factor authentication.

2 Art. 14 EU AI Act.

3 Adopted in 2019 and updated in 2024: "AI actors should implement mechanisms and safeguards, such as capacity for human agency and oversight, including to address risks arising from uses outside of intended purpose, intentional misuse, or unintentional misuse in a manner appropriate to the context and consistent with the state of the art." www.oecd.org/en/topics/sub-issues/ai-principles.html

4 Adopted in 2021. https://unesdoc.unesco.org/ark:/48223/pf0000381137/PDF/381137eng.pdf.multi

5 See for instance the UK Solicitors Regulation Authority (SRA) Principles and Code of Conduct. The courts made it clear that submitting documents containing false information, including information that was fabricated by AI, is a fundamental breach of the duty to act with honesty and integrity towards the court. Uncritical reliance on AI-generated content may constitute professional negligence.

6 A study conducted by Waymo and Swiss Re found that Waymo's robotaxis are involved in 88 percent fewer property damage claims and 92 percent fewer injury claims per mile than humans. "Unleash the robotaxi revolution", *The Economist*, 4 October 2025, page 14.

7 Schwarcz, Manning, Barry, Cleveland, Prescott, Rich: "AI-Powered Lawyering: AI Reasoning Model, Retrieval Augmented Generation and the Future of Legal Practice", 2025.

8 Herman Kahn, *On Escalation*, 1965.

9 *The Economist*, "How AI is changing warfare; An AI-assisted general staff may be more important than killer robots", 20 June 2024.

10 "The two leaders took an important step forward today with respect to AI safety and risk. They agreed, and it will be reflected in the readout, on the need to maintain human control over the decision to use nuclear weapons..." On the record press gaggle by National Security Advisor Jake Sullivan, https://bidenwhitehouse.archives.gov/briefing-room/press-briefings/2024/11/17.

11 See Planning for impact – the Pareto Principle, in chapter six.

12 Regulation 2024/1689 of 13 June 2024, OJ L 2024/1689.

13 Kaytie Ward, "What is human in the loop (HITL)", 15 July 2025, www.ai21.com/glossary/human-in-the-loop/.

Conclusion

Legal leadership is best understood not as a fixed destination but as an ongoing journey. It is defined by perpetual learning, adaptation, and personal as well as professional development. Throughout this book, we have delved into the complex and evolving nature of leadership within in-house legal teams – from the deliberate cultivation of organizational culture and the careful articulation of strategy to successfully navigating uncertainty and boldly embracing the challenges of tomorrow with both courage and clarity of vision.

What becomes clear to leaders on this path is that mastery of the law – while indispensable and the foundation for everything – is only one piece of the puzzle. True leadership goes beyond technical proficiency. Leadership demands the capacity to direct, inspire, and empower others towards a common goal, creating a sense of belonging. It means having the humility to embrace feedback, the fortitude to make difficult decisions, and the wisdom to recognize when to step aside and allow others to step forward. Leadership is about building environments in which people feel safe and encouraged to voice their ideas, take the initiative, and push the boundaries of their potential towards progress.

Communication is of paramount importance for leadership, particularly in the legal field. The ability to connect with others, to listen actively, to articulate complex ideas clearly, and to inspire confidence is what transforms legal advice from a technical output into genuine business value. This capacity for meaningful dialogue is what turns disparate individuals into a cohesive team and a team into a trusted, indispensable function within the organization. Effective communication underpins trust and enables the collaborative spirit that is essential for any high-performing legal team.

Leadership starts with a conscious decision. It begins with a deliberate and thoughtful choice that requires more than simply accepting a title or position. Leadership demands that you consciously embrace the responsibility of guiding others and overseeing the collective mission. This commitment involves a readiness to be accountable not just for your own actions, but also for the wellbeing, growth, and success of every member of your team. By choosing to lead, you signal your willingness to bear the weight of both the challenges and the triumphs that come with steering a group towards its shared objectives and common purpose. It is the intentional act of deciding to step forward and assuming responsibility for people and outcomes that lies at the very heart of effective leadership.

Leadership cannot be treated as an afterthought or a peripheral duty. For anyone with responsibility for even a single team member, leadership is the principal deliverable, the central product of your work. The way you lead sets the tone for your team's effectiveness, cohesion, and overall contribution to the broader business. Leadership serves as a force multiplier for legal expertise, amplifying both individual and collective strengths and ultimately laying the groundwork for long-term, sustainable success.

Few of us are natural born leaders. Leadership is not a mysterious gift reserved for the chosen few. It is a skill that can be learned, cultivated, and refined through deliberate effort and self-awareness. This book offers practical and insightful guidance, beginning with the cultural attributes that underpin the development of a high-performing team. From my perspective, the most pivotal values and behaviors that lay the groundwork for effective teamwork include empathy, the pursuit of excellence, taking initiative, maintaining transparency, and upholding integrity. It is important to acknowledge that the prioritization of these values will be shaped by personal conviction and the specific needs of your team or organization. Each leader must thoughtfully determine which qualities to emphasize most, shaping the team's character and approach accordingly.

Equally fundamental to successful leadership is the articulation of a compelling vision and the crafting of a well-defined strategy. These elements serve as the guiding stars for the team, providing both aspiration and a clear sense of direction. Vision inspires ambition, while strategy transforms that ambition into actionable steps. It is the leader's responsibility to chart the course, ensuring that the team remains focused on long-term objectives rather than becoming mired in the minutiae of everyday operations.

Impactful leadership involves more than simply managing tasks or resolving immediate issues. It requires the ability to step back, see the bigger picture, and oversee the collective journey towards shared goals. By setting a clear destination and fostering an environment built on trust, accountability, and shared purpose, leaders can unite their teams, drive sustained progress, and unlock the full potential of every member.

Auftragstaktik serves as a prime example of how empowering teams can be successfully put into practice. This leadership approach centers on delegating decision-making authority to team members, but within a clearly articulated strategic framework. By establishing overarching goals and boundaries, leaders provide the necessary direction while still granting individuals autonomy to act decisively. In this environment, team members are encouraged to exercise initiative and respond proactively to opportunities and challenges as they emerge. Such a system not only accelerates response times but also fosters innovation and ownership, as individuals feel trusted to make meaningful contributions. Ultimately, *Auftragstaktik* transforms teams into agile, forward-thinking units, capable of capitalizing on situations as they develop, and driving sustained progress towards shared objectives.

Leadership inherently involves the responsibility to make decisions, often in challenging and ambiguous circumstances. Few things are more disheartening for a team than witnessing anxious hesitation or indecision from those in charge. Such uncertainty can swiftly undermine trust and hinder progress. Effective leaders recognize that their role is not merely to observe or defer but to actively address issues and guide situations towards resolution if so required. They understand that leaving matters unresolved can breed confusion, diminish morale, and stall the momentum of the entire team. By taking decisive action, even in the face of complexity or incomplete information, leaders demonstrate their commitment to stewardship and instill confidence among those they lead.

Exceptional legal leaders do not stay hidden behind closed doors or limit themselves to the comfort of corporate headquarters. Instead, they are present, engaged, and highly visible, placing themselves at the heart of key business decisions and activities. They proactively seek out new challenges, tackle issues head-on as they arise, and ensure they remain approachable and accessible to their teams. While it remains vital to respect boundaries and avoid taking on responsibilities that rightfully belong to others, true leaders are always ready to offer support, guidance, and encouragement where they are needed most. They recognize that their presence and engagement can make all the difference in times of uncertainty or change.

Perhaps the most profound lesson of all is this – leadership is fundamentally about resilience. It is the art of facing setbacks with optimism, taking responsibility for mistakes and returning each time with greater clarity, deeper conviction, and renewed energy. The most effective legal leaders are not those who avoid failure altogether, but those who demonstrate the capacity to rebound, learn from adversity, adapt, and emerge even stronger. Resilience enables leaders to model perseverance for their teams, fostering a culture where setbacks are not sources of shame but opportunities for growth.

Mistakes and failures are inevitable elements of the learning and improvement process. This acceptance does not excuse carelessness or lack of preparation. Rather, it reflects an intellectually humble mindset that acknowledges human fallibility and transforms its root cause into an opportunity to improve. Black Box Thinking means openly analyzing failures to understand their causes. As a consequence, we are able to adjust and refine our processes, close gaps in our knowledge or systems, and continually raise the standard of our work. Our collective commitment as a team is to continuously improve and prevent repetition of the same errors, recognizing that to do otherwise is both frustrating and wasteful of our potential.

At its core, leadership – like the law – is a people business. Behind every contract negotiated, every compliance framework built, and every legal opinion given, there are people – colleagues, clients, stakeholders, and counterparts – whose trust is hard-won and easily lost. The time and energy invested in building relationships and nurturing trust is never wasted. It yields lasting dividends in loyalty, collaboration, and mutual achievement. The conversations we hold, the rapport we develop, and the culture we foster are as significant – if not more so – than any legal argument we set down on the page.

Leadership is about preparing your team for the future – arming them with the skills, awareness, and adaptability required to meet evolving challenges head-on. It is essential to dedicate time to considering emerging trends, technological advancements, and shifts in the regulatory landscape and to thoughtfully assess how these might impact your team's strategy and priorities.

Leaders stay abreast of technological advancements by actively seeking out new developments and taking the initiative to learn about them firsthand. Rather than passively depending on the knowledge or expertise of others, they demonstrate a spirit of curiosity, exploring emerging tools, platforms, and trends with an open and inquisitive mindset. By developing their own informed perspectives, these leaders are better equipped to critically assess which innovations are most relevant and valuable for their teams and organizations. This proactive approach not only helps them to anticipate change but also enables them to guide their teams through transitions with greater confidence and authority. In doing so, they model a culture of continuous learning and adaptability, ensuring that the team remains competitive and prepared for whatever the future may hold.

Change is rarely comfortable, but incremental, well-managed progress allows teams to adapt without feeling overwhelmed. Bring your team along with you every step of the way. True leadership is about collective progress, not solitary achievement. Attempting to push ahead in opposition to your team, or neglecting their input and concerns, is a sure route to failure. Instead, prioritize creating an environment where every member feels secure, valued, and empowered to contribute openly. Foster a sense of psychological safety, where individuals trust both your leadership and the direction you have set, knowing that their perspectives are respected and care for the team is a priority. By building trust and demonstrating genuine care for your team's development and morale, you lay the foundation for strong, lasting commitment.

At the same time, do not confuse leadership with a quest for popularity. Leadership is not about seeking approval or tailoring your actions to win favor with the majority. While it is essential to listen attentively to your team's perspectives and demonstrate genuine openness to feedback, you must also be prepared to stand firm in your convictions, even when your decisions are not universally welcomed. There will inevitably be moments when, having weighed all opinions and evidence, you must make a choice that is necessary for the greater good, despite it being unpopular or met with resistance. True leaders balance empathy with resolve, ensuring that their actions are guided by what is right and needed rather than what is simply comfortable or expedient. Be transparent and keep the team informed at every step. Explain your decision and actively seek support from the team. You will earn the respect of the team by upholding difficult but necessary decisions in the best interests of the team and organization.

As you continue along your own leadership journey, remember that your most significant impact is how you choose to lead. Lead with compassion, striving always to understand and support those around you. Lead with a commitment to excellence, setting high standards not just for technical performance, but for ethical and collaborative conduct. Lead with courage, unafraid to challenge the status quo or take calculated risks in pursuit of progress. Above all, lead with humanity and resilience – for the future belongs to those who are willing to build it, who take care of others and weather adversity with resilience, rising time and again with renewed strength and purpose.

About Globe Law and Business

Globe Law and Business was established in 2005. From the very beginning, we set out to create legal books that are sufficiently high level to be of real use to the experienced professional, yet still accessible and easy to navigate. Most of our authors are drawn from Magic Circle and other top commercial firms, both in the United Kingdom and internationally. Our titles are carefully produced, with the utmost attention paid to editorial, design and production processes. We hope this results in high-quality publications that are easy to read and a pleasure to own.

In 2021, we were very pleased to announce the start of a new chapter for Globe Law and Business following the acquisition of law books under the imprint Ark Publishing. Our law firm management list is now significantly expanded with many well-known and loved Ark Publishing titles.

We are also pleased to announce the launch of our online content platform, Globe Law Online, which allows for easy access across firms. Details of all titles included can be found at www.globelawonline.com. Email glo@globelawandbusiness.com for further details and to arrange a free trial for you or your firm.

We'd very much like to hear from you with your thoughts and ideas for improving what we offer. Please do feel free to email me on sian@globelawandbusiness.com. Happy reading and thank you for your time.

Sian O'Neill
Managing director
Globe Law and Business
www.globelawandbusiness.com

www.ingramcontent.com/pod-product-compliance
Ingram Content Group UK Ltd.
Pitfield, Milton Keynes, MK11 3LW, UK
UKHW020402210426
470205UK00005B/53

9 781837 231799